Adirondack Archangels

Adirondack Archangels

GUARDIANS OF THE HIGH PEAKS

Edited by Christine Bourjade and Alex Radmanovich

Foreword by Bill McKibben

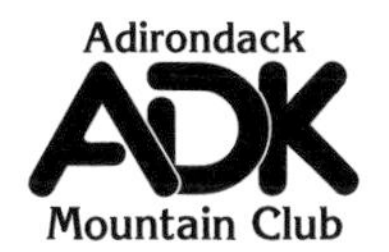

Adirondack Mountain Club, Inc.

Lake George, New York

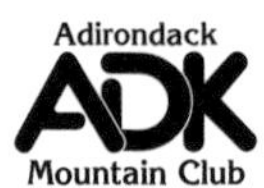

Published by the Adirondack Mountain Club, Inc.
814 Goggins Road, Lake George, New York 12845-4117
518-668-4447 www.adk.org

Cover photograph© by Nancie Battaglia: Silhouette of
Dr. E. H. "Ketch" Ketchledge on Whiteface Mountain—1991.
Back cover photograph© by Brendan Wiltse: High mountain blueberry,
on Mount Marcy—June 14, 2015.
Design by PelicanPR

First edition 2016

Adirondack Mountain Club (ADK) is dedicated to the conservation, preservation, and responsible recreational use of the New York State Forest Preserve and other parks, wild lands, and waters vital to our members and chapters.

This book was made possible with generous support from Christine Bourjade and Alex Radmanovich and the staff of their firm, Pelican Public Relations Inc.

Library of Congress Cataloging-in-Publication Data

Names: Bourjade, Christine, 1952- editor. | Radmanovich, Alex, 1950- editor.
Title: Adirondack archangels: guardians of the high peaks / edited by
Christine Bourjade and Alex Radmanovich; foreword by Bill McKibben.
Description: Lake George, New York: Adirondack Mountain Club, Inc., [2016]
Identifiers: LCCN 2016005435 | ISBN 9780996116831 (pbk.)
Subjects: LCSH: Conservation of natural resources--New York (State) |
Adirondack Mountains (N.Y.) | Adirondack Park (N.Y.) | Natural
resources--New York (State) | Outdoor recreation--New York (State)
Classification: LCC S932.N7 A35 2016 | DDC 639.909747/1--dc23 LC record
available at http://lccn.loc.gov/2016005435

ISBN 978-0-9961168-3-1
26 25 24 23 22 21 20 19 18 17 16

Printed in Canada
1 2 3 4 5 6 7 8 9 10

Acknowledgments

For over a century, a multitude of dedicated professionals, volunteers and organizations have worked tirelessly to heal and protect the Adirondack Park, a unique six-million-acre mosaic of forest lands, mountains, lakes and rivers, interspersed with human settlement. This book was inspired by one such individual, Dr. Edwin H. "Ketch" Ketchledge (Adirondack 46er #507), and the need to secure his legacy.

Each year hundreds of thousands of visitors fall in love with the Park and the High Peaks, and shortly after want to know everything about this special place. This book is an attempt to quench this thirst in a single volume. We apologize that space constraints did not allow for all Adirondack guardian angels to share their roles and perspectives.

We are grateful to every one of the authors who graciously and enthusiastically accepted our offer to reflect on their Adirondack experiences and put pen to paper. For the stunning photography, we thank the extraordinarily talented Nancie Battaglia, Yvon Daigle, Carl Heilman II, Larry Master and Brendan Wiltse. The expertise of Andrea Masters and Ann Hough of the Adirondack Mountain Club was highly appreciated, as was the artistic genius of Pierre Beaudoin and the technical contribution of Vincent Lagueux, both of PelicanPR in Montreal. Our heartfelt thanks go to Domtar Corporation for its partnership at printing time. Thanks to all of the above, one hundred percent of the proceeds from the sale of this volume will support the Adirondack High Peaks Summer Stewardship Program.

If after reading this book you are moved to contribute to the conservation and education work that Ketch began, please go to the Adirondack Foundation website at www.generousact.org and make a donation to #507 Fund for the Adirondack High Peaks Summit Stewardship Program.

Happy reading!

Christine Bourjade and Alex Radmanovich, Editors

To see more of their work, go to:
nbphotog@roadrunner.com (Nancie Battaglia)
www.lesiteayvon.com (Yvon Daigle)
www.carlheilman.com
www.masterimages.org
www.brendanwiltse.com
www.domtar.com
www.adk.org
www.rppelican.ca

This book is dedicated to those who initially protected the Adirondacks, those who have valiantly defended those protections, and to those who work to maintain the Adirondacks—so that the value of those protections is not lost.

Foreword

The Adirondacks is, truly, vast—from the top of Skylight, or up in an airplane, the green stretches on forever, the one western-scale wilderness in the American east.

But the Adirondacks is also, truly, a small world. If it has a spiritual center, it's those few acres of alpine summit described in the early pages of this book, the ones patiently restored by Ed Ketchledge and his colleagues, and now protected by the dauntless Summit Stewards. Those acres of rock and lichen and tufted grass—and of tired hikers sprawled, peanut butter sandwiches in hand, arguing over which distant range is the Santanonis—are a meeting place for the people who've fallen under the spell of these mountains. It's not uncommon to climb one of those peaks and stumble across one of the authors of this volume: Tony Goodwin, say, leading a team of young trail-improvers, or Carl Heilman, panoramic camera in hand, or Pete Fish, ready to provide sartorial advice.

And to gaze down from those peaks is to be reminded constantly of the loving work that goes into preserving the unique balance between the natural and the human that makes the Adirondacks so special and so hopeful: the work of leaders like Cali Brooks or Joe Martens or Tim Barnett or Neil Woodworth. If you're a veteran of the Park, then you'll enjoy reading about these friends of yours. If you're a newcomer to the Blue Line, then this is a handy guide to some of the people who make this place so special.

The book itself is a part of that endless process of renewing these mountains. The proceeds will help the fund established in Ketchledge's memory, providing sustenance for the stewards who in turn share the stories with the hikers who perhaps will in turn become conservationists themselves. This circle of responsibility has protected the Adirondacks for well more than a century now, and it's our job to keep it going.

Some forces are beyond the control of those of us inside the Adirondacks, of course—the specter of climate change, say, hangs heavy on these mountains as on all the world's landscapes. But that makes it all the more important that we protect the things we can protect. And that we take pleasure in and bear witness to the incomparable beauties of this big small place while we can!

NANCIE BATTAGLIA

Bill McKibben
Johnsburg, New York, January 2016

Contents

Author with his daughter on Quandary Peak, Colorado

The Original Summit Steward

By James Ketchledge

James Ketchledge

When Dr. Edwin H. Ketchledge died peacefully in his sleep in June 2010, he was survived by wife Jean, brother Arthur, sister-in-law Kathryn (who passed away in 2011), daughter Susan Mangus and her husband Gary of Hickory, KY, daughter Joan Kogut and her husband Kenneth of Potsdam, NY, grandson Keith Kogut of Saranac Lake, NY, son James Ketchledge, wife Sandra and grandchildren Garrett and Rachael, all of Conifer, CO. He was predeceased by his brother Raymond. James Ketchledge is Chief Executive Officer of Excergy Corporation based in Denver, CO. His book Successful Smart Grid Implementation *was published in 2015.*

At a young age, I was pulled into the slipstream of my father, Dr. Edwin H. Ketchledge, both figuratively and literally. Literally, in that his walking pace of 120 steps a minute, known in the military as the "quick march," was his standard gait everywhere he went. Figuratively, in that his intellect and zest for life became the major shaping force for a boy growing up and discovering what life was all about.

His students once verified that walking pace using a stopwatch as he strode across the quad at the College of Environmental Science and Forestry. It was a source of quiet pride to him that he kept his Army bearing from the 10th Mountain Division in World War II. That stride was all the more remarkable given the fact that he was missing most of his left lung from injuries during the war, when he also suffered other internal damage. The pace was the outward appearance of his inner driving force to make the most of every day that was given to him after his near fatal wounds.

The earliest shaping that Dad had, like most people, was from his parents. My grandfather, a Harvard-educated Presbyterian minister, instilled in Dad the strong moral fiber and ethical bearing that governed all his actions as an adult. My grandmother was a casual naturalist, and on walks through the woods would identify plants and talk with Dad about nature. For people who knew Dad as an adult, it may come as a shock that he did not take academics seriously as a young man. But suddenly around age 16, he matured and his focus became the outdoors and nature that my grandmother had tutored him in. My Uncle Art recalls how Dad placed signs with the Latin name of every unique plant around the summer cabin in his junior year of high school, a practice that he maintained throughout his life!

Dr. Edwin H. Ketchledge ("Ketch") (1924-2010)

His combat experience in the mountains of Italy as a sergeant in the acclaimed ski troops was the other major shaping force of his life. He volunteered because he wanted to defend his country against the fascists, and applying to join the new elite ski troops was a natural decision. Dad trained for several years in the mountains of Colorado where he built an Adirondack lean-to with another New York friend above Camp Hale. Fifty-five years later I found that lean-to, still standing above a waterfall. The Division shipped out to Italy in 1944 to break the German Gustav Line in the Apennine Mountains, which had thrown back all previous attempts to break through.

Break the German line they did, in several epic battles including Riva Ridge, which was protected by a sheer cliff the Germans thought unassailable. Six routes were planned up the cliff to be established by the best climbers, and Dad's squad was the spearhead establishing one of the routes. In the dark of night, they fixed ropes for the rest of the Company to follow, and as day started to break, they reached the top in a thick fog. Dad was the point man and as the ground flattened out he triggered a trip wire, and a German machine gun opened up on him. Taking shelter behind a small boulder, he wrote a good-bye note to his future wife Jean, my Mom, as the bullets tore up everything around him. His squad mates flanked the gun and destroyed it. Later, he counted 400 empty shells of bullets, all of which had miraculously missed him.

Dad was wounded and nearly killed in the final push out of the Apennines into the Po River valley. After coming down a steep slope, the enemy ambushed his platoon. They took protection at the bottom of the ravine where a creek flowed. Leaning against the bank for protection, they saw the snow puffing from the bullets spraying along the top. Then the mortars started raining down, and they knew they had to charge through those bullets for any hope of survival. Dad took only a few steps over the top when bullets tore through his chest, nicked the pericardium of his heart, shredded his spleen and lung, and perforated his stomach. He said he literally died that day, and felt his spirit leaving his body. His buddies, however, refused to let him go, and one medic died in the effort to save him. Forever after that day—and he had a running count of each one—he was on a mission to accomplish things before his time ran out, in recognition that he had an opportunity that many of his friends never received.

Ketch studying bog plants

Dad's military stride took me to places that were the formative foundations of life. Whether it was my first mountain (Mount Jo outside the Adirondak Loj) or what became a winter climb in August on Marcy, I was always exposed to new wonders to appreciate. In full disclosure, my Mom and my sisters did carry me part of the way up Mt. Jo. Perhaps there was a life lesson in that as well.

The climbs up many of the Adirondack peaks following him, taught me in literal fashion how any task that seems difficult can be tackled by perseverance and one step at a time. Indeed, mountain climbing is the perfect metaphor for accomplishing life's goals. Yet there was something more and deeply spiritual that was felt in ascending the High Peaks. That force seemed to hum and resonate in Dad's very being as he ascended. For him, the mountains and forests were God's cathedral, and he was seeking not only to understand and appreciate but to protect as well.

The inner force and spiritual aspect of his mission to protect the Adirondack High Peaks pulled many of his students and colleagues into his slipstream as well. It was his boundless energy and enthusiasm for the mountains and their ecosystems that was the most captivating. He exhibited the pure joy of a child at most everything involving nature and his beloved Adirondack Mountains. His greatest joy, however, was that in the process of educating the world's best dendrologists, bryoecologists and forest ecology experts, he was forging a larger community of people who respected and appreciated the outdoors and

La Garita Mountain Range, Colorado, Garrett Ketchledge had a shovel in his pack because of avalanche danger on that trip.

natural world. In that, he was eminently successful as the testimonials in this book attest. He defined his guiding principle once as:

> *The stress of the environment is shown by the irregularity of the scene: bonsai-like trees filling in the shallow ravines leading to the summit; windswept and vulnerable populations of arctic relics surviving on difficult terrain where the life zone is but two feet deep, the distance between the impenetrable bedrock below and the killing winds tearing over the surface of the ground above. This is no place for humans to lower the odds further by trampling both rare plants and fragile environment.*

His mission to protect the summits started in 1964 following an early spring hike to Wright Peak, where he found the trail in terrible shape. Along the summit trail, the thin plant life was being eroded rapidly by melting snow and the wash of spring rain. In some places, the erosion was so severe that the bedrock itself was being exposed rapidly. It was early in the season, long before large numbers of visitors would trample the summits, and this was when he first realized the impact that even a limited number of hikers could have on the fragile alpine environment. The types of plants found in the alpine zone are similar to those inhabiting arctic regions hundreds of miles to the north and were first introduced in advance of glaciers thousands of years ago. When the huge ice flows retreated, many species adapted to the surrounding summits. In the severe environment which these hardy plants inhabit, cool, windy and sodden conditions limit the growing season to about two months. The vegetation is most susceptible during the early spring and late fall when the ground is wet and easily dislodged by trampling. During the winter, as the surface layer freezes a crust forms that collapses underfoot, shearing the frozen peat and any roots contained in it.

Ketch on Algonquin

With the help of Ray Leonard of the United States Forest Service, Dad obtained a grant for the study of alpine ecosystem degradation in the Adirondack peaks. They proceeded to inventory the 46 highest summits in 1967, most of which supported one or more alpine plant species. The highest 20 peaks all showed varying amounts of trampling impact in the alpine/tundra plant community. They determined that less than 100 acres of the alpine existed, which he called "islands in the sky," and that once the plant life died, the soil quickly was swept away in the wind. Dad believed that the ancient vegetation that was being inadvertently trampled on the highest summits were museums connecting earlier times with the present—and must be preserved—just as we honor and preserve our cultural heritage in man-made museums.

Dix Mountain was chosen as their test ground for restoration experiments. They determined that the unusual summit soil cannot be re-created and that reclamation via replacement was not a viable solution to the loss of the soil mantle. Soil preservation became the chief concern. The first tests consisted of various re-vegetation regimes involving native and non-native species and fertilizer treatments. Later, Dad and his colleagues moved their studies to Mount Colden. On Mount Colden, he and team tested other high altitude grass species and different fertilizer combinations, and settled on a treatment unit consisting of several grass species, fertilizer and limestone. Once the treatment stabilized bare, exposed soil, the native plants then had a foothold to re-establish themselves, and the non-native grasses were supplanted.

On Memorial Day weekend in 1971, he and 50 volunteers from Adirondack Mountain Club and the Adirondack 46ers treated the summits of Algonquin and Wright peaks with 80 treatment units. Over the next 30 years and a thousand workdays, the volunteers preserved the ecological integrity of the Adirondack arctic-alpine landscape for future generations. I helped on several trips and in particular remember treating Iroquois Peak and Boundary on my hands and knees, carefully placing seed and lime, and trying to prevent the wind from sweeping it away.

Climbing with Dad, many of which involved his 160 ascents of Algonquin, was forever an education. For most people the focus in the mountains is purely recreational. Recreation was just a sidelight to him in pursuit of the scientific. There was almost always an academic or scientific reason behind all the outings I remember but he appreciated any person who exhibited motivation to climb, and if he could channel it into his goals of preservation all the better. Most of the climbs involved educating his students directly. Sometimes it involved science with measuring, cataloging or preserving the alpine zone but rarely was it just for climbing's sake. The only purely recreational hikes I can remember were to his favorite creek and Sliding Rock Falls near Cranberry Lake, where one could slide in the creek down a smooth rock into the waters of the pond below.

His main recreational outlet in the 1970s reflected on his love of the winter season, his desire to always be on mountains, and his enthusiasm for simple pleasures such as going fast. In contrast to today's Olympic athlete that excels only through superb conditioning and relentless focus, in that day bobsledding was the domain of interested men who lived near the only American bobsled track at Mt. Van Hoevenberg in Lake Placid. Dad was introduced to the sport and was immediately hooked, and raced until his harness broke in one competition and the force of being bounced around in the sled tore open old war wounds and led to his withdrawal from the sport. His two-man team finished third in 1971, and but for a few hundredths of a second, would have gone to the Olympics in Sapporo, Japan, to represent the United States. His affection for the sport, coupled with his natural enthusiasm and "can-do" spirit, led to the building of a quarter-mile bobsled track at his home in retirement near Saranac Lake. Six-foot high, banked turns were packed with snow and sprayed with water to create the second fastest bobsled run in the Adirondacks!

The excitement on mountain climbs and hikes also embodied a union of the macroscopic and the microscopic. The macroscopic is what most people see in climbing. The beautiful vistas, the evidence of gigantic forces at work in the past, the realization of one's trivial lifespan in the history of the landscape—are all profound and spiritual. However, he taught me, as well as countless others to appreciate the smaller aspects of nature in those climbs. As he said once:

> *All of us who climb the mountains tend to think and focus on the summits—our destination—rather than on the mountain sides we traverse on the way up. But in the process of discovery and of enjoyment of the summits, I have also learned that the variations on the mountain sides are equally as fascinating, and variable, from mountain base upwards to either open or forested summit. Each trail to each summit has its own character and its own story to tell; each stand of trees along the route displays a slightly different origin and nature; each vista out to the horizon displays a different landscape scene. The forest floor everywhere is a veritable garden of wild flowers, mosses, lichens and ferns, whose collective beauty makes separate names unnecessary for those of us who appreciate them.*

The last sentence of the quote is ironic as he *could* name virtually every plant we ever encountered. The appreciation of the smallest form of life in juxtaposition with the grand landscapes opened a completeness of appreciation of the natural world that is profound, and I use and treasure that gift even today on my climbs in the Colorado Rockies.

As a boy, I tagged along on the climbs and hikes that he conducted with his students that he taught at the microscopic levels. Through casual and repetitive listening, I picked up knowledge so that by age 12 he could call out to me if the class was stumped on a question, and there was a good chance I could answer it. Some of the answers still stick in my head today, like "*Leucobryum glaucum*" (the pin cushion moss) and "A2 soil horizon."

Many of those hikes occurred at the Cranberry Lake Biological Station (CLBS) where Dad was the Director for many years. For most of his students, the semester at Cranberry Lake Biological Station was a momentary, but special, highlight in their undergraduate curriculum. For my family, living in an isolated wilderness accessible only across seven miles of water was our lifestyle for a quarter of the year. And what a paradise that was! Only with the passing of time can I see what a special blessing we had, and how it shaped my life. The experience forged skills such as orienteering, woods craft and mountaineering. More importantly it instilled a deep love of the natural world that remains with me to this day. Dad was always there as the leader but he also knew when to step back and let me and others experiment and grow. He helped me plan with great excitement a solo multi-day backpack into the Five Ponds wilderness area at age 11, drove me in the boat across the lake to the drop-off point and then waved as I set off. My mother, Jean, of course was also supportive of the adventures. Once a graduate student came running up to my mother exclaiming he had seen me miles away in the wilderness crossing a beaver dam and that I was in danger. My mother just shrugged it off and let me be, as hiking around all day was the normal state of affairs for our family. To this day I am thankful for the skills and lessons in independence and self-reliance that I learned at Cranberry Lake. Having learned how to navigate with map and compass through the dense eastern woods and solid canopies overhead, it seems virtually impossible for me to get lost now in the rugged open vistas of the Rocky Mountains that I call home!

Not many parents grant their 11-year-olds that type of freedom to mature and grow confidence in their abilities but he had that same freedom as a child and passed it down. When growing up, he met a kid from Buffalo, NY, hundreds of miles away from his home in Johnstown, NY (near Albany). After summer camp was done, he decided to visit him and without telling anyone he hitchhiked over the weekend and showed up at his friend's door. That independence and confidence were hallmarks of his personality, along with his enthusiasm. It may also have been shaped in learning to swim by being tossed off a dock into Canada Lake by my grandfather, where he spent his summers growing up!

Cranberry Lake also indulged one of Dad's other outdoor loves, which was lakes, creeks and especially bogs. Dad was fascinated by the plethora of plant life and the ecosystems of fens. He really enjoyed floating bogs where masses of plants, often sphagnum moss, created a bouncy carpet of life over water. One of his academic specialties was mosses, or bryophytes. On the open water, one animal held his heart, and that was the Common Loon (*Gavia immer*). Once he drifted in his kayak along the shore of a lake, watching a pair of loons feeding their chicks. He said, "I wasn't more than 200 feet from them and must have appeared like driftwood to them; conversely, they were wilderness personified to me. I find that traveling alone like this produces the most rewarding experiences. And inner insights that stay with you thereafter."

Dad became an expert at loon calls with his voice and hands, and captured the warble perfectly, which he would demonstrate with delight if anyone asked. I remember him standing on a dock at Cranberry Lake conversing with a loon family in the distance. My sister Joan and I along with my two children returned to Cranberry Lake a few years ago and walked the campus at CLBS. Just as we made our way to our old cabin, several loons came around a point at the lake shore at the very spot I remember Dad calling to them decades ago. To us, it was a sure sign that his spirit was greeting us and was happy that we had come back to that special place.

Stabilizing erosion on Algonquin
NANCIE BATTAGLIA

Whether it was teaching his students, running CLBS, or his volunteer work serving as President, Vice-President or Trustee of organizations such as the 46ers and the Adirondack Mountain Club, Dad was always striving to educate professionals as well as the general public. In 1972, he wrote an article for *The Conservationist* magazine entitled Projections from a Crystal Ball. As with all forecasts of the future, some visions have not come to pass, but the majority have, and some of his insights are remarkable. He wrote:

> *The public may yet be unaware of it but there is a new generation on the scene. The youth coming through the colleges and universities today are a new breed. They are ecologically educated; they are aware of environmental consequences inflicted on the landscape by thoughtless generations before them; and they are convinced that their generation will not let it happen again. The concerned youth of today will be our aroused, informed citizens of tomorrow. They will be the conscience of society; their environmental ethic in time will become the human ethic by which all business-government actions are judged. Their "will" will become the "public will," a formal mandate giving new meaning to the concept of participatory democracy; no segment in society will be able to ignore the ground-swell of common concern for the ecological health of the world in which we live.*

In December 1989, Dad called a meeting of several citizen groups at the Adirondak Loj at Heart Lake in New York to explore new initiatives addressing the summit impacts. It was during this meeting that the Summit Stewardship Program was born. The Nature Conservancy (TNC), the Adirondack Mountain Club (ADK), and the Adirondack 46ers all sent representatives, and several concerned individuals also participated. Through great collaboration and cooperation, the Summit Stewardship Program details were finalized. NYS Department of Environmental Conservation officials eventually approved sharing administration of the Summit Stewardship Program with ADK and TNC, and also agreed to hire and pay the stewards with funds raised by TNC. The Summit Stewardship Program has been a great success. The stewards act as historians, educators and caretakers. The Adirondack summits host tens of thousands of hikers annually. Such a situation can easily create serious trampling problems orders of magnitude worse than Dad witnessed in 1964. Most summit visitors simply do not realize either the uniqueness of the alpine vegetation or the fragility of the rare ecosystem itself. My family knows that he would be deeply appreciative of the efforts of everyone still involved with preserving the Adirondacks as a wonderful and unique ecosystem, and in particular the Summit Stewards he was so fond of.

At the age of 70, and nearing the end of his climbing days as the damage of the war wounds finally caught up to him, Dad had an experience in the mountains that he called his greatest climb. In a mild winter, he was walking up Whiteface Mountain Road following his Alaskan Malamute in a 40-degree blanket of clouds. Soon the fog became impenetrable, and it was like they were walking in a bubble that kept pace as they trudged along. Suddenly they were above the clouds. The world had transformed into a white ocean with only the tops of the mountains appearing above. Dad's "islands in the sky" had become a visual reality and he was seeing the Adirondack High Peaks like he never had before. He was transfixed by the psychological impact of that vision and grateful for that profound and mystical experience. I believe his greatest climb was a gift from God, and a sign that his mission to protect the peaks had been well accomplished through his research and education efforts—reaching the ultimate expression in the Summit Stewardship Program. His mission now continues in others, guided by the principles he established and lived. As Dad said:

> *What a shame to damage them in our insensitive search for momentary vistas. Let us instead visit them both for their grand scenery and for the insights they provide us into our own natural heritage, then depart gently and leave the alpine landscape intact for our grandchildren in their time to enjoy and to learn. The real challenge is for each of us to transfer our private sense of environmental responsibility to those whom this hour we briefly share a part of God's creation.*

Dad has passed the love of the outdoors through multiple generations of his family. Both my son and my daughter are expert skiiers and have joined me on many mountain adventures in all seasons. Recently my 16-year-old daughter and I climbed 14,265-foot Quandary Peak near our home in Colorado. When in the outdoors, she always wears Dad's heavy leather belt that was passed down to her. That belt has traveled to new summits and even back to Alaska, a place Dad enjoyed immensely.

After an arduous climb in early winter conditions, we made the summit just before our previously set turnaround time. We sheltered against some rocks as the wind howled around us. I turned to her and said, "I'm proud of you!" As she smiled, I heard the echo of my Dad's voice in the wind, saying the same to me, and I knew that his dreams and joys live on in yet another generation of alpinists and summit stewards. As he once said, "I would suggest our surest guarantee for the future lies in the attitude of reverence we instill in our own children, by the example we individually set as stewards of God's creation."

My Father the Renaissance Man

By Susan Ketchledge Mangus, oldest child of Dr. Edwin H. and Jean B. Ketchledge

Because my sister Joan Ketchledge Kogut is seven years younger than me and my brother James Ketchledge is 14 years younger than me, I was able to enjoy life with my parents in their "younger days." I would like to share with you some of those experiences and memories, and especially those with my father.

First and foremost, my father was loved—and not by only us in the family—but by his students, his colleagues at the SUNY College of Environmental Science and Forestry, and by most everyone who met him. He helped students with personal and academic issues, brought many of them home for dinner—we lived only eight blocks from campus—and maintained an interest in many of them and their careers after graduation. Twice that I can remember the students at the College voted to dedicate the annual yearbook to my Dad, over other older or retired faculty members. At the time this was quite remarkable, and I recall the second time it happened the students were asked to revote—that was done and even more voted for Dad!

My Dad took a great interest in what his colleagues were doing, especially any new research, and he was the type of person to be very proud of their accolades and not just his own. He was never a self-centered person, never thought the world revolved around him. He loved it when others succeeded, whether it was us kids or his students or his colleagues. When I started my career as a high school Spanish teacher in central New York State, three men and one woman on the high school faculty were former students of my father. They loved to tell me about their own personal times with my Dad and how much he meant to them even after all the years.

Joan photographs sister Susan and their father Ketch as the three head out, June 1967

My father was a man of honor. He took his personal honor very, very seriously and taught me early on that sometimes you do something only because it is the right thing to do and no other reason. He taught me NOT to go with the crowd but to do the right thing no matter what and damn the consequences if it was the right thing to do.

One of my earliest memories of what an incredible person my Dad was—and I was only a few years old at the time when we were living in California while Dad studied at Stanford University—was of spending a day on the beach along an isolated stretch of the Pacific

Ocean. I was wading in the water when a crab bit my big toe and would not let go. Naturally I screamed and my Dad came running, got the crab off my toe, and then in what was to become typical fashion told me all about crabs and what wonderful creatures they were. I might also add that this knowledge did not prevent him from enjoying a dinner of Alaskan King Crab legs!

I too was taken camping with the family or alone with Dad when I was older. I imagine it was hard for him to slow down his "military trot" through the woods but he did, and always kept up a running commentary about all the flora and fauna around us. Once he pointed out a lovely fern and asked me if I knew the name. I replied that I did not but it was beautiful and I thought it looked just like a Christmas tree. He became very excited, patted me on the back and said that was exactly right—it was the Christmas Tree Fern! He made me feel like I had won the lottery with all the praise. Another time we were walking—at my slow pace—down Mount Marcy when I picked a large blade of grass, put it between my thumbs and blew. I had just recently learned a small child could make a tremendous noise doing that, and I exceeded all expectations with the sound I made. Poor Dad, who was walking ahead of me and had no idea what was about to happen, jumped two feet into the air, whirled around and exclaimed, "What the Hell was that?" He said later he thought the Pterodactyls had reappeared! I was laughing so hard I fell down on my fanny, to think that my little self could get such a reaction out of my Dad.

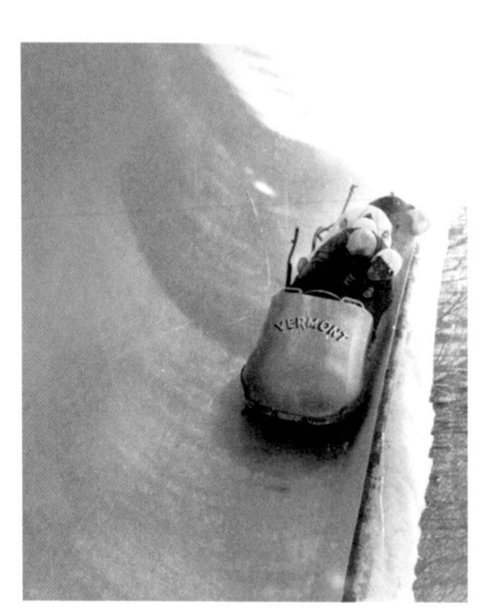

Mt. Van Hoevenberg, Ketch 3rd from front

My Dad and the whole family loved spending summers at the Cranberry Lake Biological Station where he could combine his two loves—teaching and being in the woods/mountains. Back then it was called The College of Forestry Summer Camp and was part of the required curriculum for the students of the then-called College of Forestry, now SUNY ESF. When girls first started appearing in the classes there, it caused quite an uproar in the previously all male camp. The first three girls to attend were housed in tiny rooms below the kitchen. I asked Dad if this was going to work OK, he got an odd almost pained look on his face but then straightened his shoulders and said YES, that there was no reason that "females" could not enter into the forestry world. In later years when I reminded him about that and what he had said, he laughed and admitted to more than a bit of nervousness with this big change and to hoping there would not be any crises. Before too long, girl students were common at the camp, no crisis that I remember had occurred, and Dad thought it was all great. Women's Lib found good support in my father!

I was in my last years of High School and getting ready for college when Dad started everything to do with the Summit Stewardship Program, so I was not involved like my sister and brother were, but I do remember his passion and dismay at the destruction, even if unintended, of this very fragile alpine ecosystem and his determination to save it. The time and effort he spent to get the program running and be self-sustaining was one of the biggest jobs of his life and gave him unbelievable amounts of satisfaction. He felt a great joy of accomplishing an important job well and which would hopefully live on into the future.

It gives me great delight that my sister and brother and the family grandchildren are carrying on with Dad's love of the wilderness and outdoors. I myself enjoy the out-of-doors. Being in the Adirondack Mountains in September/October when the leaves change to their brilliant reds and oranges and yellows is like having one foot in heaven but I love more traveling the cities of Europe where the family's maternal ancestors came from, trying to find "just one more" genealogy record before they disappear.

In the end, my father was a true Renaissance man, a noble man and the kind of person you rarely see these days. His illness and his death were tremendously difficult for me. It is only now, after five years, that I can feel some sort of peace, and the pain has dulled but not disappeared. His passing was a great loss on so many fronts—to the family, to friends and to the world.

An Inherited Passion for the Outdoors

By Joan Ketchledge Kogut, 2nd daughter of Dr. Edwin H. and Jean B. Ketchledge

As a youngster, I was often found scampering along behind my father on numerous hikes and camping trips, following his older students who were more than twice my size. My father's love and passion for the outdoors and particularly the Adirondack Mountains were instilled in me both genetically and by example. I became one of those students myself while attending the SUNY College of Environmental Science and Forestry (ESF), where I met my future husband Ken Kogut during my first month at college and together we continued to follow my father around on his outdoor adventures at college and in the years to come as adults. We were privileged to know many of my father's other undergrad and graduate students who have remained friends and colleagues decades later.

After my father retired from ESF, he and my mother moved up from Syracuse to near us in the Saranac Lake region of the Adirondacks, where Dad could look out at his beloved Whiteface Mountain from the front porch of their house. He spent his retirement years there in perfect contentment, until health concerns prompted a move to the Adirondack foothills in Peru, NY, and lastly to our new home in Potsdam, NY, where he lived out his remaining days and where my mother still lives under our care.

Throughout Ken's and my married life in the Adirondacks and now the St. Lawrence River Valley, our activities have always revolved around our own ongoing passions for the outdoors including hiking, camping, boating, skiing, hunting, fishing and gardening. Dad's legacy lives on in the values and appreciation for the outdoors which he instilled in us as his family and his multitude of students and colleagues over the years and decades.

I'd like to share with you this picture of our son Keith Edwin Kogut, eldest grandson of Edwin and Jean Ketchledge. Keith is shown here on October 18, 2015 with Ketch's old US Army 10th Mountain Division skis. Keith makes it a yearly personal goal to be one of the first skiers up the Whiteface Mountain Veterans Toll Road with his grandfather's skis at the first feasible snowfall of the season. When not skiing, Keith is the Saranac Lake High School Instrumental Music Teacher and Band Director, as well as the high school's Cross Country Ski Coach and active participant in many regional athletic events including Empire State Games ski races, numerous Tupper Lake Tinmans and a qualifier at the Lake Placid Ironman. He embodies his grandfather's passions of both the outdoor wilderness and of teaching; Keith is as comfortable in the Adirondack backwoods and backwaters as he is in the classroom.

Keith Edwin Kogut on Whiteface Road by Wilmington Wall

Ketch doing restoration work on Whiteface
NANCIE BATTAGLIA

Always a Few Steps Behind "Ketch"

By Jamieson R. Steele

Jamieson Steele *was born in Syracuse, NY, and lived in Fayetteville, NY. His youth was entirely about Boy Scouts of America, and he became an Eagle Scout in 1964. Jamieson attended SUNY College of Forestry, now Environmental Science and Forestry, and graduated in 1970 with a B.S. in Forest Botany and a minor in Spanish. Following a brief stint as a police officer, he started a tree and yard care service. In the 1980s, he also became involved with home restoration in the Hawley-Green National Historic District until 2005 when he remarried, and moved to the Ogdensburg area.*

Currently single and living in Dansville, NY, Jamieson is the volunteer collections and display manager at the National Warplane Museum in Geneseo, NY, where he shares his extensive WWII collection. He has, and still serves, with many volunteer, civic groups. His has two children, Andrew and Elizabeth, and Andrew and his wife blessed the family with Adelaide, now 2 1/2.

One of the best examples of everything that can be truly good about a human being was lost with the passing of Dr. Edwin H. Ketchledge on June 30, 2010. That goes for his family and friends, the State University of New York College of Environmental Science and Forestry (ESF) alumni and the natural world.

Thousands of Stumpies were privileged to have Dr. Ketchledge, or "Ketch" as he was fondly known to us, as their professor of Dendrology at our college and summer camp. He followed in the impressive and challenging footsteps of his predecessor, Dr. William M. Harlow, who taught Ketch when he was an undergrad. Ketch quickly fell in pace with those footsteps and gave Dr. Harlow reason for great pride.

To know him as professor was fortunate. To know him as professor, mentor, friend and companion was priceless. I was blessed with that priceless and unforgettable experience.

It all began for me when Boy Scouting peaked my interest and love of nature. The end result was Eagle Scout and a continued thirst for knowledge of the natural world. The College of Forestry, now ESF, was the obvious choice.

Knowing I was admitted to ESF, I borrowed a dendrology book from a neighbor who was an alumnus. That summer before my freshman year I teamed all the trees, including genus and species names. I was ready. Or so I thought, as freshman year was pretty tough.

Sophomore year meant Dendrology and introduction to the man we would call Ketch. We all know the intoxicating essence of his teaching—spellbinding. The magic was how he taught you what each tree was and why it was that tree. A sugar maple was not identified because of the bark or the leaf or the shape or the seed. No, it was a sugar maple because it looked like a sugar maple for all those combined elements. He taught us to see and know the whole tree for all the characteristics.

I did well in Dendro but in little else. All A's with Ketch but many other low C's and D's. Only extra tutoring kept me out of Harry Payne's office. But Ketch noticed my ability to master tree ID in the spirit of the way he taught the course. Except for one small problem. One day after a field quiz—you all remember those ten tree questions—he came over to me and quietly asked where I had learned some of the Latin names of the trees. I told him how I had borrowed the neighbor's Dendro book. I told him it was Kirk Buck's and he said he knew Kirk, another army veteran, from his undergrad days. He just said that some of the species names had changed since then and I should learn the new ones but that he would still give me credit for the old names.

Midway through the second semester Ketch came to me asking if I would like to join him for summer trips into the High Peaks to help him with his erosion and summit vegetation loss studies. Yeah, that took a lot of thought. So, about every other week he would pick me up and we would head into the Adirondacks. I think I even got paid but that was not the benefit.

Our mission was to use a plumb bob and ruler to measure and graph sites for advancing erosion and monitor grids of vegetation for damage or change to various sites. At times we would carry plugs of native grasses to the peaks to restore the summits where excess use had laid the peaks bare. His motive was to convince the state to change the trails to limit erosion and reduce trampling of delicate summit plants. After many years the state did make some major changes and the Summit Stewards were also Ketch's idea. Summit Stewards are folks who climb to the top every day to educate hikers about the fragile alpine plants and their protection. Each trip with Ketch was an exciting adventure, sometimes two peaks a day.

Jim Winterbottom, K-9 unit dog "Monty" and Ketch, 86th Mountain Infantry, Company F at Camp Hale, Colorado

Ketch was a quiet man and when he had something to say it was always worth listening to. That high pitched, soft voice of his was perfect for our High Peaks trips and I learned much. One early, misty morning a White Throated Sparrow was barely four feet from me, singing its familiar song. Quietly Ketch told me the bird's name. I had often heard the song but never had seen the bird. The soft song sounded like Ketch's voice. I've never heard one sing since without thinking of Ketch and that magical moment.

One time we had hiked all day up one of the many mountains and I was bushed. He was always a few steps ahead of me, rarely slowing down. I have done the math; I was about 19 and he would have been about 44 at the time. I could hardly keep up. Same as the Dendro field trips, few could keep up with him.

We began to empty our backpacks to settle in for the night. Earlier I had taken a swig from my canteen and he teased me for lugging that heavy thing along when you could just drink out of a stream. I was embarrassed. Then from his pack out came a six-pack of Utica Club Beer. As he put it into the stream to cool I said, "Hey, Ketch, you teased me about a canteen of water, and here you hauled UC all the way up here!"

He smiled and said to me, "I made a pact with myself years ago that I would enjoy three things with no limit for the rest of my life. They were ice cream, beer and pizza." I think I got one or two of those UCs.

During that memorable summer Ketch asked if I would be interested in being his teaching assistant in Dendrology during the next year. I certainly was but why me, I asked. He said because I knew my trees in the way he liked to teach tree ID, the total tree. Let me just say there were a number of ticked off graduate students when they saw a junior with his own dendro class.

Each Saturday I would meet Ketch at the site of the upcoming week's field trip for the preview. Again, I found myself steps behind him as we moved from tree to tree. However, there were always moments when he would stop and look at some natural beauty or stunning view. Come the labs I would take half the students and he the other. Me a junior, with my own class of sophomores, teaching with Ketch, what a privilege.

Ketch
ADK ARCHIVES

We all saw the railroad tracks of scars and stitches from war wounds on Ketch's back while swimming at summer camp. Ketch told me he felt nothing of being shot, just woke up months later in a hospital in the USA. He was awarded the Bronze Star and Purple Heart, and his uniform is on display at the 10th Mountain Division museum in Colorado.

He kept track ever after of how many days he had lived since being "killed." He lived every day to the fullest. It took years of recovery but he made that pact with himself to live his saved life with a few well-earned perks. One lung or not, a six-pack in his backpack, I still could not keep up with him.

Through his life Ketch was an avid backcountry cross-country skier and particularly loved skiing across the frozen Cranberry Lake in wintertime. In retirement, he skied up Whiteface Mountain Veterans Toll Road whenever possible, as well as many other places, usually accompanied by one of the family's Alaskan Malamutes.

After my graduation we kept in touch, and a number of years ago my wife and I visited him at his Peru, NY, home. He had to move to a lower Adirondack elevation as he had come down with emphysema. He still walked daily, often twice daily. When we visited him I was to take the walk with him but I was late, and he had gone on without me. As always, I was a few steps behind him.

In private he showed me a Bible he had carried in his top left pocket. It had been nicked by the bullet and stained with his blood. What role did it have in saving him will never be known!

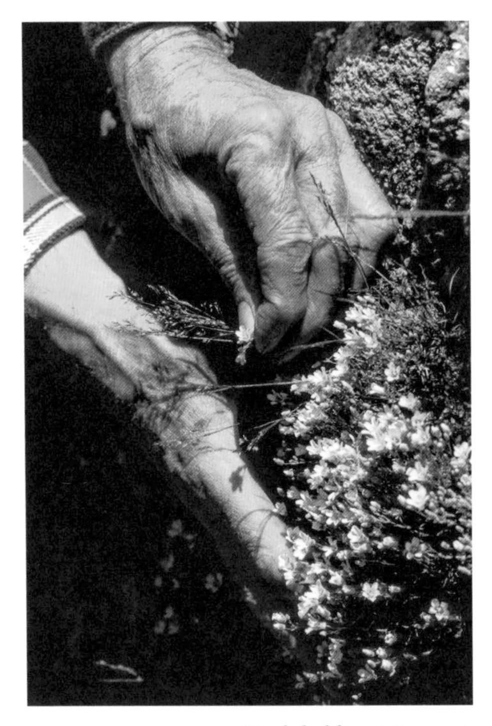

Ketch holding Mountain sandwort, a pioneer species
NANCIE BATTAGLIA

He told me that he thought of his students just as he did of his Army squad, always the best for them. He counted the days of life extended to him and gave that time to us.

He cared not to talk much of the war, as is true with most combat veterans. They will talk of funny or pleasant things. He told me that in Italy one of the nicest sounds in the Italian mountains was the wind in the pine trees. He loved that sound long before he thought about forestry school.

That was the last time I saw him in person. However, his connection to my life was far from over. When I married in 2005, as we had spent Dendrology time in Oakwood, and did volunteer work there, we chose a huge European Beech right behind ESF for the site. My dear friend, Dick Garrett, ESF'59, happened to be a justice of the peace and the knot was tied.

Garrett and I then popped open two frosty Utica Clubs, to toast our wedding, ESF and Dr. Ketchledge. When I called Ketch to tell him of this frivolity I said we got married under a "purple beech." He corrected me, stating the proper name was European Beech. That was the first time I did not get an A in Dendrology.

I have large pines in front of our home and when I hear the wind in them I always think of Ketch. When I saw his death notice I looked at the calendar to see what day that had been. I was working among my pines that day and indeed had paused to think of Ketch, his Italian pines and our wonderful times together. Was he with me to say goodbye? I think so, as I felt something different that day.

A few steps behind Ketch, I remain.

Ketch on Boundary, MacIntyre Range, May 1958

The Four Rewards of Visiting Alpine Summits

By Edwin H. Ketchledge

Boott's rattlesnakeroot

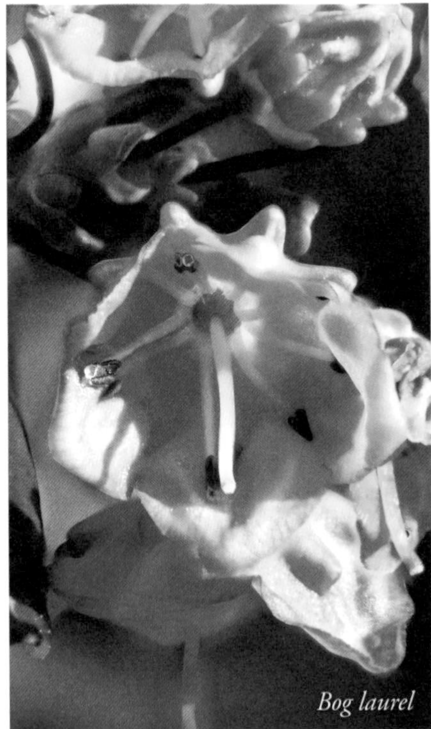
Bog laurel

Mountain honeysuckle

Meadowsweet

BRENDAN WILTSE

A version of this chapter was published in the May-June 1993 edition of ADK's magazine Adirondac.—CBR and AR, Eds.

To some people, climbing up to a high Adirondack summit sounds ridiculous—a lot of hard work just for a pretty view (if you're lucky). Better to go swimming or fishing or hike a lesser trail.

Certainly there are all kinds of things to do in the Adirondack Park. But I would also suggest there are four very real rewards for the perceptive hiker when visiting a High Peak, beyond the mindless "peak bagging" some insensitive critics once claimed such trips to be. I think I've tried most of the usual outdoor sports in the Adirondacks—including competitive bobsledding when I was younger—but none exceeds the lasting rewards you may experience from visiting the open alpine summits. Let me identify the rewards, for such they are, and suggest you may want to pursue the opportunity yourself, if you haven't already.

1. All who climb share the obvious first reward, the physical and emotional satisfaction of accomplishment. "I made it!" Climbing three or four hours is hard for everyone, certainly if you're under 15 or over 50. The climb is like a slow self-imposed marathon, going upward, for only a few miles, yes, but just as demanding of body and soul if you push it. Even though you may momentarily seem near collapse, you experience the intense satisfaction of a goal set and a challenge met. The physiological stress in both cases is similar, since you may reach the limit of your own muscular abilities in both. There is a special exhilaration, though, in a climb because of the constantly changing forests and environments along the way, which provide multiple interests and "stops" to look at the surroundings while you get your breath and learn the nature of Nature.

Most important, when you finally reach the summit, you have arrived at a totally different world from that in which you started, which fact is often psychologically startling and rewarding. You have gone from enclosing woods to vast vistas. You are in a "new place," having conquered the mountain.

Now on the summit, three more rewards may follow if you fully exploit the opportunity.

2. You gain the sensual experience of beautiful scenery and dramatic countryside in every direction, as you stand on the very boundary between sky and earth. The cooling wind in your face seems to transport distant vistas up into close proximity, as if space were erased. With fascinating views in every direction, you feel immersed and intimate with the natural world, a part of nature itself rather than a passive passenger over its surface. Climate and environment become a personal experience, a physical reality.

The cooler temperatures up here tell you this is a northern environment, as if your topographic climb to a higher elevation resembled a geographical trip to a higher latitude, into Newfoundland for example. The brilliance of the sunshine seemingly coming intensely from all directions makes you subconsciously think you are closer to the sun! The sounds here too are different: the absence of gentle echoes from surrounding trees, now left below, tells your ears you are *above* sound, alone but for the steady breeze here on the highest point on the mountain.

And all the while you are bathed in scenery whose reality and vitality exceeds the most beautiful painting or photograph you will ever see, and which seems to give life to the very landscape all about. Tired as your body may be this hour, you won't have many days as satisfying or rewarding as this intimate moment with your homeland, the planet Earth. In the natural world each day is a new celebration of life.

3. On further reflection, as you absorb the scenery, you gain appreciation of times long past, realizing that the dwarfed alpine landscape all around you is a little island relict of arctic tundra, now spatially isolated from the sub-arctic zone of which it was once a part. Here where you now stand, gigantic continental glaciers once towered half a mile high over the Adirondacks. When the glaciers melted northward some 11,000 years ago, forest followed them northward across modern New York State: throughout that entire period, though, arctic-alpine plants and vegetation hung on to these cold and windswept summits with their severe northern climates. The summit zone atop the Adirondacks is thus a living ecological museum of those past times, when vegetation quickly replaced ice as the glaciers melted northward. Those same plants growing around your feet today are both a living and visual link with the silent past, extending back genetically over 10 millennia.

Out of 30 million-plus acres of land in New York State today, only these 85 (173)[1] acres of alpine world on 20 (21)[1] separate summits survive as testimony of the great wave of post-glacial forest migration that once flowed back over this part of the continent long ago. The whole concept of stewardship for our natural inheritance in the Adirondack high country is based on this fact: the high alpine summits with their specialized plants and natural communities

1. Updated figures based on current estimation techniques / GIS.

Cotton grass on Algonquin, with nearby Wright, Heart Lake in the valley and Whiteface gracing the skyline
BRENDAN WILTSE

are surviving museums, a priceless continuum of past times into the modem, a responsibility of ALL visitors to respect during their hour or two witnessing living history.

In effect, the concept of time disappears when thoughtful people on a high summit free their minds momentarily from the dramatic impact of the distant scenery and realize that in truth the surrounding alpine meadow is a continuation of ancient times into this very day. When you reach that understanding, you can also realize why the Adirondack Mountain Club (ADK), The Nature Conservancy (TNC), the New York State Department of Environmental Conservation (DEC) and the Adirondack Forty-Sixers have joined forces to combine their ecological restoration work and to inaugurate the Summit Stewardship education program, to guarantee that heavy public recreational pursuits on the highest summits will not deprive future citizens who walk in our footsteps of *their* right to "touch" glacial history and to personalize their natural heritage atop the high Adirondacks.

Looking towards Boundary and Iroquois from Algonquin, with Santanoni Range in the distance to the right
BRENDAN WILTSE

4. Perhaps most important of all, because an hour or two on a high alpine summit is such an extraordinary psychological and intellectual experience, your visit there is an ideal opportunity to reflect upon the grandeur of the natural world here so vividly expressed and which we individually this hour can silently tune into, to the exclusion of all worldly distractions. There is an inner peace, an harmonic, to be gained in all wilderness experiences everywhere, but none exceed the intensity of contentment, of feeling at-home-at-last, as when quietly witnessing the grandeur of creation from atop a high Adirondack summit. On a clear day every scene is a beautiful and dynamic vignette, a continuing topographic tapestry wherever you turn. Under such vivid conditions, the human spirit soars, and the mind is similarly prone to explore on its own, if we only relax and put immediate concerns away, and enjoy our good fortune—and contemplate—and wonder. And perhaps sense the resonance within. Like many other folks, you may find such unstructured moments the highlight of your trip, the part you remember clearest 20 years from now.

There may be a lasting fifth reward emerging from your sojourn upon the landscape climax of the Adirondack Park: your own stimulated interest in the natural history of the region and your own commitment to protection and preservation of the endangered heritage we enjoy this day. That is why so many of us return to the summits, in all kinds of weather and at all times of the year: our brief and private recreation, reinvigoration, re-affirmation into insights best experienced and studied at those special locations where both our thoughts and consciousness fly with the wind, out over the alpine world, wherever it may take us.

A final note: if you ever hear someone disparagingly refer to climbing as "peak bagging," invite that person to go along with you the next time you climb, and demonstrate the deeper insights and rewards with the summit experience beyond the physical exertion that currently constitutes their limited horizon.

A peek at Wallface from Algonquin, with the Sewards in the distance
BRENDAN WILTSE

Bearberry willow
BRENDAN WILTSE

Vegetation Change in the Adirondack Alpine: Continuing a Legacy of Inquiry and Preservation

By Sean Robinson

Sean Robinson *grew up in Queensbury, NY, and started working for Adirondack Mountain Club in 1992. After working at the Adirondak Loj and Johns Brook Lodge during the summers of 1997 and 1998, he worked as a Summit Steward in 1999 and 2000. He then went on to get his M.S. at SUNY-ESF and his Ph.D. at the University at Albany, specializing in bryology—the study of mosses, liverworts and hornworts.*

In 2010, Sean joined the Biology Department at SUNY Oneonta in Oneonta, NY. He teaches courses in Botany including Bryophyte Biology, Vascular Plant Systematics and Dendrology. His research is focused on understanding how the mode of reproduction in plants, particularly bryophytes, affects colonization of new habitats, range expansions and gene flow within and between island populations. The alpine summits of northeastern North America have been the primary site for his work. Sean also conducts research focused on vegetation dynamics in the Adirondack alpine.

Found primarily on isolated peaks throughout the world's mountain ranges, alpine ecosystems are a small but unique part of the world. Together, land areas that constitute alpine habitat are known as the "alpine zone." Those of us who have been fortunate enough to visit the alpine know the captivating beauty of these regions.

My first encounter with the alpine zone was a hike up Mount Marcy when I was 13 years old. To this day, I remember that experience and the impact it had on me. I remember meeting a young man in uniform who taught me and my companions about the uniqueness of the small plants around us and what we could do to ensure their continued survival. The significance of these summits is something that is difficult to describe. It is something that an individual needs to experience in order to understand the drive that so many of us have to protect them and the organisms that live there.

Seen by many as biotic "museums" frozen in time, the Adirondack alpine zone is in fact an ever changing, dynamic place. Comprised of a number of plant community types, there is no one community in the alpine that can be termed a "climax community." The harsh and variable climatic conditions of the alpine zone do not produce the same linear pattern of succession on all sites. With an extremely irregular microtopography, the alpine zone is a mosaic of various microhabitats, all of which respond differently to changes in temperature, precipitation, snow cover and wind velocity. Each site, therefore, offers a varying set of climatic and physiological conditions that not all plants in the alpine are well adapted for. Consequently, each microhabitat shows a different successional trend resulting in a multitude of possible communities. Furthermore, a sudden disturbance can cause a shift in a successional trend, or a complete reversal to a previous stage by the removal of vegetation and/or soil. These disturbances can range from a sudden change in temperature and/or wind velocity to the damaging footfall of a hiker. It is, therefore, very difficult to define specific, "expected," community types in the alpine zone, where existing communities are the result of successional change, micro-climatic conditions and happenstance (Ketchledge et al. 1985).

Examples of plant growth from 1981 to 2002: A point on Algonquin transect recorded by Ketch as "bare soil" in 1981 that is now occupied by Sphagnum moss.
SEAN ROBINSON

While difficult to define, successional change is an important part of pattern and process in the alpine zone. With a great amount of exposed bedrock, the first organisms on the scene are small lichens, able to colonize this impermeable and nutrient poor Anorthosite surface. Typical northeastern lichen species that are found in great abundance as pioneers in the alpine zone include *Rhizocarpon geographicum* (map lichen), *Arctoparmelia centrifuga* (target lichen) and *Umbilicaria* spp. (rock tripe). These lichens produce acids that, with physical weathering, erode the hard rock surface to form shallow mineral soils. This, with the presence of moisture from clouds, precipitation and nighttime condensation,

Cotton grass on Boundary
JULIA GOREN

provides a suitable microclimate for the introduction of mosses. Dark colored cushion mosses like *Andreaea rupestris, Racomitrium* spp. and *Grimmia* spp. colonize shallow cracks and the periphery of exposed rock where weathered material collects and foot traffic is minimal. These mosses help to form a more substantial, organic-rich soil layer in shallow depressions by capturing and depositing airborne particles, in addition to their own decomposition. With a more ample and consistent moisture supply, more mosses are able to colonize these rock depressions, including Sphagnum mosses such as *Sphagnum pylaesii, S. fuscum* and *S. magellanicum*, creating a thick, moist mat of moss. This "Sphagnum matrix" is able to hold up to 10 times its own weight in water, thereby creating a bog-like microhabitat. This new microhabitat provides sufficient moisture as well as a thick stable network where herbaceous and woody plants can establish and grow. Slowly, plants such as *Vaccinium oxycoccos* (wren's-egg cranberry), *Kalmia polifolia* (bog-laurel), *Kalmia angustifolia* (sheep laurel) and *Eriophorum spissum* (cotton grass) appear. This is followed by the establishment of woody shrubs and heath species, whose tangled root network stabilizes the *Sphagnum* mats against the adverse effects of wind and water erosion. *Empetrum nigrum* (black crowberry), with its long thin branches, creeps along the ground, spreading over surrounding rock, accompanied by the emergence of *Vaccinium* spp. such as *Vaccinium uliginosum* (bog bilberry). The establishment of heath species is sometimes followed by the arrival of willow and birch species such as *Salix uva-ursi* (bearberry willow) and *Betula glandulosa* (American dwarf birch). By providing shaded protection, this heath-dwarf tree community facilitates the growth of boreal mosses like *Pleurozium schreberi*. These mosses, in turn, help to stabilize the community by aiding in moisture retention and soil collection.

Where deep soils collect in protected areas, larger dwarf tree communities develop including *Abies balsamea* (balsam fir) and *Picea mariana* (black spruce). These clusters of spruce and fir also facilitate the growth of various boreal moss species as well as herbaceous plants, creating island-like patches of "miniature" spruce-fir forests throughout the alpine zone. Gradually, these heath-dwarf forest communities will dominate much of the alpine. However, grasses and sedges, such

Sean and Lyndsie Robinson sampling transect #3 on Wright
SEAN AND LYNDSIE ROBINSON

Ketch on Whiteface with Lake Placid in background, 1991
NANCIE BATTAGLIA

as *Carex bigelowii* (bigelow's sedge), will also colonize the "*Sphagnum matrix*" and dominate whole areas with only a few heath and dwarf tree species present, creating a mosaic of meadowlands and small heath communities.

A smaller community type found in these more moist sites is the snowbank community. These communities form in areas where thick layers of snow accumulate in deep, protected depressions, offering thermal protection in the winter and more than sufficient amounts of water in the spring after snowmelt. Species typically found in these communities range from various alpine species to species that can be found at lower elevations, such as *Clintonia borealis* (blue-bead lily), *Veratrum viride* (false hellebore), *Cornus Canadensis* (bunchberry), *Trientalis borealis* (starflower) and *Gentiana linearis* (narrow-leaved gentian).

In drier, well-drained parts of the alpine zone, where greater exposure to wind and water erosion does not permit the growth of large *Sphagnum* mats, a coarse mineral soil remains. Consequently, a slightly different successional pattern develops. Whereas cushion mosses and *Sphagnum* pioneer moist areas, *Minuartia groenlandica* (mountain sandwort), a small white flowered plant with a cushion-like growth, pioneers dry areas. Gradually, other plants adapted to this drier microclimate such as *Sibbaldiopsis tridentata* (three-toothed cinquefoil) and *Trichophorum cespitosum* (deer's hair sedge) establish. *Diapensia lapponica* (pincushion plant) appears later, growing in dense domes, sometimes providing a favorable environment for the establishment and growth of other plants.

The need to better understand the dynamics of these plant communities and document overall changes in plant species composition and cover due to natural processes and

Labrador tea
Lapland rosebay
Clubmoss
Alpine goldenrod
Sundew
Diapensia
Alpine sweetgrass
Bog bilberry

BRENDAN WILTSE

anthropogenic impacts inspired Dr. Edwin ("Ketch") Ketchledge of SUNY-ESF to begin performing studies on the vegetation of the Adirondack alpine summits. In 1972, under Ketch's guidance, Michael G. DiNunzio, a master's student at SUNY-ESF, determined the extent of alpine vegetation in the Adirondacks as well as the composition and abundance of the species that characterized it. By mapping the area above treeline on all exposed summits, DiNunzio determined the area of each alpine summit, the percent cover of vegetated area and estimates of percent cover for each plant species he encountered (DiNunzio 1972). In order to assess changes in the vegetation over time, Ketch, along with Brian Fitzgerald, established eleven permanent line transects in the alpine zone of the MacIntyre Range in 1984. Three transects each were established on Wright, Algonquin and Iroquois, and two were established on Boundary Peak. Each transect was subjectively placed to encompass a variety of environmental conditions and vegetative community types. In 1984 and 1994, Ketch and Brian traversed each one, determining the percent occurrence of each species and substrate type encountered. In addition, in 1981, Ketch resampled a transect established on Mount Marcy in 1957 by Howard E. Woodin, a former Professor of Botany at Middlebury College.

I began working for the Adirondack Mountain Club (ADK) in the fall of 1992 stuffing maps in the back of guidebooks at the headquarters in Lake George, NY. After spending the next eight years working for ADK, including two years as a Summit Steward in 1999 and 2000, my love and obsession of the alpine grew to the point that I made the decision to devote my life to understanding its intricate nature and the plants that grow there, particularly the beautiful and captivating bryophytes (mosses and liverworts). Consequently, in 2001, I contacted Ketch to ask if I could resample his MacIntyre transects as part of my Master's thesis at SUNY-ESF. He invited me, and my current advisor, Dr. Dudley Raynal, to his house that fall. After discussing my proposal, Ketch reached down and handed me a box and asked that I take care of its contents. Inside were a number of files containing data he had collected on the Adirondack summits over the last several decades, including his transect data. As a young inexperienced graduate student, the responsibility I felt to carry out his wishes was immense. A man for whom I had tremendous respect and admiration had just shown me incredible generosity and, with one act, had set the course of my professional life.

Deer's hair sedge
BRENDAN WILTSE

In the summer of 2002, I resampled the MacIntyre transects for my thesis. After graduating in 2004, I resampled the transects in 2007 and 2012. In 2009, I resampled the transect on Mount Marcy. While there has been little overall change in the frequency/cover of vegetation along these transects, we have been able to document significant changes in the composition of species (Robinson et al. 2010). In some instances, we have seen an increase in woody shrubs while at other sites we have seen increases in grasses and sedges. A point-by-point comparison of data points along all transects has also revealed the replacement of bare soil and bryophytes by vascular plants, providing evidence that the vegetation is recovering. Most important, areas that had been severely disturbed by hiker traffic in the 1980s and early 1990s showed substantial recolonization by bryophytes and pioneering vascular plants in the 2000s. This, I feel, is evidence of the positive impact the Summit Stewardship Program has had since its inception in 1989. By simply informing the public and teaching them to care for the unique plants of the alpine, Adirondack Summit Stewards are without a doubt having a positive impact on the preservation of our alpine summits.

My last correspondence with Ketch, before he passed in June 2010, regarding the most recent publication of our transect data, included the following letter:

> *Sean – Your document certifies the worth of what I struggled so hard to start so long ago. It brings new life to the cause that drove my life.*
>
> *Reading your report, I re-lived my own efforts on that marvelous world that still reverberates within my "spirit person," which will last long after my physical person returns to "physical." My work and your work testifies to the worth of us two at different times. "Cause" is what lasts beyond our brief "presence." I treasure your document as proof of my work.—Ketch*

This letter currently hangs framed on my office wall as a daily reminder of the legacy Ketch started and the responsibility we all have to protect the alpine summits. It is my plan to continue Ketch's transect work until my legs become too frail and tired to carry me to the summits, at which point it will be my turn to hand the responsibility off to another young person to maintain Ketch's goal of Adirondack alpine preservation.

References:

DiNunzio, M. G. 1972. A Vegetational Survey of the Alpine Zone of the Adirondack Mountains, New York [Masters Thesis]. Syracuse (NY): State University of New York College of Environmental Science and Forestry. 110 p.

Ketchledge, E. H., N. A. Richards, P. F. Craul, and A. R. Eschner. 1985. Rehabilitation of alpine vegetation in the Adirondack Mountains of New York State. USDA Forest Service Research Paper NE- United States, Northeastern Forest Experiment Station. 6p.

Robinson, S. C., E. H. Ketchledge, B. T. Fitzgerald, D. J. Raynal, R. W. Kimmerer. 2010. A 23-year assessment of vegetation composition and change in the Adirondack alpine zone, New York State. Rhodora 112: 355–377.

George, James and Bob Marshall in 1939, shortly before Bob's death at age 38
COURTESY OF STEPHEN SCHOLLE

Bob Marshall: Wilderness Advocate

By Phil Brown

Phil Brown *is the editor of the* Adirondack Explorer, *a newsmagazine with a strong interest in outdoor recreation and wilderness preservation, and the founder of Lost Pond Press. In partnership with the Adirondack Council, he published* Bob Marshall in the Adirondacks: Writings of a Pioneering Peak-Bagger, Pond-Hopper and Wilderness Preservationist. *The book collects nearly 40 of Marshall's Adirondack writings and contains more than 60 photos, many taken of or by Marshall. Brown also is the author of* Adirondack Paddling: 60 Great Flatwater Adventures, *co-published with the Adirondack Mountain Club. For more information, visit* ***AdirondackExplorer.org*** *and* ***LostPondPress.com.***

Adirondack history is full of colorful characters: Noah John Rondeau, the hermit of Cold River; Verplanck Colvin, the indefatigable 19th-century surveyor; Old Mountain Phelps, the sage of the High Peaks, and Apollos "Paul" Smith, the backcountry businessman.

But few have been as influential as Bob Marshall, the legendary hiker and wilderness crusader.

Marshall left his name all over the map. You can't become an Adirondack Forty-Sixer without climbing 4,360-foot Mount Marshall, and if you do much hiking in the Rockies, you're sure to hear about the Bob Marshall Wilderness, which encompasses more than a million acres in Montana. South Dakotans send 4-H youth to Camp Bob Marshall in the Black Hills. And nestled in the Brooks Range of Alaska, north of the Arctic Circle, is a little jewel known as Marshall Lake.

We're not done yet. The Adirondack Council is pushing the state to create a 409,000-acre Bob Marshall Great Wilderness near Cranberry Lake in the western Adirondacks. The Bob, as it's called, would be by far the largest Wilderness Area in the Adirondack Park.

So who was this guy to deserve so many topographical tributes?

Bob Marshall was born in New York City on January 2, 1901, the third of four children of Louis and Florence Marshall, both of whom were the offspring of German-Jewish immigrants. Louis Marshall was one of the most successful lawyers of his time, appearing many times before the U.S. Supreme Court.

Louis Marshall also loved the Adirondacks. At the 1894 state constitutional convention, he helped secure passage of the clause now known as Article 14, which mandates that state lands in the Adirondack and Catskill Parks "shall be forever kept as wild forest lands," making them among the most protected lands on the planet. He also played an important role in establishing the state College of Forestry in Syracuse, which is now the College of Environmental Science and Forestry.

In 1900, Louis Marshall and friends purchased land on Lower Saranac Lake, where they built six summer camps, dubbing the compound Knollwood. Bob Marshall, though he grew up in New York City, spent every summer of his boyhood at Knollwood. This was his introduction to the Adirondacks and to the joys of wilderness.

Among Adirondack hikers, Marshall is celebrated as the original Forty-Sixer—the first to climb all 46 of the region's peaks above 4,000 feet. He was joined in this feat by his younger brother, George, and their guide, Herb Clark. Their first High Peak was Whiteface Mountain, which they climbed on August 1, 1918, after crossing Lake Placid by motorboat. They completed the 46 with an ascent of Mount Emmons, in the remote Seward Range, on June 10, 1925. It's worth noting that the three climbed MacNaughton Mountain a few days later. Although not on the Forty-Sixer list, MacNaughton was later found to top 4,000 feet, and so many people feel compelled to climb it as well. That means the Marshalls and Clark were not only the first Adirondack Forty-Sixers; they were the first Forty-Seveners.

Marshall and Clark on Rocky Peak Ridge
COURTESY OF SARANAC LAKE LIBRARY

When the Marshalls began their quest, they thought there were only 42 High Peaks above 4,000 feet. After climbing these, Bob wrote a booklet called *The High Peaks of the Adirondacks,* which the fledgling Adirondack Mountain Club published in 1922. The booklet notes that most of the peaks lacked trails and had rarely, if ever, been climbed before. Marshall's favorite peak was Haystack, which sits across Panther Gorge from Mount Marcy, the state's highest summit. "It's a great thing these days to leave civilization for a while and return to nature," he wrote. "From Haystack you can look over thousands and thousands of acres, unblemished by the works of man, perfect as made by nature."

Later surveys revealed that four of Marshall's 46 are below 4,000 feet, but the Forty-Sixers still cleave to the original list. In the decade after 1925, only two people followed in the footsteps of the Marshalls and Clark. Since then, climbing the 46 has become an Adirondack tradition. As of 2016, nearly 9,500 hikers had done it. Nowadays, hikers can follow marked trails or herd paths to all the summits.

Marshall did not limit his explorations to mountains. In 1920, he had enrolled in the state College of Forestry, the school his father helped found. After his sophomore year, he spent the summer at the college's forestry camp on Cranberry Lake. On weekends, he headed into the woods, often on his own, and wrote detailed accounts of his adventures. His goal was to visit as many ponds as possible. In all, he visited 94 ponds, and just as with the High Peaks, he ranked them all for their beauty.

He graduated in 1924, fourth in a class of 59. The next year, the *Journal of Forestry* published his first article in defense of wilderness, *Recreational Limitations to Silviculture in the Adirondacks.* Whereas most foresters saw the woods as a source of timber, Marshall saw them as a recreational resource that ought to be protected. He likened a virgin forest to a museum, noting that society spends vast sums on museums and parks. "But there never was a museum that had a more interesting exhibit than this last remnant of the woods that were, nor a park that could compare with them in beauty." This is a theme he developed and refined in later writings, culminating in *The Problem of the Wilderness*, his most famous article in favor of preservation.

Marshall went on to earn a Master's degree in forestry from Harvard and a doctorate in plant physiology from Johns Hopkins University. He worked, at different times, for the U.S. Forest Service and the Bureau of Indian Affairs. In both agencies, he pushed for the preservation of wilderness. In 1932, for example, he compiled a list of 38 large roadless areas that he thought should be protected in their primitive state. When this inventory was updated four years later, it included three tracts in the Adirondacks: the High Peaks, the Cranberry Lake region and the West Canada Lakes region. As a result of Marshall's work, the federal government put more of its forestlands off limits to exploitation.

In 1929, Marshall took the first of four trips to Wiseman, Alaska, a tiny prospecting community north of the Arctic Circle. The ostensible reason for the trip was to study the rate of tree growth at the northern timberline but the real reason was to find adventure. During his two-month stay, he explored the uncharted Brooks Range. He returned to Wiseman the following summer and stayed for a year. Out of this visit came his best-selling book, *Arctic Village*, a sociological portrait of the frontier community.

Bob Marshall on Wright
COURTESY OF ROGER MARSHALL

Marshall shared the royalties from *Arctic Village*, which was a Literary Guild selection, with the residents of Wiseman. In 1934, he published his second book, *The People's Forests*, where he argued that the federal government should nationalize timberlands to save them from the predations of corporate logging. In a chapter titled "Forests and Human Happiness," he made a case for preserving woodlands to provide people an escape from a crowded, mechanized world. In his view, the forest offered "the highest type of recreational and esthetic enjoyment."

After his second visit to Wiseman, Marshall returned to the Adirondacks and set a record (later broken) by climbing 13 High Peaks and one lesser summit in a single day, ascending 13,600 feet. It was just one of numerous long hikes Marshall undertook during his lifetime. In a remarkable coincidence, he met another ardent advocate of wilderness, Paul Schaefer, on top of Mount Marcy that day. Schaefer happened to be taking photographs to use in a campaign against an amendment to the state constitution that would have allowed the

Howard Zahniser at Hanging Spear Falls
PAUL SCHAEFER

construction of cabins in the Forest Preserve. Upon learning of the proposed amendment, Marshall became incensed and started pacing back and forth. "We simply must band together," he told Schaefer, "all of us who love the wilderness."

A few years later, Marshall and several colleagues formed the Wilderness Society, which became one of the nation's most effective voices for preservation. Long after Marshall's death, the Wilderness Society's executive secretary, Howard Zahniser, wrote the Wilderness Act, which President Lyndon Johnson signed into law in 1964. Zahniser, who worked on the law at his Adirondack cabin, defined wilderness as "an area where the earth and its community of life are untrammeled by man, where man himself is a visitor who does not remain." This is the same definition found in the Adirondack Park State Land Master Plan. So we have come full circle: The Adirondacks inspired Bob Marshall, who founded the Wilderness Society, which hired Howard Zahniser, who wrote the definition of wilderness now used to protect the Adirondacks.

The founders of the Wilderness Society regarded the construction of roads as one of the biggest threats to wild lands and resisted calls to open up wilderness to the motoring public. In Marshall's view, once a road is built through a wilderness area, it ceases to be a wilderness area.

When the state Conservation Department proposed constructing truck trails in the Forest Preserve, in order to speed access to forest fires in the interior, Marshall argued against the idea. He lost the debate, and the truck trails were built (today they are used as hiking trails). In an article written circa 1936 but published posthumously, he expresses dismay at seeing the truck trail along Calkins Creek near the Seward Range, where he had hiked and camped as a young man. "The tire tracks which blot out the footprints of the deer seem to symbolize the twentieth century, which has come to steal from the primeval one of its last remaining interests."

Marshall returned to Wiseman in 1938 and again in 1939. On both trips, he tried but failed to climb 7,547-foot Mount Doonerak, which he believed to be the highest peak in the Brooks Range. He did manage to get to the top of North Doonerak, where a photo was taken of him standing on the summit, surveying one of the world's wildest landscapes.

On November 10, 1939, Marshall boarded a train in Washington, D.C., and headed to New York City to visit relatives. He was found dead in his sleeper car the next morning, apparently of heart failure. He was 38. The death of such a young man, especially one as vigorous as Bob, shocked all who knew him. The next year the federal government designated the Bob Marshall Wilderness in his honor.

A bachelor, Marshall divvied up virtually all of his $1.5 million estate to three causes dear to his heart: socialism, civil liberties and wilderness preservation. He left money to only one individual: $10,000 to his old friend and guide, Herb Clark. To the rest of us, he bequeathed an enthusiasm for wilderness that continues to inspire hikers and conservationists around the world.

In August 2007, a shorter version of this chapter was published in *The Conservationist*, the outdoor magazine of the New York State Department of Environmental Conservation.

Author with Ranger Pete Fish on Marcy, 1995
COURTESY OF TIM BARNETT

The Conservation Basis of the Summit Stewards: Then and Now

By Tim Barnett

In his 44th year of working in Adirondack conservation, **Tim Barnett** *is The Nature Conservancy's longest-serving staffer—anywhere in the world. He is a vice president of The Nature Conservancy, and manages special projects and is Legacy Club ambassador for the Adirondack Chapter. Tim grew up in Westport, in the Champlain Valley, and was the Adirondack Chapter's first executive director, 1972–1997. He was executive director of the Adirondack Land Trust from 1988 to 1997. He often says that his greatest contribution is the people he's hired and encouraged throughout their careers.*

In thinking back to the origins of the Adirondack Summit Stewards, what stood out to me at the time was the fact that the Adirondack alpine was unique. What stands out to me nearly three decades later is how many people helped make the program a success.

I was executive director of The Nature Conservancy's Adirondack Chapter, and the Conservancy was interested in superlatives. In the 1980s our goal was to protect "the last of the least and the best of the rest." The Adirondacks was considered a cold, not-very-diverse habitat. But New York's rare alpine plants, found on only 173 acres spread across our 21 highest mountaintops, fell into the "last of the least" part of the mantra. Today we have discovered that "the best of the rest" is what makes the Adirondacks globally important. We no longer measure success by the number of rare plants we protect; instead, we try to conserve the integrity of whole landscapes, and it turns out that the Summit Stewardship Program is playing a key part in that as well.

New NASA land-cover imagery is providing the most refined picture ever of the Earth's ecosystems and land-use patterns. Temperate forests of mixed broadleaf and coniferous trees once encircled the Earth in a band between tropical and boreal forests, which is also where most of the world's people live. Consequently, little of this original habitat remains intact. But among the three largest and least-disturbed remnants in the world is the Adirondack Park, from just 100 feet above sea level at the shore of Lake Champlain all the way up to the mile-high summit of Mount Marcy.

In the late 1980s, Kathy Regan joined the Adirondack Chapter staff as director of science and stewardship. From her time as a student at the University of Vermont, she was familiar with a relatively new concept in the Green Mountains of deploying educators to the summits to teach hikers how their actions can help protect the habitat. She recognized how rare alpine ecosystems were in New York and was surprised there was not a similar program here.

Author by seasonal waterfall, Chapel Pond, 2004
MARK BOWIE

At the same time, Dr. Edwin H. Ketchledge was on our board. He and colleagues from the State University of New York College of Environmental Science and Forestry had demonstrated that restoration of alpine habitat was possible. They stabilized one-meter soil plots atop the High Peaks and re-established vegetation over several years. Ketch and Kathy helped our board and staff understand that it was possible to protect the larger alpine tundra zone. All we had to do was get the message to hikers to tread on the bedrock, not on the plants.

In 1989 we met with the New York State Department of Environmental Conservation (DEC) and the Adirondack Mountain Club (ADK) at the club's Adirondak Loj. Tom Wahl represented DEC, Neil Woodworth and Willie Janeway, ADK. Ketch presented his research and also represented the Adirondack 46ers. We discussed the model of stewardship in the mountains of Vermont. We all agreed we needed to do something similar to save the last 173 acres of alpine habitat in New York State.

We went around the table and talked about how an Adirondack Summit Stewardship Program would work. ADK offered to provide logistical support and living space for stewards. DEC would be able to provide equipment, including radios that were so big they were called lunchboxes. But neither organization was able to provide financial support. So the Conservancy offered to pay for the program as well as guide the science behind it. Since then the organizations have taken turns providing support in different ways. And now other groups and individuals are working to ensure that the Summit Stewards have a reliable base of funding in the future.

It was always fun to take a field trip to visit the Summit Stewards at work. One time John Sawhill, president of The Nature Conservancy, accompanied me to see the program in action. As we were preparing to hike in from Adirondak Loj I introduced him to the Forest Ranger Peter Fish. Peter looked at John and said, "Dressed like that, you're gonna die." John had on jeans and a flannel shirt.

When we got to timberline, it was completely socked in and bitterly cold, so my friend Bob Wagner, my cousin Ralph Harbison and I reached into our packs and gave John a parka, gloves and hat. We got up to the summit of Algonquin, and the steward was wearing every stich of clothing he owned.

Looking north and east from Marcy
CARL HEILMAN II

Many of those hardy early stewards returned to help train their successors, which brings me back to the people who played key early roles. Peter Zika, Kathy Regan's classmate from UVM and then a botanist with the New York Natural Heritage Program, helped shape the program and also took gorgeous photographs that helped people appreciate the diminutive beauty of mountain plants. Vinny McClelland at the Mountaineer and others got corporate sponsors to donate clothing, boots, tents and other gear. Ray Curran, chief scientist with the Adirondack Park Agency, and botanists Nancy Slack and Allison Bell

Bigelow's sedge, Deer's hair sedge and Northern bentgrass on Algonquin
NANCIE BATTAGLIA

helped train stewards in field ecology. DEC strengthened its role every year, and the Forest Rangers were always a resource. In addition to Ketch and Kathy Regan, Ranger Fish would later be honored with the Guy Waterman Alpine Steward Award, given annually to people who have demonstrated a long-term commitment to protecting the physical and spiritual qualities of the Northeast's mountain wilderness.

It was an incredible team effort. They all built something that can last forever, and that's why the movement to build an endowment today is so important. Summit protection is a never-ending project.

The stewards' photographs and data across three decades say it all: we are witnessing a recovery of a very special ecosystem. Being able to track changes in a well-documented and relatively undisturbed habitat is as valuable as the stewards' educational outreach to hikers. And despite temperature projections, indications so far are that the benefits are enduring—that this work has given the Adirondack alpine a real chance at long-term resilience.

Closed gentian, Rocky Peak Ridge
NANCIE BATTAGLIA

The Beginning of the Summit Stewardship Program

By Kathy Regan

Kathy Regan *is the Deputy Director for Planning at the Adirondack Park Agency (APA). Her responsibilities include overall direction and administration of state land policy issues and local government services at the Agency. The Planning Division at the Agency is also responsible for GIS services and coordination with Department of Environmental Conservation on implementation of the State Land Master Plan and development of Unit Management Plans for Forest Preserve lands. Kathy received her undergraduate degree in Botany from the University of Vermont and her Master of Science, also in Botany, from Miami University (Ohio).*

Kathy's work experience began with The Nature Conservancy (TNC) at the Pennsylvania Natural Heritage Program. She also worked at TNC's Worldwide office in Arlington, VA, before transferring to the Adirondack Chapter in 1989. There she developed and implemented their Science and Stewardship program, including the Summit Stewardship Program. In 2007, Kathy was contracted by the APA as a Project Coordinator for an Environmental Protection Agency (EPA) Wetland Demonstration Program. In 2008, Kathy joined the APA staff in their Planning Division as a Natural Resource Planner. Kathy was promoted to the position of Deputy Director, Planning in September 2014.

The Nature Conservancy (TNC) proposed creating the Summit Stewardship Program in December 1989. Peter Zika, botanist for the New York Natural Heritage Program, and I, the director of science and stewardship for the Adirondack Chapter of TNC, were both graduates of the University of Vermont and were familiar with a similar program in Vermont—the Ranger/Naturalist Program. In fact, Peter had spent one summer working as a Ranger/Naturalist in Vermont. We had both just started working for TNC in New York and were aware of just how rare alpine habitat was in our state. We were surprised New York didn't have a similar program. When we asked why, we were told that the alpine zone was already protected by virtue of state ownership. We eventually managed to convince people that land acquisition does not equate to species and habitat protection.

Early in this process we started working with Dr. Edwin Ketchledge. Ketch had been trying for years to get the Department of Environmental Conservation (DEC) to develop this type of program but he was told that money was not available. Ketch was a 46er and a member of the Adirondack Mountain Club (ADK). ADK was brought into these discussions early and became a critical partner.

Kathy Regan and Ketch
COURTESY OF KATHY REGAN

The program was developed rather quickly and launched in the summer of 1990. TNC paid for the program, ADK employed the stewards as part of their staff and based them at the Adirondak Loj at Heart Lake. DEC contributed uniforms, radios and the support of the forest rangers. Ketch did not favor the "Ranger/Naturalist" designation because he didn't want the stewards to have any enforcement responsibilities. He wanted them to be educators. Although not thrilled with the name "Summit Steward," he accepted it for lack of a better alternative. We did, however, agree that the stewards would be strictly educators.

The first season we hired two stewards. They worked a five-day week, alternating between Marcy and Algonquin, two of the most visited Adirondack summits. We placed the stewards here in hopes that they would teach the public—many people were hiking their first High Peak—a new ethic which could be taken with them on future climbs.

The first season went pretty well. The stewards kept data on how many people they talked to and we managed to get a fair amount of press. These articles helped spread the new hiking ethic and draw support from additional constituents.

As the years passed we managed to improve the program, hire more stewards, expand our coverage to seven days a week and add additional peaks. The money was generated from grants and private contributions. We were able to obtain equipment donated from The Mountaineer, Campmor and others as the program developed.

Some key aspects of the program included empowering individuals by showing them that they can make a difference, keeping the stewards as educators and never assuming that hikers would know they weren't supposed to walk on the alpine vegetation. We didn't criticize hikers for doing something wrong. We taught them what they could do right and that they could pass that ethic along to others and use it the NEXT time they were on a summit.

It was critical to review the program annually, to take new ideas seriously and to always assume there was room for improvement.

Further changes were made over the years. In addition to educating the public, the stewards became involved with light trail work—building cairns and scree walls—which helped speed up the restoration of certain areas. When we ran out of rocks, we placed a pile of rocks at the trailhead and asked hikers to carry a small rock to the summit. And they did! Doing so vested them in the program—they wanted to understand why they had just carried a rock to the summit and what more they could do to help preserve the alpine.

Summit Stewards Al Nejmeh (plaid jacket above) and Alix Cleveland (far left) on Marcy, 1990.
NANCIE BATTAGLIA

The stewards themselves also became vested in the program. Stewards would return for multiple seasons—although I encouraged them to limit themselves to two seasons to save their knees. Stewards would also return to volunteer as trainers, substitutes and to provide additional coverage during busy holiday weekends.

Alpine botanist Matt Scott was hired in 1999 to establish a photo-point monitoring program to document the health of alpine communities and to help gauge the program's effectiveness. Working with Ketch, Scott selected sites from Ketch's slides taken in the 1960s, 70s, 80s and 90s, and recorded their locations using GPS. This enabled Scott to have photo-points that showed a difference of up to 40 years in certain locations. What surprised me was just how fast the alpine meadows were recovering, simply by keeping people from walking on the vegetation. With the short growing season on our summits, I didn't expect to see that much improvement in my own lifetime! The stewards started showing hikers laminated cards with before/after pictures to emphasize how they could make a difference with a simple change in behavior.

I left TNC in 2003 with the program still running strong. It was hard to walk away from a program I had become so emotionally vested in but it was also time for new ideas. The connections I made with the talented people and members of other organizations remain strong.

Seth Jones summit stewarding on Algonquin
ADK ARCHIVES

The Summit Stewards and the Future of New York State's Alpine Ecosystem

By Julia Goren

Julia Goren *is an avid hiker, an alpine plant enthusiast, an Adirondack 46er, coordinator of the Adirondack High Peaks Summit Stewardship program, and Education Director for Adirondack Mountain Club. Julia has been with the Summit Stewardship program since 2006, first as Botany Steward and later as the program's first full-time coordinator. She received her M.S. in Environmental Studies from Antioch University and her B.A. in Medieval History from Williams College. Julia considers herself supremely lucky to call the Adirondacks her home and the High Peaks her office.*

ALL PHOTOGRAPHS IN THIS CHAPTER FROM ADK ARCHIVES, EXCEPT AS NOTED

The Adirondack High Peaks Summit Stewardship Program protects New York State's alpine habitat through education, research and trail work. Our job is to talk to hikers up on the highest peaks in the Adirondacks. We ask them to join in the effort to protect some of New York State's rarest plants by walking on the rocks, rather than on the fragile plants. We also complete trail work projects, preventing soil erosion by packing sensitive areas with rocks, creating scree walls to help remind hikers where to walk and where not to walk, filling trampled areas with dead brush to aid in the restoration process, and maintaining the cairns that mark the trail above treeline. Additionally, we do research to help expand our understanding of the alpine ecosystem and its recovery from human trampling.

The Summit Stewardship Program is a partnership of the Adirondack Mountain Club, The Adirondack Chapter of The Nature Conservancy and the New York State Department of Environmental Conservation. The program was created at the initiative of Dr. Edwin "Ketch" Ketchledge, botanist, hiker, scientist and steward. Collectively, in the twenty-six years of the program, Summit Stewards have spoken with over 410,000 hikers on the summits of Mount Marcy, Algonquin Peak, Wright Peak, Mount Colden, Cascade Mountain, and the fifteen other High Peaks that host alpine vegetation. One hundred and twenty-one different individuals have worn the Summit Steward uniform, either as part of the paid crew or as volunteers. We continue the work that Ketch started—that of preserving the last vestige of New York State's alpine heritage.

My first day on the peaks as a Summit Steward was on a cold, wet day in mid-May 2006. The winds were strong enough to make it hard to stand upright, and the rain quickly soaked through every layer of clothing I had, drenching me to the skin. It was about 38 degrees, and I felt as though I was taking a cold shower inside a freezer with a fan blowing. Rain turned to sleet, sleet to snow. Everything that was wet froze. My healthy lunch of carrot sticks turned into an unappetizing, frozen, tooth-breaking mass. I was cold, I was wet, I was miserable. I huddled under a rock to ward off hypothermia. I saw one group of very cold Boy Scouts that day on Algonquin; they barely stopped at the summit and thought I was crazy to be there in such conditions—I did too! I kept thinking, "What am I doing? What was I thinking? I can't spend a summer doing this!"

Not an auspicious start to a new job

Ask any Summit Steward, and they'll have a similar tale of misery and doubts about their sanity. If it's not the drenching rain and bitter winds, then it's the ferocious black flies. If not insects, it's the soggy boots that induce mold on socks and even feet. Or chronic blisters that require moleskin and duct tape every single day for three months. Or the pack rash that makes every second of wearing a pack, a shirt—anything—pure agony. Or knees that swelled to the size of grapefruits for the entire month of August because of the repeated pounding up and down the trails. Oh, it's rewarding work, too—we get to

Botany steward Patrick Murphy on Iroquois

enjoy many beautiful days of sunshine, breath-taking views from the highest of the High Peaks, glorious sunrises and sunsets, and interesting conversations with people of all ages and walks of life. But make no mistake: with the elements and the physical demands of the job, summit stewarding is not for the faint of heart. So why do we do it? Even more important, why do Summit Stewards love it?

For me, part of the answer to why I love it lies at my feet. Tiny alpine plants, relics of the last period of glaciation, continue to thrive in the harsh conditions that are our Adirondack High Peaks. They've been clinging to life on the summits since before humans inhabited the Adirondacks, and they're perfectly adapted for the harsh conditions that had me shivering on that day in May. From these alpine plants I have learned important lessons in patience and endurance. Alpine plants are slow growing. It will take a clump of *Diapensia* fifty years to grow an inch in diameter. That's a lot of days of sun, rain, clouds and insects, not to mention trampling boots. For me, the patience required is not measured in decades but in miles, ascents and conversations.

August 2013: I'm climbing the Van Hoevenberg Trail up Mount Marcy, the same trail I climbed 15 times that season, over 350 times in the past eight years. The rocks are the same, the mud is the same, the uphill climb just as exhausting. On the summit that day, I spoke with over 270 hikers, an average number for a fair weather day. Most expressed the same incredulity about my commute: "You hike this every day? Every day? Really?" Many asked the same questions: "What's that peak over there? How do I get to Skylight? Can I see New Hampshire from here?" Quite a few used the same tired jokes: "Where's the elevator? Is there a Starbucks up here? If you're a steward, are you going to bring me a drink?" I encountered hikers who were less well prepared—a gentleman wearing a sarong

Cascade on a weekend
NANCIE BATTAGLIA

and flip flops, another with a white polo shirt, dock shoes and no pack whatsoever, and one with boots and pack but a dearth of clothing. I was also asked one of my most memorable questions yet: "Can you see the Rockies from here?" The gentleman asking did not mean it as a joke.

The art of being a Summit Steward is to be fully engaged but to subtly turn each conversation about the weather, the trail, the hike, back to the alpine plants. And ideally, to do it in a way that interests the visitor in learning more about these very plants. Patience is a big part of the job: no matter how many times we've heard the same question, it's only fair to recognize that it's the first time from this particular visitor.

The endurance of alpine plants comes to me most clearly when the weather is challenging. While I'm wearing all of my rain gear, leaning into the wind above treeline or doing jumping jacks to keep warm at a trail junction, these plants are hunkered down. They are not uncomfortable and they never complain. They simply are, and

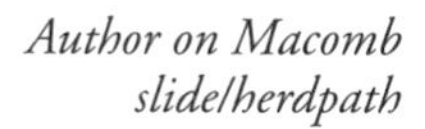

Author on Macomb slide/herdpath

Marcy 1992

Marcy 2011

I bring my best meditation skills to bear to emulate them. I count the hours in trail work accomplished, handfuls of trail mix consumed, the number of times I've wrung the water out of my gloves. I try to stay low to the ground, hide behind rocks and keep moving. Since that first weekend in 2006, I know that I can survive the conditions; looking at the plants reminds me to enjoy the challenge. On rainy days lichens and moss are at their most vibrant. Even the vascular plants seem more lush in the rain. If I look down I can remember to embrace these days rather than simply survive them.

Summit Steward John Graham on Algonquin, 1993
NANCIE BATTAGLIA

The plants have also taught me another lesson, one that keeps me going when the trail is steep or the conditions seemingly unbearable. It's why I love being a Summit Steward, no matter the weather, the trails or the questions. That lesson is that our actions matter. We can make a difference. Hikers who have been in the High Peaks for decades often tell Summit Stewards how much better things look now than they used to. Our own photopoint monitoring project confirms this. Photopoints are photographs of a landscape area taken repeatedly from the same exact position, showing changes over a set time. Our earliest photographs are from Ketch's collection, dating back to the mid-1960s. In 1999, a Summit Steward named Matt Scott figured out where all of the photographs had been taken from and repeated the photos. We've done so again and again since 1999, using the same location, tripod and camera to minimize camera lens distortion. When we analyzed the photographs, we found clear illustration of the recovery of our alpine plants since the mid-1960s. We also found that the peaks with Summit Stewards recovered better than those without stewards.[1]

Our actions matter. Collectively, we can help a fragile ecosystem recover. All of those little actions—the careful placement of a foot, each short conversation with a hiker, each moment spent placing a rock in a scree wall—add up to create a cumulative positive impact. It is inspiring and humbling to be a small part of the conservation success story that is New York State's alpine zone.

Algonquin reseeding in 1971 and results in 2011

Why has the program been so successful?

First, the Summit Stewardship program is rooted in a simple request—walk on the rocks, not on the plants. In nine years with the program, I've never come across anyone who was intentionally damaging the alpine vegetation. Hikers walking on alpine plants do so because they simply don't know how fragile these plants are. When Summit Stewards treat their interactions with visitors as an opportunity to share information, we inevitably find that hikers are happy to help protect the fragile plants. Often, the very same visitor who

1. Goren and White, "2015 Summit Steward End of Season Report"

was standing on the Bigelow's sedge a moment earlier is enthusiastically admonishing friends to "Stay off the grass!" a moment later. Hikers have put their own time, energy and sweat into reaching the summit; they are already invested in the summits.

Second, the Summit Stewardship program empowers hikers to do their part. Protecting alpine plants has to be a collective effort. Hikers who tell other members of their group to walk on the rocks are spreading the stewardship message. Those who bring a rock up from the pile at the trailhead are tangibly helping in the effort by bringing a needed resource for a scree wall, rock packing or a cairn. Volunteer Summit Stewards give that most precious resource—their time—to spend their weekends, vacations or retirements on the summits, speaking with hikers. Finally, the program is helped by those who donate to keep it running, from gear sponsors such as Campmor, the Mountaineer and OR, to organizations such as the ADKhighpeaks Foundation, the 46er Conservation Trust, and the #507 Fund, to the individuals who contributed to, produced and purchased this book. Each of these actions helps ensure that the Adirondack alpine zone will continue to thrive into the future.

Where do we go from here?

The future of the alpine vegetation requires the continued commitment of Summit Stewards and hikers. As John Muir noted, "Thousands of tired, nerve-shaken, over-civilized people are beginning to find out that going to the mountains is going home; that wildness is a necessity." In the Adirondack High Peaks, we continue to see increasing numbers of hikers coming home to the mountains. Since 2011, Summit Stewards have seen a 64% increase in the number of visitors that we speak to annually.[2] It's a testament to the Summit Stewardship Program and the visitors to the area that the alpine vegetation continues to recover in the face of increasing numbers of hikers. If the alpine plants are going to endure into the future, the stewardship of the summits must continue, and even grow, to meet the numbers of new hikers. Even to continue at the current level of coverage—weekends May through June, Labor Day and Columbus Day, seven days a week on Marcy and Algonquin, June through September, five days a week on Wright, weekends on Cascade, every other week on Colden—will require more financial resources. This book and the #507 Fund that it supports are an important step in the ongoing effort to continue Ketch's legacy by ensuring the sustainability of the Summit Stewardship Program.

The Summit Stewardship Program is making a tangible difference because of the passion we all share for this place, our Adirondack High Peaks. From Ketch, to the Summit Stewards, to the hikers, people believe in and are willing to put their energy towards the recovery of our mountain summits. These summits are the most charismatic, the most iconic part of the Adirondacks. We who are drawn to the summits as hikers want these special places to be just as beautiful the next time we visit them. We are shaped by our experiences on these mountains. We learn humility from the trails. We learn patience and endurance from the alpine plants. And, if we do what's right, we will preserve this timeless wilderness for future generations.

---

2. If you're interested in reading more about the Summit Stewardship Program's photopoint monitoring project, you can check out Julia's article in the *Adirondack Journal of Environmental Studies* here: www.ajes.org/v17/goren2011.php

Flowed Lands, Colden in background
YVON DAIGLE

Living the Adirondacks

By Pete Biesemeyer

Pete Biesemeyer, *46er #1999, has done a few more rounds since his first, which he and his wife Linda finished (on Esther) in 1985, including one winter round after age 70. His schooling includes a B.S. in Biology from SUNY Plattsburgh, an M.A.T. in Natural Sciences from Harvard, and a Ph.D. in Biology from Penn State. But his inner compass was set at a much younger age, hours of which he spent daydreaming and looking up at Spread Eagle Mountain from the elementary grade classrooms on the east side of Keene Central School and later, in high school, being further diverted from his studies by the view of the Porter Ledges from the 2nd floor classrooms on the west side of KCS.*

Pete was on the faculty of Manhattan College/College of Mt. St. Vincent's joined biology department for eight years before returning to the North Country in 1985. He has been at the Malone Campus of North Country Community College ever since, and looks forward to retirement soon after 30 years at NCCC, when every day will be a weekend, only without the crowds, and he can go outside and play with his friends anytime.

It's not what you look at that matters. It's what you see.
—H.D. Thoreau

Maybe you know the scene from the modern western, *Rancho Deluxe*. An old Navajo and a young cowboy are looking at the landscape and old guy says, "Tell me what you see." Looking off into the middle distance, then scanning the foreground, the cowboy replies, "Sky, mountains, sand." They both stand and continue staring, seemingly lost in their own thoughts. After a minute or so, the Navajo says, "Look again. Now tell me what you see."

Same thing.

No. It has changed.

The cowboy looks around, wondering what he missed, then nods. He understands. "No man steps in the same river twice. You can't go home again." From Heraclitus to Thomas Wolfe, we find similar reflections on the impermanence of nature. Entropy increases. Time is change.

Adirondackana, however, is often marked by a contrary sentiment, with such phrases as "ageless mountains," "the forest primeval" and "immemorial antiquity," evoking a sense of timelessness. Places of solitude, where only the sounds of nature are heard, and summits with views of the natural landscape unaltered by signs of human activity are still easy to find in the Adirondacks. When one compares an old Stoddard photograph such as the view of Wallface from Henderson Lake with a view of the same place today, little has changed. There are still many places where it's easy to imagine sharing the identical view with someone who stood at the same spot a hundred years ago. One would like to believe that it would still be so a hundred years from now.

Going to the mountains is going home.
—John Muir

Those who grow up in the Adirondacks and stay, as well as those who leave and later return, find in them not only a retreat from the intrusiveness and distractions of the outside world but also the peace of mind that comes from sensing that these are, as Roderick Peattie called them, friendly mountains[1]. Even some who come here for the first time experience *déjà vu*. I am reminded of a friend from California who took a first-time trip through northern New York and New England and remarked at how everything seemed familiar. He said he felt at home even though he had never been here before.

It was so for my dad. I was a year old when my parents, Walter and Marion, landed on these shores. The year was 1940, and the date was March 24, which may have been auspicious as that happened to be Easter Sunday. Timing was critical. War was on the horizon but European borders had not yet been sealed, and they were able to board the last boat out of Marseilles. Fortune played a role. Walter was an architect, and he had done some work for a client with means and connections. It was also advantageous that Walter was Swiss. When we arrived in New York City, Walter and Marion knew no one, but within a few weeks, by more good fortune, they were put in touch with a good-

---

1. Roderick Peattie. 1942. *The Friendly Mountains*. Vangard Press

hearted lady, Anne Coolidge Moore, a Bostonian and member of a summer camp in need of a resident manager and caretaker. Anne invited Walter to come and have a look at the place. It was a long drive—this was long before the Thruway and Northway, and even the Taconic Parkway only went as far as Hawthorne Traffic Circle—so darkness had fallen hours before they arrived at Putnam Camp[2]. Walter had no idea where he was but when he got up the next morning and saw the mountains and smelled the air he said, "I'm home!" That was on April 25. By May 16, they had left NYC and moved to the Town of Keene, initially to the hamlet of St. Huberts, never to leave again.

We lived at Putnam Camp for three years, then moved to Keene Valley where we lived until 1948. But once a Putnam Camper, always a Putnam Camper. I have been told that I was the first Putnam Camper to become an Adirondack 46er. Now I believe there is at least one other.

However that may be, last year I walked down from the Garden to my car at the Rooster Comb trailhead and was bemused at finding myself walking along Market Street, retracing the exact same steps I had taken so many years before on my walk to school every day. The neighborhood has not changed much. The sidewalk looks the same, the houses look the same and the front of the school looks the same.

Pete, Walter and Marion Biesemeyer, Putnam Camp, 1941

There is a comfort in finding old, familiar things years later, whether it is the parent rediscovering a long-forgotten favorite childhood book, or the college alumnus at homecoming weekend, showing his embarrassed wife where he once scrawled his name on a barroom wall. Transient entities that we are, touchstones to the past make us feel connected to something more permanent. They echo in the soul. And there is a similar comfort in finding, here in the Adirondacks, scenery and vegetation that evoke memories of cattle-grazed meadows of the Alps, the tilled fields of the Low Countries, or the sheep-grazed commons of English villages. But there's something more going on than an absence of change. Total lack of

2. Putnam camp is a private family colony located on Putnam Brook, formerly Beede Brook, at the south end of the valley just east of the AuSable Club. Founded by a group of young Bostonians—Drs. James and Charles Putnam, Dr. Henry Bowditch, and William James in 1891—on property they purchased from Smith Beede, one of Keene Valley's earliest hoteliers, its most famous visitor was Sigmund Freud, who arrived Sept. 16, 1909, accompanied by his German colleagues Jung and Ferenczi. Freud also visited Glenmore School at the other end of town at that time. Though the founders were all dead by 1920, the camp continues with second and third generations spending pleasant hiking summers here in the rustic, simple accommodations their parents deemed adequate—James Bailey, *History of the Town of Keene*

change is death without decomposition; it would be like a wax museum. That, surely, is not our view of the Adirondacks nor what characterizes our love for these mountains.

House of memories and trail blazers

Walter and Marion bought the property on East Hill which became the Mountain House before the war ended but not long before. My father took me along when he went to a lumber yard in Peru for some building materials, and while we were there, a man came out of the office shouting, "The war is over!" A siren sounded, people started tooting their horns and my dad laughed and said that's it; we're going home. Nobody's doing any more work today!

The Mountain House is still in the family. My brother Bob runs it now but that's another story. This story is about the Adirondacks then and now, and more particularly how things have changed in the Home of the High Peaks—the Town of Keene—from the postwar years to the present, and how they have stayed the same.

Indian Falls lean-to, 1950
RUTH TALMADGE

The Mountain House figures into this story because of some tie-ins with the history of the Adirondack Mountain Club (ADK) and the Adirondack 46ers. Nearly every one of the earliest, single-digit 46ers were regular guests. ADK was smaller then and many members came to Mountain House and became close friends. The Hurricane Mountain Chapter of ADK had its first meeting there and continued to hold annual meetings at the Mountain House for many years. Walter and Marion were founding members, and Marion at one time or another held every elective office in the chapter.

My dad, together with fellow ADKers and neighbors Alfred, Murray and Wallace Jones; Wayne Byrne; and Burns Weston, Sr. rediscovered and cleared the abandoned trail to Lost Pond. Walter and Burns also explored the Soda Range, which later came to be known as Nundagao Ridge[3]. They marked the route of the original path from Big Crow over Weston

3. The origin of the name Nundagao can be traced back to the late 1940s/early 50s when my father, Walter Biesemeyer, and our East Hill summer neighbor and Hurricane Mountain Chapter co-founder, Burns Weston, laid the route of today's herd path over the so-called Soda Range and its then unnamed highest point, now officially designated Weston Peak. Borden Mills was an Albany attorney and incumbent president of ADK at the time, and a frequent guest at the Mountain House. He and my dad thought the range deserved a better name. Borden had supposedly found, in some archive in the State Library, that Hurricane Mountain was the white man's mistranslation of its aboriginal name, nun-da-ga-o, meaning "hill of the wind spirits," a bit more poetic than "soda range." Changing the name of Hurricane Mountain was out of the question but few people knew about the Soda Range, so that was a better candidate for a name change. Borden, Burns and Walter were prime movers in lobbying to rename the Soda Range Nundagao, and its highest point Weston Peak. So far as I know, no one has ever authenticated the term Nundagao. It does not appear in William Beauchamp's Aboriginal Place Names of New York State. However, Beauchamp (in NYS Museum Bulletin 108; Archeology 12) says that No-de-ne-o, meaning hill of the wind, was a name given to Hurricane Peak by Charles Fenno Hoffman, and Rogh-qua-non-da-go, child of the mountain, was a name Hoffman formed and applied to Schroon Lake. Lewis Morgan is cited therein for the name Nun-da-o, meaning hilly, as in O-non-da-o, place where many hills come together, from which we derive Onondaga. It seems likely, therefore, that Nun-da-ga-o was based on one or more of those earlier place names which, while not establishing a truly aboriginal provenance, nevertheless gives it at least a patina of authenticity. In short, we owe the name Nundagao to two most dubious cartographers—an Albany lawyer and a Swiss architect.

Peak to Lost Pond. The unmarked trail of today sticks pretty close to their route, with only minor detours around patches of blowdown.

The 46ers started with a group of hikers from the Capital District who made the Mountain House their informal headquarters in the North Country, and used it as the jumping-off point for their adventures into the wilderness. Ed and Grace Hudowalski (46ers #6 and #9) live in my memory as the real spark plugs of the organization[4], usually planning the next hike while the others were still recounting the last. Grace was first president (1948-51) and legendary correspondent for decades thereafter. All 46ers fortunate enough to have known Grace surely treasure the personal replies from her as she recorded our progress. Her letters were usually encouraging and filled with her joy in vicariously reliving each climb as it was described. It has been told, however, that sometimes her letters were more acerbic, when details of someone's report didn't jibe with her knowledge of the mountain or didn't match up with previous entries in the summit register, making it evident that they had not actually attained the summit. That could happen easily when wishful thinking clouded the mind of an exhausted and confused bushwhacker before the well-defined herd paths of today. But Grace would have none of it. They had to go back and do it right before she would enter their names in the ledger!

I was only a kid then, eavesdropping on the adults in the living room, through the floor register in my bedroom, as they talked about mysterious places like Ouluska Pass, Panther Gorge, Shattuck Clearing and Duck Hole, yet old enough to remember Ed and Grace and the several other single- and double-digit 46ers who stayed at or visited the Mountain House, as well as most of those who lived in the Keene/Keene Valley area[5] or moved there later.

Herb Clark (46er #1), who finished on Emmons with the Marshall brothers, George and Bob (46er #2 and 46er #3) on June 10, 1925, made his "final ascent" in 1945. That was about three years prior to the events recounted here, so first in numerical order of the pioneering 46ers that I actually knew was George Marshall, a friend and mentor even while I was just a stripling. I still have the book he gave me for my high school graduation, his brother Robert Marshall's *Arctic Wilderness*. I never met Bob (46er #3), so the next of those early peak baggers, and one of the first leaders and promoters of Adirondack back-country ski touring, was Fay Loope (46er #4). He was instrumental in the establishment of the ski trails at ADK's Heart Lake property and his winter ski trips up Marcy in the 1940s inspired generations of followers. Fay had served as executive secretary of ADK and was

---

4. On October 9, 1948, the 46ers emblem, designed by Ed Hudowalski, was officially adopted at a meeting at the Mountain House. Grace, of course, is a legend for whom it would be beyond the aim of this essay to give due recognition.

5. It may be of passing interest to students of class distinctions that Keene Valley and St. Huberts have historically been the upscale end of town where most of the artists and intellectuals gathered, and Keene was a mill-town and blue-collar community. In my school years, there were well-delineated tribal boundaries between summer people and locals. In recent years the downstream end of the valley has become gentrified. Many former seasonal residents have retired and now live here year-round; a significant number of talented and energetic young people have relocated to the area and either are able to work out of their homes or have established local businesses; their F1 and F2 generations attend the local school; and there has been gene flow among the populations. For those and a dozen other reasons the boundaries have become blurred. But do not confuse Keene and Keene Valley; each takes pride in not being the other, and residents of either will take umbrage if you mix them up. Outsiders could be forgiven, considering that, in addition to the hamlet of Keene, there is the Town of Keene, which includes Keene Valley and St. Huberts.

Flowed Lands before dams were removed, 1973
GARY KOCH

just preparing to enjoy his retirement in Gabriels when he was called to the helm again to oversee the Club's acquisition of Adirondak Loj in 1958.

A few other low-number 46ers were neighbors. Many were, of course, also ADKers. Among them were the Plum sisters, Dorothy, Elizabeth and Eleanor, whose home overlooked the valley from the crest of East Hill. Nellie (46er #26) was the most avid mountaineer of the three, while Dorothy and Betsy were active in other ways. Dorothy, former librarian of Vassar College, compiled the 1958 ADK publication, *Adirondack Bibliography*, the definitive source for Adirondack materials at the time. And Betsie, mindful of the many who preferred to explore the valleys and lower mountains, was the founder of an unofficial organization, the Non-46ers. She selected a rocking chair as their symbol. But this was no virtual symbol. It was a real rocking chair, with cane seat and armrests, which they carried to the top of Little Crow where for a number of years it welcomed the non-46er and 46er alike.

The Dittmars, Mary and Adolph (46er #29 and 46er #31), who served as Johns Brook Lodge (JBL) hut crew in the late 1940s, lived in AuSable Forks. Many will remember Dit as the long-time 46er treasurer. This 46er's memory of Dit goes deeper. After Linda and I (46er #1998 and 46er #1999) finished, Dit was the one to whom we sent our dues. But for a time, many years before that, he was also my dentist.

Other memorable 46ers from that era were Werner Bachli (46er #33), Morgan Porter (46er #69), Harry Eldridge (46er #90, and 6th recorded winter 46er), and Herb Allen (46er #96). Werner, a founding member of the 46ers, and Walter especially enjoyed each other's company as they could converse in their native dialect, *Schweizerdeutsch*, nearly incomprehensible to anyone else. Morgan, as Maps and Guidebook Committee Chair of ADK in the early 1950s, recorded the first accurate trail mileages by pushing a measuring wheel, calibrated to the hundredth of a mile, over the mountains. Harry Eldridge was the first winter mountaineer I ever knew, at a time when winter mountaineering was considered a sport only for heroic alpinists. Herb Allen (46er #96 and fourth president of the 46ers, from 1956 to 1957), a retired forester who used to come over from Vermont and stay a few days at a time, liked to go off by himself and work on the path over Nundagao, which in those days was seldom hiked and hard to follow. Herb was soft-spoken and always had a slight smile, as one who is either mildly amused by hasty, noisier people, or totally at peace with himself. Think of a sinewy Dalai Lama in work clothes. With a brush axe.

Of the early 46ers who lived in Keene and Keene Valley, probably the best known and most fondly remembered of all was Jim Goodwin (46er #24). In addition to leading many youngsters on hikes and overnight camping trips, Jim also took some of us to the cliffs at Chapel Pond where he introduced us to the fundamentals of rock climbing. Bob Denniston (46er #40) taught Latin and history at Keene Valley High School and, as scoutmaster, led Troop 4 on various outings, sometimes to do side-cutting, sometimes just for fun. He also led many of us on our first overnight camping trips to JBL and Heart Lake. Bill Endicott (46er #80 and third 46er president, from 1953 to 1956) and John Siau (46er #94 and unofficial maintainer of the Nundagao Ridge Path who followed Herb Clark's stewardship) round out the double-digit 46ers who lived in Keene or Keene Valley and whom I knew well enough to advert to on a first name basis, if not then, at least after my formative years.

Whiteface from Connery Pond
CARL HEILMAN II

Father Peter Ward (46er #72) didn't live in Keene. He used to come over from Saranac Lake. He was not only an ardent hiker and bushwhacker but also a rather unpriestly *bon vivant*. He kept a speedboat on the Saranacs and had a black T-bird roadster, the first car I ever rode in with seatbelts. The hierarchy was perhaps not entirely OK with Peter's lifestyle—everyone in our family called him by his first name and, sharing the same name, I was privileged the same liberty—as he was later assigned a more rustic parish somewhere in the hinterlands of northern Clinton County.

Moving down the roster into the three-digit 46ers, I find many more familiar names, starting with Carolyn and Mary Schaffer (46er #104 and 46er #105) who had the mountaineering shop in Keene and from whom I purchased my first pair of Vibram-soled boots, and our East Hill neighbors, the intrepid Trudy Healey (46er #148) and her adventuresome family, daughters Karen and Sandy (46er #149 and 46er #158) and sons Thomas and Michael 46er (#150 and 46er #164). Trudy and Carolyn inspired a lot of young kids to climb the High Peaks and led them on camping trips as well as the occasional unplanned bivouac in the Sewards, Santanonis and trailless Dixes when those peaks were truly trailless, route-finding was an order of magnitude more difficult than it is today, and equipment consisted of clunky army-surplus gear and hand-me-downs. They sometimes had to make do with wet clothes, no fire and cold hot dogs for breakfast. They would come home dirty, scratched-up, bug-bitten and tired. And in a week they were eager to do it again! It is good to learn at an early age that it doesn't have to be fun to be fun. My sister, Anne Bailey, was one of those kids. She is 46er #163.

Turning from reminiscences of people and looking at the Adirondacks in a broader aspect, I'm moved to consider what once was and is now gone or in decline, and what's new or becoming more common. If one were to make three lists; going or gone, new or increasing; and generally the same, which list would be the longest? Let's see how this turns out…

Remembrance of things past; fading trail markers

- Lean-tos above 3500'
- Litter on trails
- Garbage pits behind lean-tos (which used to be accepted practice)
- Balsam boughs on lean-to floors placed there by rangers. I'm not making this up up; they really did that!
- Tire chains in winter
- Bats
- Monarch butterflies
- Gas stations. There were at least six in Keene/Keene Valley—three Mobil stations, one Texaco, one Sunoco and one Gulf. And three of those were real garages that could do an entire engine rebuild. Now the only place to gas up is Stewarts and if you need anything more than air in your tires, you have a problem.
- Service stations. Also a thing of the past. No one comes out to pump your gas, clean your windshield, and check your oil anymore. And they had free road maps and clean rest rooms.
- Bars/taverns. There were at least six in Keene and Keene Valley. Now there are two. But some of those old ones were rather disreputable dives. The two that remain cater to a more cosmopolitan clientele and are places you could take someone to.
- Ski centers. Jeremy Davis's *Lost Ski Areas of the Northern Adirondacks* provides histories, maps, photos and descriptions of more than fifty, fourteen in Lake Placid and the High Peaks region alone. When I was a teen we used to ski at Scotts Cobble, Fawn Ridge and Paleface, and the original Whiteface Mountain Ski Center on Marble Mountain with an upper ski area on Lookout Mountain.
- Rope tows, T-bars, J-bars and Poma-lifts
- Views. The top of Giant used to be open to the east and the view of the Jay Range from Nundagao has grown in considerably. Windstorms and fires will open new views but succession closes them off. On balance, I think the trees are winning.
- Fire towers[6]. Jack Freeman's *Views from on High* identifies 33 towers that still exist. He says that from about 1910 to 1990 there were more than 60 observer-staffed towers. Today there are none.
- Forest fires. When I was growing up, a summer without one was rare. Today, forest fires have become not only less common but are also more quickly brought under control when they do occur.
- Passenger trains. Westport and Lake Placid had daily trains, as did AuSable Forks. Trains still pass through Westport but rail travel in the North Country is only a memory, except for a couple of limited tourist trains which function only as nostalgic trips to the past, not as practical transportation.
- Town dumps. They used to be gathering spots for neighborly chit-chats, handy places to recycle old appliances and furniture, and great for watching bears. Many of those old dumps have been closed and capped. Some have been converted to transfer and

6. Marty Podskoch's *Adirondack Fire Towers: Their History and Lore, The Northern Districts* describes 26, of which 11 have either been removed or relocated, and his *Adirondack Fire Towers: Their History and Lore, Southern Districts* describes another 32, of which 14 have either been removed or relocated. That's a total of 25 towers gone. Of the remainder, 11 have been adopted and restored or restoration is pending, 11 are abandoned, 2 have been or are being used for communication, and 4 are privately-owned.

recycling stations. Nevertheless, when I do a garbage run, I still like to say I'm going ta-da-dump.

- Young kids on ADK chapter outings. Maybe it was different for other chapters, but there were many youngsters on our chapter hikes. I don't see that anymore.
- Canisters with registers on trailless peaks
- Ridge Runners (forerunners to the Summit Stewards)
- Bear bags
- The cable and pulley across Johns Brook to Winter Camp, a fun way to get across and even more fun to watch when someone took off with insufficient launch speed and was left dangling in the middle!
- The road to Crow Clearing extended beyond the clearing another half mile, from where it was only a brisk five minute walk to the junction of the Hurricane and Lost Pond trails at the former site of the Gulf Brook Lean-to. My dad often took guests up in the bed of the pickup and dropped them off there.
- The stone shelter on the summit of Marcy, a nonconforming structure under the State Land Master Plan which had to be removed for that reason, and also because it had become a nuisance, attracting the wrong sort of people to misuse it—as the wrong sort of people will.
- Summit markers and summit signs. After the canisters were removed, it was considered a good idea to mark the highest point of each formerly trailless peak with a yellow summit marker, or in some cases a wooden sign. They are something new. Why are they on this list? Because, although over the years those markers and signs occasionally disappeared, that problem has gotten much worse in the past two or three years. They have become even more favored targets and souvenirs for vandals[7].

Anne Bailey, author's sister, Tabletop summit, 1981
PETE BIESEMEYER

- Glenmore, the Philosophers Camp on the Hurricane Road, was still in operation when I was growing up at the Mountain House. Today nature is reclaiming it. Those who gathered at the camp were inspired by the Scottish-born philosopher Thomas Davidson. A large cottage down the road, known as Summerbrook, also hosted famous guests, including Maxim Gorky and Thomas Mann. It was said that Gorky was booked into a hotel in NYC with his mistress, and was asked to leave by the shocked sophisticates of the big city. Apparently he found the rubes in the sticks more tolerant and welcoming.
- The Dewey Cottage, where education guru John Dewey summered, barely 1/2 mile from the Mountain House, is long gone. It was the summer camp of Wayne and Peggy Byrne, ADKers from Plattsburgh. (Wayne was related to the founders of Glenmore.) The cottage had a screened porch with a magnificent potential view. I say potential, because it was on

7. Barbarians have always been the bane of civilization but it's hard to understand why Vandals get all the credit. Didn't the Huns and Visigoths do their share?

a steep bank and the tops of the tall conifers below were exactly at the level of the porch. Wayne and Peggy told us that Dewey kept the trees because he didn't want to be distracted from his work. I guess you could say they shared his view.

- The Rondeau hermitage. A sign at the site on the Northville-Placid Trail commemorates Noah, Mayor of Cold River City, Pop. 1. In his later years he came out of the woods and wintered with relatives in AuSable Forks. My mom received Christmas cards from Noah written in a beautiful calligraphic hand. His brother Alec lived at the junction of Bartlett Road and Lacy Road in Keene. His Model T lacked a fuel pump so the engine was gravity-fed with the gas tank mounted on the firewall and when he came up East Hill he had to turn around and back up the steepest grade. One spring our school bus slipped into a ditch on Alstead Hill Road and while the bus driver went to get help Alec happened by. He stopped to see if we were OK and one of the kids said, "The bus got stuck in the damn mud!" Alec's face took on a serious look and he bent down and picked up a handful and said, "Oh no. This is good earth. This grows our food." That lesson stayed with me about as well as anything I ever learned later.
- The floating hitch-up-Matildas
- Red spruce near the alpine zone. Some fieldwork in the 1990s[8] has shown that there has been a loss, and historic records from before then confirm it. Where there had been a significant admixture of red spruce in the boreal forest above 3500', today it is mostly balsam.
- Friday evening bonfires at the airfield on Fall Outing weekends in Keene Valley
- And let's not forget Nubbins, the fractious burro of JBL. Some guests once walked in to JBL and one, wearing a straw hat, stood by the corral for a photo. Nubbins started nibbling the hat. The guest took exception and grabbed the hat. Nubbins took exception and grabbed the guest. The guest returned minus hat and with a nasty bruise on his arm.

Waypoints of the new; novelties and nuisances

- Pavement. Once upon a time the road to Heart Lake was gravel all the way from Route 73, and the road to Newcomb was gravel all the way from Route 9. The Upper Works seemed as remote as Ultima Thule. The pavement on East Hill ended at the top of the hill and it was dirt—and in the springtime, mud—from there all the way to Spruce Hill. Today all those roads are paved.
- Eagles. It's still a thrill to see one, but no one will drive far out of their way to see one anymore.
- Wild turkeys
- Canada geese. It's hard to believe but as recently as in the mid-1960s, on a college field trip to Lake Alice on the Miner property in Chazy, our professor was excited to see a flock.
- Summit Stewards
- Armed forest rangers. There used to be less emphasis on the law-enforcement aspects of a ranger's job.
- Alpine flora. The restoration by Edwin H. Ketchledge (a.k.a. Ketch) has been wonderfully successful, as has the continuing effort by the Summit Stewards to protect the habitat by artful rockwork and, most importantly, by educating the public.
- A penchant on the part of many for technical jargon over plain language. Back in the day, we sometimes got *cold* and *wet*. Now we get *hypothermia*. Then, we *drank* to slake our *thirst*. Now, we *rehydrate* to avoid *dehydration*, and can even purchase gadgets or

---

8. For anyone who wants to dig into the literature, a quick and easy point of entry would be to go to Google Scholar and search under "apical dieback in red spruce." ("Evans and Biesemeyer" will also get you there.)

Lower Wolf Jaw and the Lower Range, 2013
BRENDAN WILTSE

program our smart phones to remind ourselves when to do so. La!

- Cleverness with gadgets is replacing basic woodcraft and common sense.
- Trails. A number of new trails over the past fifty or sixty years come to mind; the Zander Scott (Giant Ridge) Trail, Jay Mountain, Nundagao Ridge, the Jim Goodwin Trail to Porter from the Garden (Jim cut the old trail. There is a commemorative plaque on the new re-route), and the Rocky Peak Ridge (RPR) trails. My first climb of RPR was a bushwhack from Giant. I was 16 and by myself. A thunderstorm was imminent as I approached the top but I felt compelled to sign the register and had to beat a fast retreat down into the cripple brush, totally drenched—did I mention I was wearing jeans and a T-shirt?—with electricity zapping above. The teen-age prefrontal cortex is not yet fully myelinated; those who survive presumably make better decisions later.

Bennie's Brook Slide, Lower Wolf Jaw, 1973
GARY KOCH

- Official unmarked trails where there used to be just plain herd paths, as on Street and Nye (where people often got lost on the descent and ended up at Last Chance Ranch)
- Lyme disease and giardia
- Giant hog weed, Eurasian milfoil, the spiny water flea, the emerald ash borer and dozens of other invasive aliens, not to mention the most invasive alien of all, *Homo sapiens*
- Lean-to relocations and reconstruction by the Lean-to Rescue crew. Watching them work is like watching the Harlem Globetrotters. They make it look so easy! They are a team and they are pros.
- Bottled water. Why people will pay for water is a mystery to me. Don't they know it's just coming out of someone else's tap?
- Professional crew trail construction and maintenance done to a very high standard. They believe in only doing the job once.
- More secure funding for the Summit Stewardship Program (to wit, the #507 Fund, named for Ketch's 46er number)
- The public's remarkable buy-in to the leave-no-trace ethic
- Notwithstanding the previous item, one dismaying trend is that, although ordinary litter such as candy wrappers and the like is rare, signs of human bio-waste are becoming

Marcy Dam, in background Whale's Tail Mt., 1967
PETE BIESEMEYER

more evident. Even more dismaying, those signs—soiled tissues and worse—are often found not just on or near the trails but, worst of all, on the summits! Did they really have to hold it in until they reached the top?! Ernest Choate's *Dictionary of American Bird Names* gives us *shite pote* as a common name for the green heron, explained as "an attempt to render more delicate by a change of spelling a name for [a] bird derived from its habit of ejecting effluent when making a startled departure." It's unlikely these subhuman offenders are ejecting effluent when making startled departures but what can explain such behavior? Maybe their fear of being unable to find their way back to the trail is greater than their sense of decorum. Whatever moves them to their disgusting practice, shite potes would seem a fitting sobriquet.

- The use of trekking poles
- The summit cairn on Skylight. Hikers still carry rocks up to add to it, though it seems to be growing more at the base than at the top, and is spawning off smaller cairns in the vicinity.
- Rescues of hikers in distress for trivial reasons, lost on well-marked trails, caught by nightfall without headlamps, dehydrated (sometimes walking next to a stream!) and similar foolishness
- Bear canisters
- There seems to be a steady increase in the proportion of hikers and campers in the

Adirondacks from out of state and from other countries, of which a super majority are our northern neighbors.
- Lastly and definitely, the trails have gotten steeper. Climbing out of the col between RPR and Giant and between Blake and Colvin was a lot easier half a century ago.

Plus ça change…

- The vast acreage of natural habitat seen from almost any summit
- All those distinctive, instantly recognizable profiles and features—Indian Head, Sawteeth, Big Slide, Noonmark, Shepherd's Tooth, Indian Pass, Allen, the Beckhorn... one could go on and on.
- Scenic vistas. There are three which I think are particularly outstanding—the view of Whiteface from Route 86 between Saranac Lake and Gabriels; Marcy, Colden, and Algonquin from the Loj Road; and the view from the High Peaks overlook in Newcomb.
- The ease of finding solitude. Even on the busiest summer weekends, all it takes is getting off the trail.
- The adventure of discovering new things practically in my own back yard. After decades of hiking in the Adirondacks, almost every off-trail exploration is still rewarded with a new waterfall, flume, cliff or other hidden gem. And going back in a different season, different weather, or time of day transforms it and also makes it new.
- The regularity of natural cycles and rhythms of nature—*phenology* in scientific jargon
- Predictable patterns of ecosystem structure and function, as in the vertical stratification of forests with their canopy, midlevel and ground-level communities; and altitudinal zonation as one climbs from the hardwood forest through the boreal forest up into the alpine and tundra zones
- Large and leisurely geological movements. Glacial rebound is still happening. Ten thousand years ago this region was under the weight of a mile of ice. The mountains really are getting higher! And North America and Europe continue to move apart at about the same rate as fingernails grow. Just think, if your arm were long enough to reach the cliffs of Dover, you could scratch your nails on the chalk for a thousand years without moving your hand.
- Relatively rapid and localized geological movements. The North Country experiences occasional tremors, frequent landslides and floods, the seasonal downslope movement of soil creep due to frost jacking and thawing, and mass wasting from stream erosion. All are evidence that the present is the key to the past. The same processes that shaped the landforms of the past are still in play today.
- The stars at night. I have taken students from the city on camping trips to the Adirondacks and they were absolutely amazed by the Milky Way. They just had no idea.
- The basic principles of ecology. In one thumbnail lesson: energy flows, materials cycle, every square mile on earth contains material from every other square mile, everything is connected to everything else, you can't throw anything away, and there's no free lunch. These principles are, of course, inviolate, but are not always as evident as here, where the natural world has not been overwhelmed by the artificial world.
- The peace of mind a green place gives me!

...see, and ask for the old paths, where is the good way, and walk therein.
—Jer. 6:16

Of course change is constant, even in these most ancient of mountains, but changes occur over vastly different time scales. Measuring time in hours and days, even months and years, offers a limited and abstract knowledge of changes that take place over millennia. As I approach my eighth decade, I find that I am only now beginning to truly understand even such a simple thing as stream erosion. Gulf Brook, where as a boy I spent many languorous hours as a self-appointed examiner of stones and riffles, is very different now. I used to be able to lie on the bank and stare at the water and see the fishes so close I think I could have touched them if I had been patient enough. Now the stream bed is a good six to eight feet below the edge of the bank and I don't recognize any of the boulders. The old ones have been displaced and interlopers have taken their place. I realize now, of course, as I did not then, that the old familiar rocks of my youth were themselves transported from elsewhere in an earlier age. Clearly the deep gulf behind the Mountain House was carved by running water. I learned that as a student and knew it as hand-me-down, book-knowledge. Now I know it in a deeper, more personal sense—I feel it in my bones. How long did it take to create that valley? Extrapolating at the rate of one foot per decade, it's easy to understand that it happened in just a few thousand years, the blink of an eye in geologic time.

Author on Whiteface, 1945
COURTESY OF PETE BIESEMEYER

The mayfly has its morning, noon and evening. Think what changes we can see that a mayfly would miss! Yet think too, what changes occur over longer spans of time, to which we are oblivious.

Modern life is movement. Compared with natural rhythms, the artificial environment is frenetic and kaleidoscopic, and the developing brain becomes programmed to process that information efficiently, with the consequence that movement in the natural world, whether it be the fall of a pebble or the flight of a bird, does not easily escape the eye. But there are more subtle changes—night sounds, the smell of fallen leaves, the charged air before a thunderstorm. It takes a while for most people to stop making noise and open their senses to the natural world, and even so, our senses are limited.

Nothing shows the limits of our senses as easily as getting lost in the woods. Every experienced hiker I know has gotten turned around at some time, walked in a circle, come upon a stream that wasn't supposed to be there or that should have been flowing in the other direction, or been stumped by a ridge or valley that wasn't on the map. Even Christine B., one of the most experienced off-trail adventurers I know, will say that she does not get lost but has sometimes found it necessary to reconnoiter. I have been confused in so familiar a place as my own property when, after a heavy snowfall, the bent-over trees obscured the trails and the woods looked equally strange in every direction. On truly

The High Peaks from Cascade
YVON DAIGLE

trailless hikes with no herd paths whatsoever, and especially on cloudy days, I've learned the hard way to trust my compass and check it constantly. Which prompts the question, how often do animals get lost?

The home ranges of many mammals are large enough that it is not possible that they could familiarize themselves well enough with the terrain to navigate by familiar landmarks. It is known that the homing and orientation of many amphibians is by sun compass. Red efts return to the same vernal pools where they were bred, after a three-year sojourn on land, over distances up to three miles. Birds migrate thousands of miles, apparently sensing Earth's magnetic fields *en route*. Bees track the changing position of the sun in relation to food resources and the hive, and can also distinguish the polarity of sky light. Many insects detect UV light. Bats, whales and elephants hear sounds far beyond the frequencies of our acoustic range. And humans cannot even imagine the role of olfaction in the animal kingdom.

How often does the deer get lost? How often does the bear collapse from dehydration? How often does the coyote get benighted in the woods? No one knows. That it happens is not unlikely. That it happens a lot, is. But where is the deer's map and compass? Where is the bear's water bottle? Where is the coyote's headlamp? The log of DEC search and rescue calls is replete with reports of people taking wrong turns and getting lost even on marked trails. People usually survive one emergency overnight bivouac, even in bad weather, if they are uninjured and in good health, but they're lucky to make it through a second night without a complex apparatus of clothing, foot gear, camping equipment, food and first aid supplies.

The Adirondacks and people's relation to them reveal two measures of human limits. One is the frequency with which people get in trouble in the woods. The other is the flawed perception of the apparent timelessness of the mountains. There is a mismatch between the tempo and spectrum of the signals that nature emits, and the ones to which our senses are attuned. We miss things that happen too slowly—and which would be apparent to eyes more watchful and minds with longer attention spans—and we are blind to phenomena that fall outside the range of our senses, which are further diminished by being blunted by the coarseness of an increasingly hard-edged and clangorous artificial world.

Nevertheless, one needn't become a hermit to get in tune with nature. How long does it take for the soul to catch up with the body? For some, fifteen or twenty minutes of quiet meditation may suffice; for others it might take a day on the trail. Going into the woods provides a sense of restoration, a sense of being made whole, which is largely coincident with becoming focused on the path and the natural environment, and leaving behind the noise of the outside world. Then, being in the moment, one can begin to let go of thoughts about work, household chores, and coffee cups and teaspoons. The mind is free to wander toward those peripheral matters but in a more detached way. Walking in the woods promotes cogitation, and those who are at home in the woods find serenity there. I suppose that's why it's *re-creation*. It's not just an excuse for grownups to play outdoors. It's something more.

The essence, I believe, of what grounds our sense of place is not constancy but predictability. Having insight and imagination, we find patterns in nature, and being reasoning animals, can ascribe reasonable causes for what we observe. The more familiar the natural world and the better we understand it, the more we find ourselves at one with it. And what better place than here?

Almost anywhere else, you have to be careful where you sit and what you touch and watch out for things that bite or sting. We like to complain about bug season but elsewhere the bugs are out all year round, and carry things like malaria and yellow fever. Apart from brambles and poison ivy, our woods and fields are populated by user-friendly native flora. And the fauna? City people, flatlanders and newbies worry about snakes and bears. Bears can be dangerous but incidents are rare. Everyone has seen campground and dump bears but in a lifetime of hiking in the Adirondacks I have met a grand total of three on the trail, and as soon as they sensed me they went a different way. Snakes? Reports suggest that most people who've been bitten were trying to kill the snake. Fair is fair. The most dangerous animals are the most unpredictable. The behavior of wild animals is adaptive and largely ruled by instinct, and therefore predictable. Humans are much less predictable. Moreover, as Cesar Milan the dog whisperer has pointed out, humans follow unstable pack leaders.

Truly the Adirondacks are friendly mountains, the plants and animals for the most part are inoffensive, too, and so are most of the human inhabitants, provided they're not provoked.

Great Range and Johns Brook Valley
BRENDAN WILTSE

The Adirondack Forty-Sixers: The Transition to Stewardship

By Phil Corell

Phil Corell*'s introduction the Adirondacks began in 1956, when he first attended Camp Pok-O-Moonshine in Willsboro as a ten-year-old. He completed his first round of the 46 High Peaks in the summer of 1962 (# 224W) and continued his involvement with the Pok-O-MacCready Camps for the next 50 years. Phil began his winter climbing in high school and, despite wrestling at Franklin and Marshall College, found time during vacations to make cold weather trips to the Adirondacks. He completed his first winter round of the 46 in 1985 and still continues to actively climb. After graduation he began a 33-year career at Saranac Central School, initially as an elementary teacher. He retired in 2001 as Pupil Personnel Director and Director of Special Education.*

His wife of 43 years, Mary, and both of his sons are also 46ers. While the boys were growing up, Phil was active in coaching and officiating wrestling, working with Scouting, teaching Wilderness Recreation courses at Plattsburgh State University and serving as a Licensed Adirondack Guide. Phil served four terms as 46er President, spent over 40 years on the staff of the Outdoor Skills Workshop, and is currently the Club's treasurer. His most gratifying memories during the past 60 years of climbing are the family and friends with whom he has shared his experiences in the mountains.

Whether it's a small hill in one's back yard or an impressive peak on the distant horizon, the lure of climbing a mountain and conquering its heights has motivated countless individuals through the years to "reach for the summit." Each individual possesses his/her own personal motivation—exploration, the physical challenge, something new, a social experience or just the personal satisfaction of getting to the top.

The first recorded completion of the 46 High Peaks was by Robert and George Marshall and their guide, Herb Clark. They finished their quest on June 10, 1925, on the summit of Mt. Emmons. Subsequently, Bob Marshall published his booklet, *The High Peaks of the Adirondacks*, which began to generate interest in the Adirondacks and climbing the 46 High Peaks. One of the individuals who became interested was Russell Carson, who researched the history of the High Peaks and penned his book, *Peaks and People of the Adirondacks*, in 1927. Carson focused on the story behind the naming of the peaks, the history of first ascents and information related to each mountain.

Members of Grace Methodist Church in Troy, NY, were particularly inspired by the Marshalls' accomplishment and Carson's book. The Reverend Ernest Ryder and a group of his parishioners began taking regular hikes to the mountains and decided to work on completing all 46 peaks. They formed the "Forty-Sixers of Troy," requiring members to climb at least one peak each year and submit a report on their climb to remain active. Included in their group were Ed and Grace Hudowalski, who would later become founding members of the current Adirondack Forty-Sixers.

By the end of the 1930s, 17 climbers had completed the peaks. Then, in 1946, 15 more joined the ranks bringing the total list of finishers to 46!

On May 30, 1948, a meeting was held at Adirondak Loj and the Adirondack Forty-Sixers (46ers) organization was created. Grace Hudowalski was elected its first President and Dr. A.G. "Ditt" Dittmar became Treasurer—a position he was to hold for the next 53 years.

As the Adirondacks were "discovered" by recreational enthusiasts, the number of individuals completing the challenge began to explode.

By the Year	# of Finishers
1960	179
1970	590
1980	1,591
1990	2,723
2000	4,655
2010	6,733

By 2016 there were 9,425 registered members and the Class of 2015 included 606 new climbers—the largest new class to date. Where will it stop? When will it peak? Who knows!

Climbing was impacted by a major event in 1950 when a huge hurricane hit the Adirondacks and devastated parts of the High Peaks region. Many of the summits and open ridges were leveled by the severe winds. "Blowdown" from the storm—huge fields of downed trees resembled the old game of pick-up-sticks—was so extensive that the Department of Environmental Conservation (DEC) banned hiking for two years due to the increased risk of fire. In support of this action, the 46ers organization refused to recognize any climbs completed during the ban. But, once climbing was allowed, hikers were faced with an additional obstacle beside the fallen trees. New growth had sprouted between the downed timbers obscuring the climbers' view of where to place their next step. Hikers often tight-roped six feet in the air on top of downed trees hoping not to fall and become impaled on a jagged branch.

One blowdown-related story worth sharing involves legendary Adirondack guide Jim Goodwin. In August 1962, our group was climbing the Seward Range accompanying future 46er President Jim Bailey on his 46er finish. Just as we were leaving the summit of Seward we heard a noise in the brush and out popped Goodwin, who was guiding a Keene Valley client. We briefly discussed our route and headed off to Donaldson, confidently expecting to see them at our next stop. By the time we dragged ourselves through the tangle of downed trees we discovered that they had arrived—and left—long before us and were on their way to Mt. Emmons. Their time recorded subsequently in the Emmons log book indicated that they had left the summit hours before, leaving us to question how that could be possible!

Looking west from Marcy summit
CARL HEILAMN II

Many years later I attended Jim's memorial service and listened intently to all the speakers. One individual, who had been guided by Jim years before, shared the secret to his success. On several trailless climbs he recalled Jim saying, "I think we should drop down this valley for about 500 feet and see what we find." Each time after following his suggestion, the blowdown ceased and the woods surprisingly opened allowing easy travel. Jim skirted the confusion of downed trees to the next valley and led the group to the next summit. It seems that right after the 1950 hurricane a friend had flown Jim around the High Peaks. Jim took photos and noted where the blowdown fields started and ended, and where conditions were least affected. If you're curious why the existing herd path everyone uses today to Donaldson drops immediately off the side of Seward and skirts around some cliffs before climbing back up to Donaldson, I think I know the answer!

With the number of climbers beginning to explode in the 1970s, their mere presence began to impact the High Peaks area. Litter increased on trails, heavy use accelerated erosion and the development of herd paths on the trailless peaks—and the degradation of camping areas—became more prevalent. The old ethic of "leaving the campsite better than you found it" was no longer followed. The use of wood for fires and cooking had always been sustainable. Now "dead and down" fuel was nowhere to be found in the heavily used camping areas. The new breed of inexperienced camper was often unprepared and untrained in the woods skills of the "old timers." Garbage was left at sites attracting animals, fires were started on forest duff or in the middle of trails with "green" wood, and the overall impact became clearly visible to others who cared deeply about the mountains and their condition.

Large groups—summer camps, Scouts, and various organizations—arrived in increasing numbers. Their impact on the environment was directly proportional to the experience and training of their leaders. The 46ers responded by creating the Outdoor Skills Workshop in 1972. One of the leading proponents of this effort was Jim Bailey, who had been a summer camp counselor for many years. His committee invited camp, Scout, YMCA and 4-H leaders to a weekend training session where skills and philosophy could be stressed to minimize the impact of the groups on the High Peaks. I attended the first workshop as a participant and became a member of the staff the following year. The program has continued for the past 44 years, staffed by 46er members and offered for only $30 per participant. Additionally, the 46ers sponsor four campers each year to attend the DEC Summer Camp. The earlier we can introduce campers to the tenants of "Leave No Trace," the better!

Through the years the 46er organization has experienced many phases and changes in philosophy as it grew from a recreational and social group to embracing a leadership role in the stewardship of the High Peaks, stressing education and environmental awareness.

Jim Goodwin, Railroad Notch, 1986
COURTESY OF TONY SOLOMON

In the 1970s, 46er presidents Glenn Fish and Dr. Edwin H. Ketchledge spearheaded the change in the organization's focus and outreach. They helped organize efforts to remove lean-to garbage pits, promoted the "Carry it in, Carry it out" philosophy, joined with local search and rescue groups, instituted summit reseeding projects, fostered a litter bag program, distributed trowels to combat the pollution of water sources, and increased hiker education and trail maintenance efforts.

As litter on the trails increased, the 46ers purchased thousands of plastic litter bags for distribution at the trailheads. With the 46er logo on one side, the original bags had a picture of a pot hanging over a rock fire circle. Subsequently, with the changing philosophy, the "Pack it in, Pack it out" message replaced the camp fire on later models. The bags were popular with hikers. They helped to get the message out and greatly reduced the presence of litter on the trails through the years.

In 1978, Jim Goodwin became the Club's first Trailmaster. Working with the DEC, he organized volunteers who donated hundreds of hours on trail improvement projects each season. In the last 15 years, 1,328 individuals have donated 20,786 person-hours of voluntary trail work. In 2010, the 46ers began supporting the work of the Lean2 Rescue group both financially and through member volunteers. Through their efforts the famous Adirondack shelters have been rebuilt and relocated to more environmentally sound locations.

Large groups of inexperienced campers, who lacked knowledge about the proper techniques to store food at campsites, led to a problem of nuisance black bears. Uninformed or lazy campers often left their food in lean-tos or hung it improperly in trees. This led to the habituation of the bear population. In effect, the bears were "trained" to seek human food as a primary source. Why forage for berries and natural foods when humans left sumptuous treats available for such easy pickings? As the bear population became emboldened, the fear of attacks grew and popular campsites became littered with chewed packaging and the remnants of meals. In response, the Wilderness Conservation Society (WCS) stepped in with their Bear Education Program. After surveying campers and working with the DEC to assess the issues, the WCS turned to the 46ers to assist with the funding of their educational efforts. Since 2006 our organization has invested over $55,000 in WCS efforts to educate wilderness user groups, to place a backcountry steward at the Upper Works trailhead, and to enable the distribution of bear canisters to unprepared campers.

Increased usage of the High Peaks has also led to more hiker rescues, and the need for a well-trained and outfitted group of wilderness responders. Lack of experience and poor decision-making generally create most rescue situations. How to get training and resources to the hikers to prevent issues from arising is a challenge. In addition to the previously mentioned Outdoor Skills Workshop, the 46ers have also donated funds to purchase rescue equipment for the Keene Valley and Wilmington Back Country Rescue Groups. To motivate climbers to learn the skills necessary to be prepared for emergencies, the 46ers instituted the Wilderness First Aid Tuition Reimbursement Program. The Club offered to pay up to $100 of an individual's tuition upon the initial completion of a wilderness first aid certification course.

Personal recollections

I have many personal recollections from my early years climbing and camping. My first round of the 46 High Peaks was completed between 1956 and 1962. As touched on earlier, conditions, equipment, philosophies and the people themselves were very different in the 1950s and 60s. With the lack of herd paths, map and compass skills were mandatory with no GPS, cell phone or internet to rely on for trail updates or emergencies. Cooking was done over an open fire—if you couldn't start a wet wood fire in the rain, you didn't eat. Now fires are illegal in many areas of the High Peaks and stoves and fuel are a necessity. The pack weight and volume of the food required to feed a group of 12 for four days was daunting. Instead of carrying bulky cans and foods, dehydrated meals can be purchased in camping stores and light, easy to prepare alternatives can now be found on supermarket shelves.

David (in pack basket), Ditt and Mary Dittmar, 1940s
COURTESY OF TONY SOLOMON

Groups used tarps rather than heavy canvas tents. Blanket rolls and pack baskets gave way to the Boy Scout Yucca Pack and the Army surplus pack board. The novice hiker who hadn't mastered the diamond hitch to securely fasten their gear to the pack board could expect to see it strewn along the trail. Then in the 1960s the external framed Kelty pack came on the market to begin the revolution in light-weight backpacking. Flimsy plastic and surplus Army ponchos were replaced with the new, light coated nylon garments. Early generation fiber filled bags were heavy and bulky to carry. Lighter down sleeping bags—if

Approaching Marcy
JAMES APPLEYARD

one could afford them!—began to appear. Soon next generation, more compact fiber-filled bags became available. Army surplus gear from the Korean War was popular with those who could find it.

Until nylon and polypro fabrics arrived, cotton and wool were the only clothing available. Again, secondhand Army surplus clothing was substituted when available. With camp groups, sneakers, jeans and sweatshirts were commonplace since that's what parents had sent with their children. With most climbers there was a quick learning curve when you came back from your first rainy trip.

Camping in general was a totally different experience. There were fewer people in the woods, so the opportunity to find an open lean-to was much better. From the inception of lean-tos, the accepted ethic was to cut balsam boughs to place on the lean-to floor. Not only did they soften the surface but the odor was fantastic, especially since your fire often smoked out the inside of the lean-to. This wasn't all bad since the smoke often kept the mosquitoes and those dreaded no-see-ums from driving one crazy. Through the decades the needles fell off the boughs and gathered on the floor. By the 1950s you could place the end of the fresh boughs down into the bed of dry needles and form a hip or shoulder hole to sleep more comfortably. But as the numbers of campers increased, the surrounding forest could no longer sustain the cutting and replenishing of balsam boughs. Lean-to floors were replaced with boards and foam pads became a necessity.

The presence of a garbage pit at every lean-to, where campers were encouraged to deposit their refuse, was the accepted practice until the 1970s. They were removed with the advent of the "Carry it in, Carry it out!" philosophy. Garbage pits did have an interesting positive. During the night you might catch a glimpse of a bear, raccoon or other scavenger picking through the debris looking for a meal. Common practice was to leave any unwanted food on the lean-to shelf for the next individual or group. Since animals were conditioned to scavenge through the garbage, they tended to leave the food in lean-tos alone. Imagine the hiker who arrived to find a can of beans, hash or beef stew ready to heat up! In fact, there were individuals who spent their summers hiking from lean-to to lean-to living off the leftovers of other hikers. Freeze dried and dehydrated foods were not available and many of the new items on the market weren't extremely palatable. You could freeze meat, wrap it in newspaper and eat it the second night out but options after that were limited, especially in a camp group of 10 to 14.

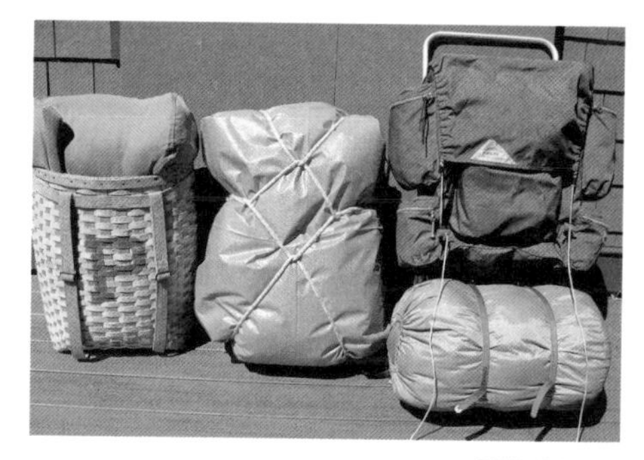
PHIL CORELL

Water was another story. Drinking right out of the stream was the norm. No purification was required but you always knew to get your drinking water upstream. No one understood the importance of hydration. "Don't drink too much or you'll get cramps!" was a common philosophy. Often on hikes we had a limited number of canteens, which were shared by all. The Health Department would have a "fit" about that but we seemed to survive. I remember more than once squeezing water out of moss to quench a raging thirst. As numbers increased, incidence of *Giardia*, a microscopic parasite found in contaminated water that causes the diarrheal illness known as giardiasis, began to surface. The 46ers stepped up and purchased 10,000 trowels to be distributed with an informational sheet explaining the importance of burying one's waste and staying 150 feet away from water sources. Now smart climbers depend on water filters, chemicals and UV pens to purify their drinking water.

Winter climbing had its own set of challenges, many of which have been forgotten with the advent of new clothing materials and equipment. Wool was the primary fabric for warmth but snow easily stuck to it and needed to be constantly brushed off. No Gore-tex or polypro existed but Army surplus gear from the Korean War was popular. The double layer, rubber Korean boots—later generation were the white "Mickey Mouse" variety—were heavy and could be tough to get on and off when damp, but kept your feet warm well below zero. The original cotton waffle long johns were later replaced by fishnet underwear. Snowshoes were wooden and usually had leather bindings which soaked through, stretched and often broke on the longer trips. Long, narrow shoes gave great flotation but were difficult to use in thick woods and when bushwhacking off trail. Bear paw snowshoes were very maneuverable but didn't keep you afloat in deep, powder snow. It would be many years before neoprene bindings, crampons, quick release straps and heel lifters arrived in the stores.

Fewer hikers on the trails gave more solitude but also meant fewer broken paths. There were times in the 1970s and 80s when only one group might successfully climb some of the major trailless ranges during the entire winter season. Water was and still is a challenge. Camping near steams offered running water to heat as long as you had an axe to make a hole in the ice. Otherwise you had to melt snow, which was time consuming and tedious while producing a less than desirable final product to drink.

The recent banning of fires in the eastern High Peaks has a secondary consequence. When it gets dark at 5:00 pm in winter the climber isn't ready to go to bed. In the 1960s, while sitting around the light and psychological warmth of a roaring fire, one could while away several hours before courageously climbing into that cold, nylon-lined sleeping bag. Drinking hot chocolate or soup next to the fire while you reminisced past exploits or planned the next day's trip is no longer legal!

My winter climbing began at the age of 16 when my father placed me on the train and sent me up to the Adirondacks to climb with my camp counselor, Jim Bailey. My father had spent cold nights camping during his military training and had me well clothed and geared up for the winter conditions. Later, in college, I took a yearly January trip with college friends and Mark Gibson, with whom I attended camp and finished my 46. We would usually convince our unsuspecting friends that spending four days in below-zero conditions and fresh snow would produce the "time of their life." I look back now and question my sanity—a snowshoe race on Wallface Pond, packing over Marcy in four feet of fresh powder, or spending four nights at Lake Colden never seeing the thermometer go above zero. But there are also memories of beautiful cloudless skies on open summits and of many cups of tea and climbing stories shared with Charlie Nolan at the Ranger's Cabin at Lake Colden!

Summer camp brought me to the Adirondacks and my climbing experiences introduced me to the 46er organization. During my 53 years as a member, I have served as President, Treasurer and Outdoor Skills Workshop coordinator. I personally witnessed and participated in the Club's growth and its transition into the role of mountain steward. No matter what each member's background may be, we are all bound by the journey we have taken, the experiences we "survived" along the way, and the spiritual bond we have developed with the Adirondacks. We look at our Club with pride as we continue to commit ourselves to protecting the mountains we love.

For a more detailed description of the birth of climbing the 46 and the creation of the 46er organization, please refer to *Heaven Up-h'isted-ness* published by the Forty-Sixer Club (www.adk46er.org). This reference book includes a complete history of the Club as well as historical background on each of the Adirondack High Peaks.

Common merganser
LARRY MASTER

Doing Right by Wilderness

By Tom Martin

Tom Martin *is Regional Supervisor of Natural Resources, Region 5, for the NYS Department of Environmental Conservation (DEC), based in Ray Brook, NY. He is a Certified Forester, Chair-elect of the New York Society of American Foresters and 46er #2237.*

Tom is a graduate of the NYS Ranger School (1976) and holds a B.S. from the College of Forestry, Syracuse (1979). Early in his career, he worked as a Wilderness Area Park Ranger in the Pharaoh Lake area (1979-1980) and as a forest fire observer at the Pharaoh Mountain fire tower (1983). Prior to his current position at DEC, Tom was successively Pesticide Specialist (1983-1988), Forester (1988-1998) and Region 5 Regional Forester (1998-2012).

I have an almost lifelong appreciation and deep and abiding love for the Adirondacks. I say "almost" lifelong because I plan to hang around quite a few more years! Anyway, in retrospect, my feeling for the Adirondacks began at a very young age. Like many Baby Boomers, I first visited in the early 1960s. I initially saw the area through the back window of our family station wagon—I'm still not sure why I always had to sit in the back—as we drove to and visited places like Story Town, Frontier Town, Enchanted Forest and Land of Make Believe. As a kid, I always thought that the Paul Bunyan statue in front of Enchanted Forest was really cool. To be honest, I still think Paul Bunyan is cool. And who knew that this feeling was a precursor to a 35+ year career with the New York State Department of Environmental Conservation (DEC)?

My next visit to the Adirondacks and my first trip up a High Peak came when my family stayed in a Wilmington campground in order to visit Expo 67 world exhibition in Montreal. It seemed like quite a long ways to drive to get to Expo but it provided some time to tour around Wilmington. One of the things we did was drive up Whiteface Mountain. So even though I didn't climb the mountain that trip, my first view of the Adirondacks from up high was on Whiteface. We also visited Mystery Spot, another place that piqued my interest in natural phenomena. Even though I now know most of what they said was bunk, it was quite plausible to me as a young kid.

In 1975, I entered the New York State Ranger School. Edwin H. Ketchledge ("Ketch") had started his summit restoration work and in the spring of 1976 had encouraged folks at the Ranger School to allow him to take the students up Algonquin. The class was split into two groups, about 40 people each day. Ketch hiked both groups up Algonquin, with each student carrying five pounds of limestone, five pounds of fertilizer and a pound of grass seed. We were instructed in which areas of bare soil we were to spread the materials we had carried up the mountain. I was incredibly impressed not only with Ketch but also with the view. It wasn't a great day, a bit rainy and overcast, but still really outstanding views.

Author on Saddleback, August 1978

I then went on to the College of Environmental Science and Forestry in Syracuse. There I met a young lady who I ended up spending quite a bit of time with. Her last name was Dittmar and her father was "Dit" Dittmar, Executive Secretary and Treasurer of the Adirondack 46ers, and her mom was Mary Dittmar. Dit and Mary were well known in the hiking community and were 46ers #31 and #29, respectively. Mary's sister, Helen Menz, was also a 46er, so being part of that family it was sort of required that I spend time climbing mountains in the Adirondacks.

Helen C. Menz (46er #42) and sister Mary C. Dittmar (46er #29), Cascade summit, 1934
COURTESY OF TONY SOLOMON

Later, I worked a summer on the Pharaoh Mountain fire tower. I would spend five days on the mountain and then, on my two off days, I would come off the mountain, repack my pack and go backpacking and climbing. I spent several years backpacking, hiking and climbing the 46 High Peaks. I finished my 46 on Allen Mountain with a group of people. From what I recall, it was a first round of the 46 for three of us, a 2nd round for another three, her 3rd round for Helen Menz and her 4th round for Mary Dittmar. It was a pretty amazing experience!

I've had several jobs with DEC over the years mostly in Region 5 but I did work five years in Albany when the office was at Wolf Rd. I have lived and recreated in the Adirondacks my entire career. Having spent years as a hiker and enjoying the mountains as a member of the public, my work at DEC has afforded me a different perspective—that of land manager. I was now tasked with protecting and managing the resource I so dearly enjoyed and respected[1].

When I came back to the Region to work in the spring of 1998, we were at the tail end of getting the High Peaks Unit Management Plan (HPUMP) across the goal line. Stu Buchannan was the Regional Director at the time. The Department had been working for some 27 years on getting a plan in place for our management of the High Peaks Wilderness Area—the largest wilderness in New York State. Jim Papero at DEC and Chuck Strafford at APA were the prime authors of that document. There was a large citizen advisory committee and lots of reports, lots of writing and lots of controversial issues that came up through that 27-year period. Some of these issues we were able to deal with and move forward on and some still remain to be dealt with today.

Serving the public

One of the fun things about working at DEC is the kind of telephone calls we get. Most public servants and employees of DEC truly believe that we do work for the public and we always try to be polite and provide good information whenever someone calls. It's always interesting to find that many folks who call the DEC have an incomplete understanding of how big the Adirondack Park really is and what six million acres truly means. (Helpful hint: The state of Vermont is about 6 million acres.) I think some of the following examples will illustrate that point and more.

One of the most common calls we get is from people who are on their way to the Adirondacks and are running late. They want to know when the Park closes—when do we close the gates! Now that folks have cell phones and the service in the Adirondacks is improving, the other type of call we get routinely is from people who say they are on the Northway or on the Thruway and "I'm on my way up there and I'm coming up for the weekend"—these are usually Friday afternoon calls. They proceed to tell us that they are heading up to hunt, fish, hike, camp, or any number of those things that we love to do in the backcountry. So far so good but then they follow that up by asking "Where should I go?" or "Where should I camp?"

A true classic was when one of our fisheries biologists received a call from a woman who informed him that her husband was in the Park fishing and would he please shout out the window and ask her husband to call home—she needed to speak with him! A while ago, a fellow who was keeping pigs called to let us know that a black bear was attacking his animals. When we asked how he dealt with the situation, he said that he attempted to shoot the bear but unfortunately shot one of his pigs instead!

Conservation measures

The HPUMP, completed in 1999, brought in new measures like the requirement to have dogs on leashes on the trails, as well as the limit of eight people for overnight groups and 15 for day groups.

Probably the most controversial was the ban on campfires in the eastern High Peaks. When hiking around in the eastern High Peaks in the 1970s and 80s, you could stand at Marcy Dam and see just about every tent site that was there. At Lake Colden, you could see day glow from groups of tents lit by lantern and candles. You could see all through the woods because there was no undergrowth, everything had been picked over and burned in campfires. If you go into the High Peaks today, it looks vastly different. I think the single most destructive thing that we allow in the backcountry is campfires. And I think that the way the camping areas around Marcy Dam and Lake Colden look like today is strong evidence to support the decision to ban campfires there. You no longer see any areas that look like an open park. Seedlings, saplings and bushes have grown back so most of the tent sites are now screened by young vegetation.

Outstanding issues

We continue to struggle with many backcountry issues today—issues that we wrestled with in the late 1990s and frankly punted (as in postponed until next time.) One example is permitting in the backcountry or permit restrictions on camping or day use, and the issue of restricting the numbers of people allowed in the backcountry at any given time. We continue in many ways to love the woods to death. Over the recent Columbus Day/ Canadian Thanksgiving weekend, a three-day holiday period, 2,600 people registered at the Cascade trailhead. Think about it for a moment, a 3-mile trail with 2,600 people in three days! That seems a bit extreme. Wilderness is defined in part as an area that has opportunities for solitude and primitive and unconfined recreation. I would argue that if you were on that 3-mile-long trail on any one of those days there clearly was not any opportunity for solitude.

We often see full parking lots at Adirondak Loj. We see trailheads for Dix, Giant and Rocky Peak Ridge along Route 73 jammed beyond capacity. We've had to institute a parking fee at the Garden parking lot and the Town of Keene has instituted a hiker's shuttle because the number of people exceeds

Johns Brook Outpost, April 1974
GARY KOCH

The High Peaks Wilderness
CARL HEILMAN II

parking capacity. Folks suggest that we should just increase the size of parking lots but that doesn't solve the issue or give us any handle on the number of people. If we continue to build bigger and bigger parking lots, I believe that the numbers will just continue to grow and we will get to a place that is far, far away from what was intended by Bob Marshall and others when they pondered the idea of wildness. I expect Howard Zahniser would be quite surprised at what he would see in the High Peaks Wilderness today in terms of the number of visitors.

The issue of dams in wilderness areas is also something that we struggle with. Wilderness is supposed to be an area that "...appears to have been affected primarily by the force of nature, with the imprint of man's work substantially unnoticeable." So by definition, I question whether dams are structures that should be allowed in wilderness. Clearly, an impounded pond or lake is a landscape that is created by the work of man. Yes, we love to paddle. We love the opportunities to traverse the backcountry by watercraft. We love the open views provided by water bodies. But I wonder if we should have dams in the wilderness. What should they look like? How should they be built? How should they be dealt with when there is a need to repair them? Should we be using large motorized equipment

Haystack Trail, 1981
PETE BIESEMEYER

or have motorized intrusions into the wilderness to do major rehabilitation projects? The federal government allows that in their wilderness areas. They go through a process called "Minimum Requirement Decision Guide" that often results in a decision to use a helicopter to fly heavy equipment into these sites to rebuild dams and other manmade structures. These are questions that we still need to think about and address.

Progress is being made

The good news is that our backcountry areas, particularly the High Peaks, are in much better shape today than they were when I started spending time there in the 1970s. This has been achieved thanks mostly to dedicated and committed individuals who share a love for the mountains—from groups like the 46ers and Adirondack Mountain Club (ADK), the Adirondack Trail Improvement Society (ATIS) and the Summit Stewardship Program, as well as individual volunteers, trail adopters and lean-to adopters. We've also had significant funding through the Environmental Protection Fund, which has allowed us to enter into stewardship contracts with ADK, ATIS and the AmeriCorps/ Student Conservation Association. These programs put trained trail builders into our backcountry. We had lean-tos replaced, relocated and repaired through the incredible efforts of Lean2Rescue and other individuals who have adopted lean-tos.

We do have some issues we still need to resolve but I firmly believe that people who care about and love the mountains and the High Peaks deeply, people who recreate here, advocacy groups, DEC staff and other smart, committed and dedicated individuals will find the answers in the future to continue to protect this very special place.

---

1. I've read many good books over the years and I'd recommend three for those who love wild places and the backcountry. The first is *The Big Burn* by Timothy Egan, a story about the fires in Idaho and Montana back in 1910. But more importantly, it's a story about Gifford Pinchot and Teddy Roosevelt and how those two individuals were the impetus for our National Park and Forest systems. And that ties back to NY and their work here and the fact that the Adirondacks were the place that helped them to develop their beliefs and conservation ethic.

   The other two books are *Wilderness Ethics* and *Backwoods Ethics* by Guy and Laura Waterman. They discuss the way we should treat the backcountry and how we should conduct ourselves when we're in the woods. They speak about numerous issues that are of concern, or should be of concern, to all of us. They write about snowmobiling, fires in the backcountry, off trail hiking, dogs, aircraft, radios and other modern technologies that often take the wild out of wilderness. They also contemplate a number of issues that are really important for us to tackle and talk about as our population continues to expand, and as the number of people who come to the Adirondacks and other wild places continues to grow.

Elk Lake from Macomb, May 2009
YVON DAIGLE

Elk Lake: When Conservation Makes History

By John Ernst

John Ernst *is Chairman and President of Bloomingdale Properties, a private investment company in New York City. He is Chairman of Adirondack Foundation and Treasurer of Lochland School. He serves on the boards of the Adirondack Council, the Adirondack Landowners Association, the Adirondack Lakes Survey Corporation, the Open Space Institute and the National Museum of the American Indian, NY.*

Margot Ernst *for twenty years was a curator of Japanese art. She has been working in the museum and environmental nonprofit sector since then and lives in New York City and North Hudson, NY. Her current board affiliations are: National Public Radio Foundation, Island Press, National Museum of the American Indian, NY, and Audubon, and active emeritus of the Adirondack Museum in Blue Mountain Lake.*

Margot and John own and run Elk Lake Lodge in the High Peaks.
www.elklakelodge.com

Elk Lake features prominently in Adirondack lore for many reasons, not least of which are its strategic location as a gateway to numerous points of interest and mountaintops, natural beauty, magnificent views of several High Peaks and the presence of Elk Lake Lodge. The nearby Elk Lake state trailhead provides access to the Dixes, Marcy and, soon, Boreas Mountain, among others. Clear Pond, a pristine body of water visible from many surrounding peaks, is located where the Elk Lake Road transitions from public to private property.—CBR and AR, Eds.

My family history at Elk Lake began when my grandfather, Bernard M. L. Ernst, spent part of the summer of 1907 on Clear Pond with his fiancée and returned the next year, after they were married. That started a tradition in which my grandparents spent their summer vacations in the Adirondacks, ultimately switching to Elk Lake and lodging that was marginally less primitive.

Tradition led to more permanent status when my father, Richard, bought the land around Clear Pond nearly 60 years ago. Some years later, he persuaded his father-in-law, Samuel J. Bloomingdale, to purchase the vast forestland surrounding Elk Lake.

This was a heritage I received with little enthusiasm. My childhood memories are of getting hopelessly lost in woods swarming with black flies; of my cousin falling into the Branch while fishing and knocking out his front teeth; of toiling up mountains whose views were obscured by clouds. Returning to the city was bliss!

Eventually, I stopped fighting it and looked around and was amazed. But I never did a complete reversal. My favorite Adirondack sport is still sitting in a chair reading, or watching the light change in the mountains. But I began to value the precious thing that others had thought to preserve, and my wife Margot and I resolved to do likewise.

But first some history about Elk Lake, Clear Pond and Elk Lake Lodge.

The earliest map of Elk Lake (née Mud Pond) and Clear Pond shows the owners as Peter Smith, John Ireland and John Kiersted. When Peter Smith died, his land passed on to his son, Gerrit Smith, who became a well-known abolitionist, friend of John Brown, and donor of the land in North Elba for the settlement of former slaves called Timbuctoo.

The first permanent resident was Israel Johnson, who took out a mortgage on 195 acres at Clear Pond from the Smiths and ran a sawmill there from 1832 to 1846 but never completed his purchase. For years it was the last house on the road east of the Boreas Range and was the overnight stopping place for travellers going to or coming from the ironworks. William C. Redfield stopped there on his trips to the headwaters of the Hudson in 1836 and 1837.

Clear Pond and the High Peaks from Clear Pond Mountain
CARL HEILMAN II

In the early 1830s, Ebenezer Emmons stayed with Johnson while working on his *Natural History of New York*, during which time he made the first recorded ascent of Mount Marcy on August 5, 1837. In 1873, Verplanck Colvin, in the course of writing his topographical Adirondack survey report, *The Adirondack Wilderness*, changed the name Mud Pond to Elk Lake "in memory of the stately Alpine deer once abundant in the vicinity." On August 26, 1871, the *Albany Evening Journal* published a letter from Colvin: "From Mud Lake (Elk Lake), I visited Johnson's Clear Pond, and another day was occupied in ascending Dix's Peak."

By the 1870s, Myron Bruce, who was postmaster at nearby Blue Ridge and ran a general store that still stands (although unfortunately no longer in business), was operating an inn at Elk Lake where his son, Will, was born in 1874.

This inn is advertised in S.R. Stoddard's *The Adirondacks Illustrated* (1874) as follows: "Mud Pond House located in the immediate vicinity of the Adirondack Mountains upon the nearest and most direct route, from the South, to the Ausable Ponds and Mount Marcy, distant only 9 miles, over a good trail, 4 miles of which can be made on horseback. Terms, $1.50 per day, will accommodate 30."

After Finch, Pruyn and Company (Finch) bought the bulk of the land from a Washington County speculator named Phoebe Bloomingdale for $25,000 in 1891, they continued the practice of leasing the summer Elk Lake operation to a succession of innkeepers. The leaseholder in 1903 was Henry Pellitier "Pell" Jones, who began construction of the present day lodge. An earlier structure at a different spot was swept away when the dam washed out in 1888. Its replacement, "Hunter's Rest," burned to its foundation in the 1930s.

In *Friendly Adirondack Peaks* (1924), Robert S. Wickham recounts an August 1923, multi-day trek over 16 high peaks: "A long walk over the tote road around Elk Lake brought us to Elk Lake House for dinner, a place of beautiful view. Elk Lake House was built of peeled spruce logs years ago, and artistically built, by Pell Jones, its guardian angel. I suspect it took a long time to build it, even as time is measured in the woods."

My grandfather was said to have helped construct the lodge's original fieldstone chimney. His two daughters and my father lost little time before neatly carving their names and their annual dates of occupancy on the varnished interior logs of the building, where these graffiti remain to this day, half-hidden by a trestle table discreetly moved to the spot to discourage others from following their bad example.

In 1956, my father bought the 1,000-acre Clear Pond property from Finch for $50,000. Seven years later, he persuaded his father-in-law, 90-year-old Samuel J. Bloomingdale (no relation to previous owner, Phoebe), to purchase the 11,000-acre Elk Lake Tract, also from Finch, and to donate a conservation easement to the state. It covers a fringe of 1,000 feet around most of Elk Lake and includes the lake's 30 or so islands, ensuring that nothing will ever spoil the views of Dix, Macomb, Nippletop and the Colvin Range.

This was the first conservation easement in the history of the State of New York. At the same time, my family donated an easement for a small parking lot near the end of Elk Lake Road that has since provided thousands of hikers a takeoff point for state trails into the High Peaks.

Fisher
LARRY MASTER

Nearby Elk Lake Lodge still operates as a resort, much as it has since the 1870s. Many of the guests who use the main building and eight cottages during the summer months are families who have been coming for several generations. The Lodge can accommodate 40 guests.

Every effort is made to manage the preserve in such a way as to maintain its wilderness character. A service forestry program with Finch provides light winter cutting to improve the timber stand and to reduce the danger of fire and disease. Temiscamie hybrid trout were introduced under Dr. Dwight Webster's Cornell program to strengthen the native strain, which a recent study indicates is now genetically distinct. No gasoline motors are allowed on either Elk Lake or Clear Pond in order to protect loon habitat. Guests may not bring in their own boats to either body of water because of the risk of contamination from invasive species.

Elk Lake looks much the same now as it has since 1875, when E. R. Wallace's *Descriptive Guide to the Adirondacks* referred to Rufus Fiske's "Secluded lake-side inn… (that) can accommodate 40 visitors." It looks much the same as it did when Charles Ives composed parts of his symphonies No. 3 and No. 4 there between 1909 and 1911. It looks much the same as it did when my father was carried around its shore in a homemade knapsack by his father, when both of my daughters were married at water's edge, and when my grandchildren splashed each other at its beach. That, after all, is the point.

Protected forever

As the sole owners of the Elk Lake/Clear Pond property, Margot and I faced a two-fold problem. First, how to protect this land forever, which has clearly always been our family's intent and second, how to pass the property to our children in a way that would allow them to afford to hold it.

The answer seemed simple: why not extend permanent protections over the rest of the property with a new easement to the state? The property would be protected forever. We would retain enough rights to operate Elk Lake Lodge and provide house sites for our family. The appraised value of

Wagon Wheel Landing, Elk Lake, 1986
COURTESY OF TONY SOLOMON

Boreas Range, Colvin Range, Nippletop and the Dix Range from Elk Lake Lodge
CARL HEILMAN II

the property would be reduced by the value of the gift. We would earn a tax deduction for the gift. And the state would pay some of the annual property taxes in proportion to their ownership of rights.

The answer may have been simple; the execution was a bit more complicated. The original easement document protecting Elk Lake's shoreline covered one and a half pages. The easement we signed several years ago covering the rest of the property runs 70 pages and comes with a baseline description of the property and recent environmental studies on the property requiring 437 pages of text, photos and maps.

We started the process in the Pataki Administration. Four Governors and nine years later, we reached the finish line in the Cuomo Administration.

The first step along the road was in choosing Land Planner Vinny McClelland to do a Master Plan for the property that attempted to look out a hundred years. This was the critical and difficult process of thinking through all the variables that affected running the business and accommodating family needs. Teaming with

Elk Lake Lodge, 1973
GARY KOCH

Vinny was Attorney Tim Smith, who provided the expert legal and agency guidance that illuminated the journey.

Our partners throughout were the staff of The Adirondack Chapter of The Nature Conservancy (TNC). They provided environmental guidance, expertise in the process, key links with state government, especially the Department of Environmental Conservation (DEC), and they arranged and administered meetings involving as many as ten or 15 DEC officials, lawyers and TNC personnel.

In addition, an important part of what we did was swap about 1,600 acres of Elk Lake land at Casey Brook that separated two state wilderness areas with an equal-sized parcel that TNC had purchased from Finch that ran up one entire side of the Elk Lake Road. Land that had been timbered and would have been inaccessible to us once the land around was re-classified, was exchanged for land that came with a fiber supply agreement to Finch, insuring it would remain in production. That protected our entire road frontage from development, since the other side was to be acquired by the state. Mike Carr, Executive Director of the Adirondack Chapter of The Nature Conservancy / Adirondack Land Trust, and Todd Dunham, Director of Land Protection TNC Adirondack Chapter, were an integral part to every step of the easement process.

The other key partner was the DEC, led by Joe Martens, DEC Commissioner. Without his support of the easement nothing would have happened. The talented and dedicated team he assigned to work with us, led by Frank Dunstan, Natural Resource Planner (DEC), was a pleasure for us to deal with. We never had a serious disagreement about what we needed to accomplish.

Although the easement was a gift, it brought benefits to us as landowners and therefore the state understandably expected to achieve benefits for the people of New York. We strengthened the public rights to the Dix and Marcy trails and we agreed in principle to a new public trail to go up Boreas Mountain to replace one that had been closed.

In the final agreement, approximately 280 development rights were extinguished permanently. Elk Lake retained five development sites and the right to build several remote camps with no water or power. Remaining outside the easement is the land immediately adjacent to the Lodge and cottages and to the gatehouse and support buildings, as well as the five acres surrounding our residence.

For us this is a win/win for private stewardship and environmental protection. A beautiful piece of land is protected. The Lodge will operate as it has for 150 years. Timber harvesting continues. And our children are the new owners of the property, effecting the generational change that was one of our objectives. We couldn't be happier with the result.

View from the Adirondak Loj Road
CARL HEILMAN II

The Adirondack Landowners Association: Private Lands with Public Benefits

By Ross Whaley

Since October 2007 Dr. **Ross Whaley** *has served as Senior Advisor to the Adirondack Landowners Association. He started this position after serving the Governor of New York as Chairman of the Adirondack Park Agency for four years. He brought to these positions more than 30 years of experience as a university teacher, researcher and administrator. He also served as Director of Economics Research for the US Forest Service for six years. From 1984 to 2005 Dr. Whaley was associated with the SUNY College of Environmental Science and Forestry, 16 years as its President and subsequently as University Professor.*

He has been awarded the USDA Superior Service Award, the Pinchot Medallion by the Pinchot Institute for Conservation, the Professional Conservationist Award by the New York Conservation Council, the Heiberg Memorial Award by the New York Forest Owners Association and Honor Alumnus of Colorado State University. Dr. Whaley holds a B.S. in Forestry (1959) from the University of Michigan, an M.S. from Colorado State University and a Ph.D. in Natural Resource Economics (1969), also from the University of Michigan.

Some would argue that when the *Blue Line* was drawn around the Adirondack Park in 1892 the intention was that all the lands would eventually become Forest Preserve. Therefore, did the Adirondack Park of today with slightly over half of its land still in private ownership miss its full potential? Or is it a terrific example to the world of how people and wild lands can coexist in close harmony? As the old adage goes, "The proof of the pudding is in the eating" and I would argue that this pudding is exceptionally tasty.

Along with its 130,000 people living in 103 towns and villages scattered across the Park, one finds 1.2 million acres of wilderness or wilderness-like Forest Preserve, another 1.3 million acres of public lands available for more intensive public recreational use and 2.9 million acres of private lands that are ecologically indistinguishable from the Forest Preserve. Combined, these lands form the largest protected area of temperate deciduous forest in the world.

Perhaps most impressive about the Park is how well it illustrates the recuperative power of nature. Here we see a land which today looks quite different from the time when timber and minerals were being exploited to facilitate the early growth of the northeastern United States. Evidence of this is not only seen in the Forest Preserve but also on the private forest lands. Today, if you have the pleasure of flying over the Adirondack Park almost all that you see is forests and water in valleys and mountains. With the exception of the highways, hamlets and houses along the shores of some lakes, one cannot distinguish between private lands and the Forest Preserve. All these lands have contributed to the return of the bald eagle, peregrine falcon, moose, beaver and other animals that had disappeared from the landscape or were headed for extinction.

R. J. NOWICKI

The owners of much of the non-industrial private forests of the Park came together in 1990 to form the Adirondack Landowners Association (ALA). It was founded to encourage continued stewardship and sound resource management of the land; to promote public awareness of the valuable role played by private landowners in the Park; to advocate for laws, regulations and governmental policies that promote and facilitate good stewardship by private landowners, and recognize and preserve their land rights. Its members own more than 150,000 acres of land, a small but significant portion of the Park. There are 32 members of ALA made up of clubs, extended families covering several generations, groups and private preserves, some with ownership dating back to the mid-1800s. Counting club members, joint owners and family members, ALA represents about 1,500 people. More about ALA can be learned from our website adklandowners.org.

NANCIE BATTAGLIA

The contribution of private lands and their owners can be seen in three distinctive ways. First, is their contributions through the ecological services that they provide—protecting stream habitats from siltation and warming, carbon sequestration and its role in reducing the advance of climate change, a critical role in protecting ecological corridors for the migration of species, and a privacy that makes them ecologically some of the most protected lands in the Park.

Second, in some instances the private lands have been sought out for forest, fisheries, wildlife and acid rain research because of the ability to separate the research protocols from public intrusion while at the same time being relatively accessible to the researcher. The results of this research have played an important role in informing forest and wildlife management practices and regulations in the state. Notable is the relationship between Cornell University and the Adirondack League Club, a collaboration that has focused on fish habitat and genetics since 1950.

In addition to the ecological services and research opportunities provided by private lands, ALA members as well as other private landowners contribute directly to the economy of the Park.

A survey of ALA members conducted in 2011 revealed that:

- ALA members employ several hundred full and part-time employees ($6 million in annual payroll).
- ALA members pay nearly $3.4 million in annual property taxes.
- ALA member timber harvest programs contribute significantly to the Adirondack economy every year. Our members have over 135,000 acres in active Forest Management and some are Forest Stewardship Council (FSC) and/or Sustainable Forestry Initiative (SFI) certified for "green" harvesting and management practices.
- ALA members purchase over $5 million in goods and services annually in the Adirondacks.
- ALA members are active in a wide variety of organizations that work to support wise resource management and sound environmental conservation.
- Additionally, many of our members work closely with state and local officials to help promote better communication among the various stakeholder groups in the Adirondacks. Their participation in workshops, discussion groups and various not-for-profit advocacy organizations highlights the contribution and concern ALA members have for the economic and environmental health of the Park.

In 2013, the ALA initiated an education program to help reduce the spread of aquatic invasive species. Working in collaboration with the Department of Environmental Conservation and the Department of Motor Vehicles (DMV), we were instrumental in creating an educational insert to be included in all mailed renewals for boat and trailer registrations. In addition, local DMV offices operated by the County Clerks throughout upstate New York have partnered with ALA to help with the education effort. The County Clerks agreed to provide space for signage and educational brochures on aquatic invasive species. The ALA supplied the signage and brochures to the approximately 30 County Clerks, who are deserving of high praise for their enthusiasm and the way they have embraced ALA's request to assist in this education program.

This year, in addition to celebrating our 25th anniversary, ALA has been exploring new ways in which it can contribute to private land stewardship by setting an example of high standards for best management practices on our own lands, contributing to our neighboring communities, and being active participants in the long-term nurturing of the people and lands of the Adirondack Park. Through this effort we intend to be a major contributor to the Park being a world-class model of sustainable land use in rural wild land areas.

The Color of Water

By Mary Thill

Ed Ketchledge was a botanist, but he was a keen observer of things other than plants. On one of his many hikes in the Adirondack High Peaks, he told me that nowhere in his mountain travels had he seen water the color of these gray-green streams.

High Peaks water *is* unusually gray-green, but not in the cloudy way of absinthe. It is as clear and cool as a martini garnished with lichen. Water has apparent color and it has true color. Tap water appears clear because algae and other suspended material have been filtered out. True color is hard to perceive in a glass-sized sample, but dissolved minerals and other components lend a subtle cast.

In the Adirondacks we have thousands of lakes, some of them true blue, some green and many classically Adirondack tea-brown. That brown can indicate iron or dissolved organic carbon—basically life in its most micro, decomposed form. Green water can also indicate organic matter in the form of algae—and the return of life to water once rendered clear by acid rain. Or green can indicate pollution from too many lawns and too much fertilizer, or from nitrogen rained in from Midwestern power plants. Blue is the default color of the ocean and other large bodies of water that don't contain much suspended material. Clear water absorbs colors on the red side of the light spectrum, leaving us to see blue.

If you've been to Niagara Falls, you may have been startled by the semi-opaque teal of the Niagara River above and below the falls. It comes in part from tons of dissolved limestone. The erosive power of the river scrapes a rock flour from the bedrock.

In High Peaks streams, the tint comes from a smaller-scale relationship between water and mineral. The underlying rock of the High Peaks is Mount Marcy anorthosite, which is dominated by a greenish-gray feldspar. A 20-ton block of Marcy anorthosite mined from the Cold Spring Granite Quarry, south of Au Sable Forks, is the cornerstone of the Freedom Tower at Manhattan's One World Trade Center.

This stone is rare on Earth but common locally, occupying more than 3,300 square miles, according to SUNY Plattsburgh geologists. This rock is the underpainting of the High Peaks forest, coloring the water and, sometimes, it seems, the air.

This essay appeared first at AdirondackLife.com in 2013.
Mary Thill is a science writer and editor working with The Adirondack Chapter. of The Nature Conservancy.

Ranger Pete Fish on Marcy, August 2008, the day of his 700th ascent.
NANCIE BATTAGLIA

Ranger Pete Fish: A Legacy of Stewardship to the High Peaks

By Seth Jones

Seth Jones *is the Adirondack Mountain Club's (ADK) Education Programs Coordinator. He has worked for ADK since 2008 and is a former High Peaks Summit Steward and Johns Brook Lodge Hutmaster. Seth is also on the board of The Waterman Fund, an organization dedicated to preserving the spirit of wildness and the alpine areas of Northeastern North America. He enjoys a variety of outdoor activities, including paddling, fly fishing, hiking, skiing and photography.*

Seth holds a B.S. in Conservation Biology from the SUNY College of Environmental Science and Forestry.

Protecting a wilderness like the Adirondack High Peaks has always required the dedication of individuals willing to put their boots on the ground to get the work done. One such individual is the legendary Forest Ranger Peter "Pete" Fish. For over 20 years Pete patrolled the High Peaks educating the public and protecting this beautiful Adirondack landscape.

I had the privilege of hiking with Pete this past October, when we climbed Baxter Mountain, a small peak outside of Keene, NY. Most of the foliage had already dropped but the reddish browns of the oaks still held some color. At one point along the trail Pete spotted an abandoned energy drink container peeking out of the downed leaves. "You know what I find interesting with these energy drinks? The consumers never seem to have the energy to carry them out after they drink them." I helped Pete put it into his bag.

Fred LeBrun described Forest Rangers as "men and women of the woods, sentinels in the wilderness. They watched for forest fires and fought them, and still do. They rescue lost and injured hikers, and are best known to the public as trail and outdoors educators, informing rather than enforcing—a reassuring and knowledgeable presence in the backcountry, generally welcomed by all." Pete Fish summed up his role as "protecting the people from the environment and protecting the environment from the people, so that they could coexist, thrive and do well together."

From 1975 to 1998 Pete Fish was one of the official stewards of the Adirondack High Peaks, working as a Forest Ranger for the New York State Department of Environmental Conservation (DEC). By the start of his tenure, hiking and camping were gaining mainstream popularity bringing flocks of new recreational enthusiasts to the Adirondack High Peaks. This sudden heavy usage had a toll on the region.

Marcy, fall 1984
PETE BIESEMEYER

Pete describes the High Peaks in 1975, his first season on the job, as a mess.

"While driving along Adirondack Loj Road there was litter on both sides," Pete recalled. "If you went down to South Meadows the whole place was a pig pen… people camping anyplace they wanted to. If you hiked into Marcy Dam from the Adirondak Loj you could fill both pockets with ordinary, lightweight litter. At Marcy Dam, there was litter all over the place, garbage in the fire pits. Litter was the name of the game."

Pete remembers the trail registers being in poor shape as well. Many were missing pages and lacked information about regulations. "It was as if there had never been a Forest Ranger in the area before," he explained.

NANCIE BATTAGLIA

Pete seized the opportunity to help clean the place up and provide a consistent DEC presence in the High Peaks. "I've always had the feeling that you can't stand knee-deep in garbage and pretend that you care," he said in an interview with North Country Public Radio's Martha Foley in 1999.

Throughout Pete's tenure he made recommendations to the state about how the High Peaks should be managed, many of them included later in the High Peaks Unit Management Plan. According to Pete, the bureaucracy of DEC meant that it was sometimes more efficient for him to work around existing regulations than to strictly follow procedure. For example, he wanted to start enforcing his idea of a maximum group size but wasn't allowed to discourage large groups on his own authority. So he asked his supervisor to write a memo explicitly instructing him not to issue camping permits to groups larger than 20. This marked the beginning of the now familiar High Peaks group size regulation.

Another clever work-around shows Pete's dedication to the job. As a Ranger he was expected to patrol a specific region during his normal working hours. But Pete thought he should be patrolling other areas and routes. To fulfill the requirements of his job and remain true to his personal convictions, he'd do what was expected of him during his workweek but on his days off he patrolled areas and routes that he believed needed to be covered.

Marcy from Colden

CBR

It was characteristic of Pete to speak with every single hiker he came across. Many people have a story about running into him on the trail or in the parking lot where he would accost people with his customary humor and directness. Pete describes his backcountry education style as "nagging, endless nagging." He wouldn't wait for someone to ask him a question or until it looked like they needed help; he would just talk to everyone and would often give very blunt advice. His extra patrolling and consistent contact with hikers significantly increased the DEC presence in the backcountry and gave him the reputation for being everywhere. You'd always see Pete when you were in the High Peaks. True to form, this reputation still stands.

I was working as a High Peaks Summit Steward on Mount Marcy when I first met Pete who had long since retired and was on a quest to hike Marcy 777 times. That particular June the black flies were relentless but Pete seemed unaffected. Clad in a tan shirt and shorts, Limmer hiking boots (without a speck of mud on them), quality wool socks and a walking stick, he started a conversation by complaining about a hiker aerating the sides of the trails with trekking poles. After some discussion, I eventually confided in him that I was having a hard time with the black flies. He looked at me and said, "I have the perfect remedy." He went into his pack, pulled out a small plastic bottle of single malt whiskey and poured me a shot. "This usually helps," said Pete.

Being unprepared for blackflies is one thing, but during his Ranger years Pete became passionate about educating hikers on preparedness in the backcountry. He realized early on that the bulk of search and rescue activity came from poorly prepared hikers. One of his educational techniques was a classic, well-known lecture he provided around the state about backcountry essentials. In these lectures, he would use his own meticulous backpack to demonstrate not only what to bring to the woods but how to organize it. With his deceptively small pack, he would pull out stuff sack after stuff sack, neatly and efficiently organized with all of the essential items needed for a hike. On this list was wool clothing. Pete is still preaching the many benefits of wool and other non-cotton clothing materials to this day. His mantra is, "Our best dressed corpses all wore cotton; if you feel the itch you must still be alive."

Continuing our fall hike up Baxter, I was feeling the itch of my own comfortable wool pants. We continued past the summit and made a stop to take in the beautiful view of the High Peaks. Pete opened his pack to grab a sip of water—a neatly organized pack made up of smaller stuffed sacks that perfectly fit in his mid-size daypack. Not much has changed.

A well-planned and organized pack wasn't the only part of backcountry know-how that Pete was dedicated to preaching. As Pete continued his work as a Ranger, cleaning up the High Peaks and forging connections with visitors, he saw an opportunity for a formal backcountry education program. He got the idea when he met an Adirondack Mountain Club Ridge Runner on top of Marcy. Started in 1974, the Ridge Runner program was a backcountry stewardship initiative under which individuals patrolled the main trails giving advice and information. He saw the Ridge Runner's great enthusiasm and positive interactions with the public, especially the younger crowd. In Pete's opinion, this kind of interaction would have been strengthened if provided by state employees. This inspired Pete to start the Assistant Forest Ranger Program, which continues to this day.

Pete's legacy of stewardship in the Adirondack High Peaks is one that lives on with us. If you take a trip into the High Peaks for an overnight you probably couldn't fill both your pockets with litter. You probably won't come across a group that has more than 15 people in it. Most people will be camping in DEC designated sites. Pete helped protect the High Peaks region at a time when it was very vulnerable. His charismatic, outspoken personality helped educate a generation of outdoor recreationists on being stewards of the Adirondacks. There is still work to be done but Pete laid a foundation for all of us to continue to be stewards of this beautiful place.

Before we turned from the summit of Baxter Mountain, Pete told me that this spot was where he wanted his ashes spread. This deep connection to Baxter and the Adirondacks did not surprise me. True to his usual fashion, he cut the severity of that statement with a question: "Would you like a drink?" I accepted the offer and out of his pack came the stainless steel shot glasses and the single malt whiskey. Looking out at the High Peaks we sipped our drinks, taking in the beautiful fall scene. "So how do we get the next Pete Fish?" I asked. Pete replied, "You aren't going to and a lot of people will be very grateful for that."

Giant from the Ausable Club (AMR) Golf Course
YVON DAIGLE

Gateway to the High Peaks

By Margaret Bartley

Margaret Bartley *lives in New Russia, NY, on the East side of Giant Mountain. She spent 26 years teaching History and Government, and then served as the Supervisor for the Town of Elizabethtown, NY. She has a Master's of Creative Writing from Johns Hopkins University and her book* GRISHA: The Story of Cellist Gregor Piatigorsky *won the 2005 Adirondack Literary Award. As the editor of Otis Mountain Press, she was a frequent contributor to* Adirondack Life Magazine. *She currently serves as a Trustee for the Essex County Historical Society where she spends her time documenting Essex County history.*

Every year over a million drivers head North on I-87 to exit 30, drive down the ramp and turn left under the interstate onto Route 9, the north-south road that connects New York City to the Canadian border. Route 9 is the oldest road into the Adirondacks—since the 18th Century—and the best way to reach the 26 High Peaks surrounding the Town of Keene.

After just two miles, drivers reach "Malfunction Junction," an intersection that is a modern engineering puzzle. Staying on Route 9 will take you past Split Rock Falls and the trailhead to Rocky Peak Ridge, through the Hamlet of New Russia and into Elizabethtown, the Essex County seat. To get to the Town of Keene, you need to navigate the junction to reach Route 73, also known as the Chapel Pond road. Route 73 offers some of the most dramatic landscapes in the region as it climbs gradually above the headwaters of the Boquet River before making a steep drop into the Ausable Valley.

A trip through Keene, established in 1808, takes visitors past towering vertical rock walls, mirror-like ponds and hanging waterfalls. The same trip taken in winter can be both spellbinding—trying to catch a glimpse of a frozen cascade—and downright scary—driving at night in a snow squall. Unnoticed by most travelers are the 26 bridges, 252 culverts and several dozens of miles of pavement that make this journey possible.

Travelers heading to points northwest, weekend hikers and summer residents assume that some unnamed, faceless government entity makes the Adirondack Park a safe and welcoming destination.

In reality, what makes it happen is more like a melting pot of residents, visitors, governments, public agencies and non-profit organizations. Each group has its own agenda—often in conflict with one another—but it takes the efforts of all these bodies to make the Park accessible and enjoyable. The point person who brings it all together at this time is Bill Ferebee, the elected Supervisor of the Town of Keene since 2006. As one of 18 Town Supervisors in Essex County, he is not only the leader of the Town of Keene— population 1,105 residents in 2010—but he is also the Chairman of the Essex County Board of Supervisors, which serves as Essex County's legislative body.

"My family came here in 1968," said Ferebee from his small office in the Keene Town Hall. "I was 14 and went to school at KCS (Keene Central School) in the Hamlet of Keene Valley. It was a lot different than Norfolk, Virginia, where I had grown up." Ferebee joined the U.S. Army in 1971 and didn't return to the Adirondacks until 1986, when he, his wife and several relatives came back to Keene to start a restaurant and grocery business.

By definition Ferebee is a "*blow in*," a local term used to describe people who are not born and raised in Keene. But, as he explains, "it's these '*blow ins*'—people who come from elsewhere—that have expanded and sustain the local economy. We need new people and the money they bring to keep our town and local businesses growing."

The number of people who pass through Keene in a given year is staggering—over one million cars according to a recent official count. Sometimes traffic is so unrelenting that residents complain about the noise. But Stewarts, the lone gas and convenience store in Keene Center, does an enormous business. Almost everyone who visits the High Peaks will stop at Stewarts sooner or later. Average number of weekly customers—5100!

Ferebee has been the Town Supervisor for 10 years and he has learned how to navigate the layers of bureaucracy. "The State of New York and the federal government are the most difficult," he said. "Especially when one organization doesn't get along with another, and they are both part of the same government." When that happens, Ferebee has to act as the diplomat, trying to satisfy both parties, and make sure the outcome of governmental decisions doesn't hurt his town.

Visitors might be surprised to learn that one of the biggest problems in a Town of 157 square miles, with only 1,100 residents, is—of all things—parking! But anyone who has driven past Chapel Pond, Roaring Brook Falls or the Cascade Lakes on a holiday weekend can't help but notice hundreds of cars spilling out from small parking lots along both sides of Route 73. Even more congested is the parking lot in what is called the Garden, which is the access point for Johns Brook Lodge (JBL) and a large number of High Peaks. The narrow dirt road and the sharp-angled, one-lane bridge make getting in and out of the trailhead an adventure.

Linda Biesemeyer at the Garden, 1981
PETE BIESEMEYER

In 1998, the Town had to face the problem. Hikers parking at the Garden trailhead overwhelmed the small parking lot. Neighboring landowners found their driveways blocked and cars on their property. Even the Garden access road is on private property. Faced with the possibility of having the Garden lot closed to hikers, the Town Supervisor at that time, Tom Both, borrowed a bus on a Columbus Day weekend, to test the idea of a hiker shuttle. It was an immediate success.

Seventeen years later, bus service using a 12-passenger van paid for with money from the NYS Department of Transportation (NY DOT), runs from Marcy Field airfield on Route 73 to the Garden trailhead. The cost to maintain this service is split between hikers—$5.00 round trip—and Keene taxpayers. A five-year cooperative agreement between the Town and the state was signed and is renewed every five years. The state program known as "Adopt a Natural Resource" allows the eastern access to the High Peaks to remain open to the public, and also protects private landowners. Money from shuttle tickets also helps cover the cost of plowing snow from trailhead parking lots in the winter. Other services the Town provides include port-a-potties at the airfield for visitors. Emergency services, both on the trails and the roadways, are provided by the Keene EMS, and the Keene and Keene Valley volunteer fire departments.

1940 Chevrolet, Jim Brown, Pete Hall and Hubert Nye
COURTESY OF ADIRONDACK HISTORY MUSEUM IN ELIZABETHTOWN

"Meeting the need for tourist services in a town with so few residents is difficult," said Ferebee. "But tourism is our most important industry. It provides jobs to many people in Keene."

The Town also owns and maintains a swimming area along the Ausable River, a visitor's center at the Holt House and a public gathering space at Marcy Field, a wide, level expanse of grass. Marcy Field is used by small private planes as a landing strip, and it serves as the site for the weekly farmers market, as well as arts and crafts fairs. In the summer the Town-owned Holt House offers the Back Porch Concert Series for the entertainment of residents and visitors alike. And in July, Marcy Field provides a viewing place for the Town-sponsored annual fireworks show.

One best-kept secret in Keene is the transfer station located on the western slope of Hurricane Mountain. While providing a necessary place to deposit refuse and recyclables, it also serves as the site of an annual Easter Sunrise service. The view from the dump is a panorama of the Dix range to the south and is one of the best scenic views in the area.

One of the most memorable and often photographed vistas in the Adirondacks is a view of the High Peaks taken from the west side of Spruce Hill (Route 9N). Driving down the long slope, it's hard for drivers to keep their eyes on the road. No matter what the season or the weather the view is breathtaking.

At the foot of Spruce Hill is one of the most important and popular places in the High Peaks region. It's in the middle of Keene but is owned by the state. The location is less than a

half-acre of dirt and gravel, with not a single amenity or improvement. This busy spot is where truck drivers take a lunch break, state troopers set up speed traps and commuters park their cars before hitching a ride with others heading south. This scrap of dirt is also the Town's billboard. Signs announcing upcoming public events are planted in the grass and gravel.

In all seasons, rain or shine, this pull-off area is a coveted spot for artists and photographers. They frequently set up tripods and easels, as they try to capture the image of the old red barn, the expanse of golden grass and beaver ponds, all with a backdrop of the Cascade Range.

After Hurricane Irene in 2011, this unassuming dirt lot became the staging area for enormous road graders, double tandem dump trucks and mountains of tree trunks, stumps and wooden debris that were deposited in the most populated parts of Keene by the Ausable River and its tributaries. More recently, this parking area was filled with giant steel I-beams, concrete decking and galvanized railings as several new bridges were installed on Route 73 by NY DOT.

The importance of this space in his Town is not lost on Bill Ferebee. "The Department of Environmental Conservation (DEC) owns all the land on the west side of that parking lot and NY DOT owns the shoulder of the road. And now DEC is worried that DOT and the multiple uses of that parking area are encroaching on DEC property." Ferebee realizes he will have to find a way to solve the problem and keep the area open.

Electronic communication is another area that all Adirondack communities struggle with. Most visitors assume that there will be cell service and Internet available wherever they

Chapel Pond
BRENDAN WILTSE

go but that is not always the case in the High Peaks. The need becomes quickly apparent when people are hiking and get lost or injured. A new Verizon tower was recently built in the Hamlet of Keene but coverage does not extend into all of the state forest land. In 2011, the Town of Keene completed a grassroots project to bring Internet service to more than 97% of the homes in Keene. The goal was to make available Internet service in the home of every child who attended Keene Central School. Bringing this level of Internet coverage to such a small mountain town was a unique accomplishment in the Adirondack Park. It was only possible because the Town along with the people of the community pulled together to make it happen.

The ability of all the different layers of government, residents and visitors to work together was put to the test on August 29, 2011, when Hurricane Irene visited the High Peaks. The enormous volume of water that fell on the steep mountain slopes was immediately funneled into the Ausable River and its tributaries. In less than 24 hours the water tore through Saint Huberts, Keene Valley and then into Keene. Flowing down the steep terrain, the water picked up speed and in just a few hours

Whiteface ski area
BRENDAN WILTSE

destroyed bridges, roads and swept away homes. So intense was the deluge that Gulf Brook, a rivulet that is easy to walk across most of the time, tore through the Town's commercial hamlet in Keene Center, sweeping homes off their foundations and cutting the Keene firehouse in half.

In the mountains, where damage was less easily seen, the bridge over Marcy Dam was gone, Duck Hole pond was washed away and many mountainsides were stripped of vegetation. Trails and back roads were impassable, parking areas disappeared under piles of sand and gravel, and all hiking in the High Peaks was suspended for several weeks. When the DEC opened some trails on September 8, even experienced hikers found that the High Peaks landscape they had known was changed forever. New trails had to be cut around mountains of debris left by the rock and mudslides. Familiar ponds had disappeared, drained of their water, footbridges were reduced to splinters and wide swaths of bare rock exposed.

Two months after the flood, Bill Ferebee shared his feelings with the press:
The first step was to reopen the Town. Route 73 is the main artery. This was like a heart attack. We called in the best of the best, the Governor operated on us three times and made his repairs, and now we're in recovery.

Governor Andrew Cuomo's operating tools included suspending DEC and Adirondack Park Agency guidelines, which require a permit to do construction of any kind near a river or stream. "About 60 homes in Keene and Keene Valley were evacuated when the storm hit, at least 15 of which are currently uninhabitable," Ferebee said. "Several businesses have also been drastically affected, and there are 35 roads that still need repair. We are lucky no one died."

Four years later, much of the visible damage from the storm is gone but the memory is still very fresh. The Town of Keene is back in business, serving residents and visitors alike. Trails into the High Peaks are open and an improved Hurricane Mountain trail takes hikers from the top of Spruce Hill on Route 9N up the south side of the mountain.

On November 3, 2015, Bill Ferebee was re-elected for his fifth term as Town Supervisor. Every day he has to balance his job as diplomat, negotiator and leader. While most hikers, tourists and vacationers may not even know who he is, Bill Ferebee is an integral part what makes the High Peaks around the Town of Keene available to all.

Dix and Hough tower over Elk Lake
CARL HEILMAN II

An Uncommon Bond

By Alex Radmanovich

Alex Radmanovich *is a former journalist, corporate type and, for the past twenty-seven years, partner in PelicanPR, a Montreal-based corporate communications/graphic design firm he co-founded with his wife Christine Bourjade. Alex and Christine, respectively 46ers #4968W and #4967W, discovered the Adirondacks in 1999 while climbing the 46 High Peaks, and now divide their time between Canada and New Russia, NY.*

In 2014, they established and seeded #507 Fund for the High Peaks Summit Stewardship Program with a $10,000 donation that was followed by grants from the Adirondack 46ers ($15,000), the Adirondack Chapter of The Nature Conservancy ($10,000), Adirondack Mountain Club ($5,000) and other organizations and numerous individuals. The goal is to reach one million dollars, with annual investment income earmarked exclusively to support outdoor education, research and conservation efforts by Summit Stewards on the Adirondack peaks that host alpine vegetation. #507 Fund is administered by the Adirondack Foundation. To make a donation, please go to ***www.generousact.org*** *or for more information to* ***www.507fund.org****.*

Vincent McClelland has forged a unique connection with the land and people of the Adirondack Park and with generations of outdoor enthusiasts who stream into the mountains each year. This bond is the product of his many talents and interests, combined with a natural ability—uncanny may be an apt characterization—to relate to, engage and transact with people from all walks of life as one of them. It is made stronger by McClelland's deep sense of community, determination and, as the 65-year-old says, the good fortune to catch a break or two along the way.

The Keene Valley resident is perhaps best known as the manager and one of the owners of The Mountaineer, the venerable outdoor gear mecca located on Route 73 in the middle of the hamlet, at the confluence of Johns Brook and the East Branch of the Ausable River. But McClelland is also a Board member of Champlain National Bank, past co-Chair of Adirondack Foundation and former Board member of the New York Ski Educational Foundation; co-Chair of the New York Rising Community Reconstruction Program; successful land use and site planning consultant; philanthropist; youth soccer and hockey coach.

Growing up in the Adirondacks was fun. When he talks about the 1950s and 60s, the nostalgia of long, fun-filled, barefoot summers, summits with no people, trailless peaks that were real bushwhacks, 30-below winters with deep snow, giardia-free water that you drank without a filter, skinny dipping in all the now-popular swimming holes, is palpable. Many of the best adventures in the wild were led by his father George, and George's close friend the legendary Jimmy Goodwin, with Vinny, his three brothers and the Goodwin brothers in tow.

In the 1970s, McClelland completed his B.S. in Forestry at the University of Vermont and, with his brothers, helped George fell the trees that were to become The Mountaineer. As he remembers, "Everyone thought my father mad to open an outdoor/climbing shop and try to purvey fine outdoor equipment and supplies in a town of 700 year-round residents that literally shut down after Labor Day all the way to Memorial Day."

Vinny's father George in Alaska

But that is exactly what George and his wife, Jane, and then partners Sid Miller, who designed the original building, and his wife, Kay, did in 1975. The business enjoyed an auspicious start selling half of its inventory on the opening weekend. The mountaineering shop continues to attract climbers, skiers, hikers and other outdoor enthusiasts from all over the Northeast to this day. The early years were difficult but as the lure of the outdoors grew stronger, bringing more and more people into the mountains, and as new pursuits emerged, such as ice and rock climbing and, much later, trail running, the recreation seasons grew longer, the customer base expanded and the store in the middle of nowhere found its groove.

The McClelland family about to reach the summit of Marcy
NANCIE BATTAGLIA

It was never smooth sailing, however, and never is inside the Blue Line. In fact, earning a living in the Adirondack Park can be an ongoing struggle. "Life in the Adirondacks isn't quite like visitors imagine," says McClelland. "The people here often work more than one job to raise their family. Many drive long distances to and from work every day. You have to be resourceful to live here." McClelland knows the drill. After helping to build the store and working at the Adirondack Park Agency, he moved to Alaska where he honed his skills in land use planning, site planning and construction management, all the while getting a taste of real wilderness by plane, sail, on foot and backcountry skis.

Twelve years later, McClelland headed back home and was lucky to land a job with a landscape architectural firm, The LA Group. In 1994, his father asked him to help run the store, which developed into his primary occupation. "At that time the store was struggling and I was lucky to hold onto some consulting work at LA Group, he recalls. "The work commute—round trip well over a hundred miles—was exhausting but it helped pay the bills. When Internet service became available in Keene Valley and as telecommuting became more acceptable, there were fewer back and forth days." McClelland also found time to add to his resumé a Wetland Delineation Certificate from Rutgers University and a real estate brokers license.

More than a decade after McClelland returned from Alaska, opportunity knocked again. In 2005, based on his expertise, McClelland was approached by LandVest, headquartered in Boston, which provides services to owners of and investors in high-quality real estate assets, specifically land, estates and distinctive homes, and investment timberland. He has since worked with many of the Adirondack Park's large landowners and advised on

The Mountaineer (www.mountaineer.com), Keene Valley in 2015...

significant conservation easements and ownership transfers. "It has been very rewarding to be able to take advantage of my land planning expertise and forestry background to not only help families and large landowners plan the future of their properties—many of which were generational family assets—but also to work with Landvest's timberland group and, as a real estate broker, handle some significant transactions," says McClelland with typical understatement.

... and 1975

However, you can't do much about *Wall Street Journal* headlines, no matter how modest you might be. And so it was that the whole world—and that includes the global conservation movement—found out that a man known locally as "Vinny" was part of the team that in the summer of 2015 sold a property for the highest price ever recorded in the Adirondacks. The buyer was none other than Chinese billionaire Jack Ma of Alibaba fame and the property was the 28,120-acre Brandon Park estate belonging to the DuPont/Ross family. McClelland hastens to point out that the land remains under a conservation easement granted to The Nature Conservancy by the original owner and will continue as such.

How is it possible to operate a retail business while holding another time-consuming job, volunteering in the community and being a husband and father of three children? McClelland credits the healing powers of the wilderness and the reliable professionals who run the day to day operations of The Mountaineer—Chuck and Nick; Carolyn and Jeremy; Drew, Kaz, Brittany and Holly, some of whom have been with him for 20 or more years. "They are an amazingly accomplished, passionate team of pros who take ownership of the store's performance and take pride in managing the various departments. They share responsibility for providing the best customer service, one of the store's hallmarks."

Under McClelland's leadership and dedicated staff, The Mountaineer has become a fixture in recreationist circles in the High Peaks and beyond. The many events it hosts—from the annual mountaineering festival that celebrates its 20th anniversary in 2016, to the fly fishing camp, backcountry ski fest and Adirondack trail run—attract hundreds of outdoor enthusiasts from around the Northeast and generate welcome funds for local charities, by McClelland's count over $150,000 to date.

There isn't much time for rest and relaxation but McClelland takes solace in living in Keene Valley and the Adirondacks, "an oasis and refuge in this increasingly complicated and hectic world. For me, this is a place of familiarity, where our best friends and memories reside and where the trail runs, hikes, canoes, overnight camping trips, backcountry ski adventures, great views and the smells of the forests help us get refocused, recharged and energized."

McClelland's life adventures, travels and experience in the outdoor industry, real estate and land use planning have instilled a deep appreciation for wild and protected places, especially in the Adirondacks. "The Adirondacks have helped shape my life and my children's lives and our perspective and appreciation of the environment, the mountains, the world and our sense of community. We have been blessed with both this great place and visionaries like Tim Barnett, Peter Paine and Mike Carr who continue to shape and protect its future."

The third generation of McClellands, the G3 in the 1980s in Johns Brook

Author with measuring wheel
NANCIE BATTAGLIA

The High Peaks: The Family Business

By Tony Goodwin

Tony Goodwin *was raised in Hartford, CT, but spent every summer in Keene Valley. He climbed all 46 High Peaks by age 11, and then worked seasonally at Johns Brook Lodge (1966-1968), and as Adirondack Mountain Club (ADK) "Ridge Runner" (1974), and chief of ADK's first professional trail crew in 1979.*

From October 1979 through April 1980, he worked for the Lake Placid Olympic Organizing Committee as Venue Manager at Cross-Country and Biathlon, and from 1981 to 1985 as manager of the Mt. Van Hoevenberg Cross-Country and Biathlon Area.

Since 1986, Tony has served as Executive Director of the Adirondack Trail Improvement Society and Executive Director of the Adirondack Ski Touring Council, which he founded. He is also editor of guidebook High Peaks Trails, *published by ADK through four editions from 1985 to the present. Tony was a member of the Citizens Advisory Committee to the High Peaks Wilderness Unit Management Plan in 1990-1992.*

Tony graduated from Williams College in 1971 with a B.A. in History and from Plattsburgh State College in 1980 with an M.A. in History.

One could say that in my involvement with the Adirondack High Peaks I have simply continued in the "family business." My father guided clients up Marcy at age 12 and cut his first trail (Little Porter from Keene Valley) at age 14. So I guess it was no surprise that I was out with my father at age 12 helping him to maintain the Hedgehog trail, another one of the trails he cut.

My father's motivation for both his guiding and trail work was his desire to help others enjoy the same mountains and forests that gave him so much pleasure. Over the course of his career, he saw the number of users of the High Peaks go from very few to today's heavy use. Not wanting to be selfish, however, he never wanted to do anything to reduce the numbers of users. He did recognize that early practices such as pitching tents on Mount Marcy's alpine vegetation had to end but he didn't want to deny anyone the chance to experience what he had always enjoyed.

My own philosophy isn't a whole lot different. Despite the significant increases in use of the High Peaks—beyond the use levels seen by my father—I am still pleased to see that so many choose to get out and appreciate the lands that have been preserved for all to use. That said, I have always been willing to work to maintain trails and educate users so that this use does as little damage as possible.

After constructing the trail to Little Porter in 1924, my father went on to construct a number of other notable trails. These included extending the trail from Little Porter to Porter, the Giant Ridge Trail, Big Slide from the Second Brother, and Hedgehog, which connected Keene Valley to the Great Range. His final new trail, and perhaps his best, was the Pyramid-Gothics trail with the spur to Sawteeth cut in 1966. His final role in trail maintenance came when in 1978 he accepted Ed Ketchledge's request to become the first Adirondack 46er Trailmaster, a position he held for five years.

Jim Goodwin, Marcy, 1985
ED HALE

Early observations

At age 16, I worked for two weeks on the Pyramid-Gothics trail before starting my first of three summers on the Johns Brook Lodge (JBL) crew. From that perspective, I saw the whole range of hikers—both those who stayed at the lodge and those who passed by. As is the case today, there were those who were supremely well-prepared and those who had no idea what it meant to hike a mountain trail. Most telling were the hikers who arrived at JBL and asked, "Where's the top?" They somehow thought they had already hiked nine miles from the Garden and that Marcy's summit must be nearby. The numbers were, of course, much smaller, but unprepared hikers have been out on the trails for at least that long.

Also worth noting is the general condition of the trails, campsites, lean-tos and summits in the era before "Carry it in, Carry it out," trail hardening and Summit Sewards. Even with many fewer hikers in the 1950s and 60s, the trails tended to be muddy, wide and getting wider. Just below timberline on Marcy was a major quagmire 100 yards long by

25-30 yards wide. (My father called it "Nine Yahds Deep Swamp" after the comment by an Englishman he guided in the 1920s. His client tried to go straight across and became mired practically to his hips.) Each lean-to had an open garbage pit with the contents often strewn around by foraging animals. The summit of Marcy had a trash can (usually overflowing) in the remains of the stone shelter. A sign in the stone shelter said, "This is not a latrine" but your nose told you otherwise. And of course everyone walked, sat and sometimes camped on the alpine vegetation.

ADK Ridge Runner Program

The late 1960s and early 70s (think hippies and "back to the land") saw the first big increase in the number of hikers and campers nationally, and the High Peaks likewise saw a significant increase. This increase caused considerable concern among backcountry managers and casual observers alike. There were suggestions that access should be limited or perhaps that competence should be increased by requiring potential users to pass some sort of test at the trailhead. Fortunately, neither of these "solutions" was implemented, and finally there was a consensus that better education was the best way to reduce the perceived problems. Thus it was that in 1974 the Adirondack Mountain Club (ADK) initiated the Ridge Runner program. Modeled after a hiker education program of the same name in the White Mountains, ADK's effort put three ridge runners out for 10 days at a time to patrol, observe and educate users. This was at a time when no forest rangers regularly patrolled the trails and campsites and the interior caretakers tended to stay in their "ranger" cabins and then clean up after the campers had left. I was hired as one of the three that first summer.

While the Department of Environmental Conservation (DEC) had initiated "Carry it in, Carry it out" in 1970, there remained many who clung to the old ways. That included the Lake Colden caretaker, Charlie Nolan, who continued to keep a garbage can at every lean-to. Deciding that this was not the correct approach if campers were expected to carry their trash out, I spent several days collecting all of the garbage cans. Charlie was skeptical but I promised him that I or another ridge runner would be at Lake Colden to patrol the campsites and lean-tos every weekend to educate campers in the proper handling of their trash. If the lack of garbage cans resulted in more trash on the ground, I promised to replace all of the cans. Fortunately, the new system worked, aided in part by Charlie's supply of 46er litter bags that we could hand out each evening as we went through the camping areas contacting and educating campers.

At that time there was no limit on the size of camping groups, nor were there any restrictions on where one could camp. I and the other ridge runners therefore could only appeal to the better judgment of leaders of camping groups of 40 or those preparing to pitch a tent on the tundra. While the trash can and stone shelter on Marcy were gone by then, there was still trash stuffed into seemingly every little crevice, so a general clean up was in order on each ascent.

The following year, the first DEC "wilderness rangers," including Pete Fish, were assigned to patrol the High Peaks in much the same way that we ridge runners had been doing the year before and were again doing that year. In 1977, DEC Commissioner Peter Berle declared that the non-conforming interior cabins at Duck Hole, Shattuck Clearing and in

Eastern end of Upper Preston Pond, looking west
NANCIE BATTAGLIA

other designated wilderness areas had to go. The Lake Colden cabin remained because the Adirondack Park State Land Master Plan (APSLMP) specifically excluded it from removal. The removal of the other cabins caused a huge hue and cry that without the cabins the DEC couldn't properly manage the land or ensure user safety. Commissioner Berle responded to these criticisms by promising more rangers in the field as better than one sitting in a cabin.

The result was a large number of park rangers (now assistant forest rangers or AFRs) who would patrol in uniform with the authority to issue warnings and a radio to summon a forest ranger if the situation warranted. These rangers also had greater authority and could enforce compliance with several new regulations enacted the year before. These regulations included a nine person limit on camping groups (permits could be written for larger groups) and a ban on camping above 4,000 feet. Additionally, there were park attendants, also in uniform, who greeted users at trailheads, had them fill out a survey, and began the educational process. With the ADK Ridge Runner program still going, one tended to meet a lot of official and semi-official individuals on the trail that summer. The park attendants did not return the next season but seasonal assistants to the full forest rangers continue to this day to be a useful presence in the High Peaks.

ADK Professional Trail Crew

By the following year, 1979, it became apparent that much of the funding for the park rangers had come at the expense of the DEC's trail maintenance budget. ADK thus decided that the best "division of labor" was to let uniformed DEC personnel educate and enforce in the backcountry while ADK tackled the backlog of deteriorated trails. The Ridge Runner program was thus downsized to one (and none after 1979) with ADK establishing a professional trail crew for the first time. I became chief of that five-person crew, and we started out to see what we could do to improve the Van Hoevenberg Trail to Marcy.

For the first week, we had a veteran from the Appalachian Mountain Club's trail crew instruct us in the basics of water bar construction and other trail hardening techniques. We worked mostly with wood (as did crews for the next few years), so that only a few of the water bars we placed are still assisting in draining water off the Van Hoevenberg Trail. Nevertheless, our work that summer did show that Adirondack trails could be improved beyond their previous muddy and eroded state. It was also very apparent that fixing all of the deteriorated trails would take many, many years; but the fact that such improvements were possible helped blunt any demand that use be limited in order to preserve the trails.

Author working on guidebook/map, 1985
NANCIE BATTAGLIA

In 1985, the DEC issued a directive that, pending a review by the Attorney General's office, no trees on the Forest Preserve could be cut for the purpose of trail maintenance. That pretty much ended work for that year but by the next year new leadership with experience working with rock instead of wood had changed for the better the way ADK trail crews hardened trails. In 1986, the Attorney General ruled that, if properly controlled, wood could be cut for trail maintenance when necessary; but the ADK crew has continued to work mostly with rock.

Guidebooks

In addition to maintaining trails and guiding clients, my father had a hand in every edition of ADK's *High Peaks Guide*—at least since the Sixth Edition in 1956. He wrote the trailless peak section starting in 1962, while also editing the topographic map that accompanied the guide from its first edition in 1969 to my assumption of that responsibility in 1985. He did all of this work for free in the name of making "his" mountains available to all those who wanted to enjoy them. While I have been a bit more "mercenary" in continuing that tradition, I have done it for the same reasons.

My first guidebook contributions were a few descriptions for the 10th Edition of the *High Peaks Guide* in 1980. The next year I researched and published a ski touring guide *Northern Adirondack Ski Tours*, which has led to two expanded versions since then. In 1984, I took the summer off from my then position as manager of the Mt. Van Hoevenberg Cross Country Ski Area to research and write a wholesale revision of the ADK's *High Peaks Guide*. I felt that the existing descriptions were overly detailed—500 words to reach JBL from the Garden—with the result that important information might be overlooked. In most cases, I achieved my goal of reducing each description by a third to a half. I also wanted to reorganize the sections and include recommended hikes for first-time users. Store clerks had, for instance, reported frequent instances of selling a guidebook to a customer, only to have that customer return with the question, "Where should I go?" I believe that I was successful in producing a more user-friendly guide, and subsequent editions have included further improvements.

In working on the guidebook, to this day I still trust a measuring wheel over GPS to determine distances. The wheel measures every twist and turn of a trail plus the distance as the trail slopes up or down. Beyond that, the process is pretty basic—push the wheel, take notes and convert those notes into a description that is useful to trail users. Landmarks for which a distance is provided should be obvious so that users can easily plot their progress. If a relatively easy trail later becomes steep and rough, that should also be communicated. The goal is to provide guidebook users with the information needed to not only follow the trail but also to decide if it's time to turn around.

Bartlett Ridge Trail after Hurricane Floyd, 1999
TONY GOODWIN

Over the years there have been requests that the guidebook reflect a "standard" time for each trail as well as the distance. Such a designation is possible when one is describing a single hike but in a network such as exists in the High Peaks there is no way to come up with a standard for each section of trail. A hiker on the Shorey Short-Cut may be fresh, having just come up the three miles from JBL, while another hiker may be exiting from a Great Range traverse after hiking for ten or more hours. The Introduction to the guide—there but not often read—gives a formula for estimating time based on a two-mile-per-hour pace plus an additional 20 minutes for each 1,000 feet ascended. Truly prepared hikers can thus "do the math" to determine how their pace varies from the formula.

Over the years, I've also realized the ways that users access the information contained in the guidebook. As noted above, many never bother to read any of the introductory material—either at the front of the book or at the beginning of each section. Many just look in the index and then turn to that page. There has thus been a need to "idiot-proof" some of the descriptions so that users are referred to any additional important information. In particular, the trails starting from the Adirondack Mountain Reserve's road to the Lower Ausable Lake had to each have a line directing users back to the general introduction to that section of the guidebook. I realized that this was important when I encountered a confused-looking hiker on the Lake Road. I asked if I could help. The reply was to the effect that, "We've figured it out now but the guidebook wasn't any help...." I asked which

Backcountry skiing
NANCIE BATTAGLIA

guidebook the group had and of course it was mine. That's when I realized that the group had just turned to the page for Sawteeth where the description said, "The trail starts at the west end of the bridge below the Lower Ausable Lake dam...."; but no mention that one had to hike the Lake Road to get to the dam.

Another unanticipated source of confusion was the numbering of the trails so as to make it easier to refer from the map back to the book. The numbering did achieve that goal but it also led many novice hikers to expect the same numbers to be posted on the trails like highway route numbers.

Adirondack Ski Touring Council

The year after my initial guidebook effort, I left my position at Mt. Van Hoevenberg and became executive director of two trail organizations. One was the well-established Adirondack Trail Improvement Society (ATIS); the other was the Adirondack Ski Touring Council (ASTC), an organization I helped to found.

ASTC's mission was to improve cross-country skiing opportunities in the Keene-Lake Placid-Saranac Lake area by constructing a ski trail that linked the three towns. ASTC named it the "Jackrabbit Trail" after Herman Smith "Jackrabbit" Johannsen, who had lived and skied in Lake Placid early in the 20th century before moving to Canada. In his era, one could ski right from the towns to the mountains and ASTC hoped to re-create that experience. For a time, ASTC even tried to groom those sections outside of

Led by the author, ATIS outing climbers on Cliff posed for the traditional summit picture.
NANCIE BATTAGLIA

designated wilderness as a means of encouraging greater use. In the end, grooming didn't seem to add that much value to the local skiing experience, so ASTC later rechanneled its efforts to improving and maintaining other popular ski routes that needed some winter-specific care.

Right from the start, however, ASTC set out to reopen the Wright Peak Ski Trail. Constructed in the late 1930s, that trail had been popular for a few years until lifts became prevalent and skiers seeking a steep, challenging down mountain run stopped climbing for their skiing. By the 1980s, a new generation of skiers—aided by a new generation of equipment suitable for both climbing and descending steep trails—was looking for opportunities beyond the ski trail on Marcy. ASTC thus went ahead and secured permission from the DEC's regional forester to reopen the trail. Two days of intensive work by volunteers accomplished that in the spring of 1987.

Unfortunately, there were others in the Adirondack Park Agency (APA) who believed that trail had been abandoned for so long that reopening it was akin to cutting a new trail—something that could only be done if included in a completed Unit Management Plan (UMP). Our situation wasn't helped when a forest ranger reported that the hasty clearing job had left six inch "pungi" sticks in many locations. The volunteers apparently figured that these would be well-covered by the snow and there was no need for greater care. Additionally, at places on the upper part of the trail it was not clear exactly where the trail had originally been. Thus a long-time protector of the Forest Preserve, Barbara

McMartin, using a hand lens reportedly found cut stumps with enough tree rings to make that tree older than the original trail. Ed Ketchledge also expressed concern that this route would lead to hikers traversing the alpine tundra to access the trail. We easily dealt with this concern by pointing out that we had stopped clearing well short of the summit because we were equally interested in not having any summer traffic on the trail because that would result in erosion.

I had not been involved in the original clearing but I organized several groups to return and fix some of the sloppy original work. After that, however, ASTC performed no further maintenance for another 10 years until the controversy died down. Now firmly established as part of the High Peaks, the Wright Peak Ski Trail sees considerable use when conditions are right. There is some conflict with the snowshoe traffic on the section shared with the Algonquin trail—so much so that a whole new finish to the ski trail has been proposed. There is enough interest that there will likely be no shortage of volunteers to construct that trail but that will probably just have to wait for a revision of the High Peaks UMP.

Adirondack Trail Improvement Society

In addition to maintaining 90 miles of trail (1986), ATIS also hired counselors to lead local children on hiking, camping and canoe trips. The challenge with this side of the organization was to make sure that the counselors were teaching both wilderness skills and a wilderness "ethic." The skills component would hopefully allow participants to later on be both comfortable in the woods and skilled enough to survive without doing any damage to their surroundings. The ethic component hopefully instilled in participants a love of wild, undeveloped spaces so that they would not only treat these areas with respect but also later advocate for their continued preservation. I am not going to claim that every participant was so educated but I do feel that ATIS has made an important contribution in this regard.

Cameron Doman and author completing a stone staircase on Deer Brook Trail, 1999

On the trail maintenance side, I inherited a trail system with a lot of maintenance not done in previous years. The first priority was to just get the system back in good shape with regards to clipping, bridge maintenance and ladder construction. As of 1986, ATIS had also assumed maintenance responsibility for the Elk Lake-Marcy trail up through Panther Gorge. For the DEC, this was a very long and remote trail coming in from Elk Lake. Consequently, very little maintenance had been done between Marcy Swamp and Four Corners. Given its access through the Upper Lake, it made sense that ATIS would have an easier time maintaining and improving this trail. This was the first of several trail "takeovers" from formerly state-maintained trails that have brought ATIS's total to 115 miles.

By 1991 I felt that ATIS crews had taken care of the backlog of trail work and we could turn our attention to the sort of hardening (true "improvement") projects that ADK had been doing. So after one day in service with some members of the ADK crew, the ATIS crew set to work building rock staircases and water bars on the heavily-used Stimson Trail to Noonmark. Devoting three to four weeks at the end of each season, ATIS crews ultimately worked for seven years, finishing the hardening practically to the summit by 1997. With the Noonmark trail now in "modern" condition, I thought that a recognition of this accomplishment could be made part of the ATIS's Centennial celebrations going on that year.

The "founding" story for ATIS is that in 1897 three gentlemen, S. Burns Weston, W.A. White and Felix Adler, were climbing Noonmark when they encountered a large log. As Adler struggled to get over that log, he announced, "Gentlemen, we must at once form an Adirondack trail improvement society," and so it was that a 19th century organization still operates under a 19th century name. For the recognition I had the trail crew build, but not quite complete, a final water bar a short distance up the Stimson Trail. We then had a brief ceremony, noting how much trail maintenance had changed in 100 years. The ceremony concluded with descendants of all three founders placing scree rocks to finish the water bar.

In 1998, ATIS and ADK teamed up to construct a wholly new trail up Rooster Comb that demonstrated what could be achieved when a trail is designed and constructed to modern standards right from the start. Since then, ATIS has continued hardening work on the trails to Giant, Elk Pass, Indian Head and Gothics, with the most recent work on the Beaver Meadow Trail to Gothics.

One interesting observation is that, when I started with ASTC and ATIS in 1986, the DEC was not particularly easy to deal with regarding the efforts of our "private" organizations to build and maintain trails. I think the DEC remembered when their funding allowed them to do this work themselves and they were hoping that this funding would somehow return. After many years of continuing cuts in funding, however, the DEC acknowledged that they could not fulfill their mission to maintain these backcountry facilities unless they worked with and indeed encouraged these volunteer trail organizations. The current system has the private groups enter into a Volunteer Stewardship Agreement (VSA), a relatively simple document that outlines what is and is not permitted on the Forest Preserve. These agreements run for five years with each organization responsible for annually providing a general work plan. Major changes require approval but for the most part organizations can work as they see fit. And significantly, most volunteer organizations that have made a commitment to maintain one or several trails have stuck with their commitment. Such was not always the case. My father noted that in his initial discussions regarding the 46er Trailmaster program, the DEC officials were skeptical that this initiative would last. Both my father and the DEC had seen similar volunteer efforts fizzle out after the initial enthusiasm wore off. The 46er program has of course continued and grown. Perhaps that can be attributed to a more evident need for good trail work coupled with a larger pool of potential volunteers; but it didn't hurt that the program was initiated by Ed Ketchledge as the way to justify the very continuance of the 46ers.

Citizen's Advisory Committee to the High Peaks UMP

Finally, my involvement with the High Peaks wouldn't be complete without saying something about my service on the Citizen's Advisory Committee (CAC) to the High Peaks Unit Management Plan. Between August 1990 and June 1993 the full committee met 16 times with many additional meetings of the 10 subcommittees. I was identified as representing ATIS and as the guidebook author but by the end I was by default also representing the 46ers as their representative was no longer able to attend the meetings. The members of the Committee included representatives from each town, every interest group and individuals with knowledge and interest. At one end of the spectrum were those who wanted to restrict use and reduce the interior facilities to create a "true" wilderness experience. Others like myself favored a plan recognizing that the High Peaks were a popular destination. Existing and future use should be controlled with the minimum amount of regulation needed to preserve the resource while continuing to build and maintain facilities such as bridges and hardened trails that accommodated this use. There were also sportsman's representatives who wanted to ensure that permits for extended stays at interior campsites could still be obtained and that dogs could still be used for hunting when that use was otherwise not permitted.

Beaver Meadow Trail's new staircase, 2014
TONY GOODWIN

Ultimately, the plan provided for the existing use levels and sanctioned the construction and maintenance of facilities to allow these levels of use. Control of the numbers of users would only be exercised by not expanding parking facilities and, where possible, pushing any overflow parking back a considerable distance from the trailhead. This method of control would, it was hoped, reduce the peaks of use. In practice, this system seems to have achieved its goal, although cars parked on the narrow shoulders of the Loj Road and at various points along Route 73 makes this a somewhat messy solution on the peak weekends.

There were two issues on which I felt I had a direct influence. One was that of the so-called "herd paths" on those 4,000 foot peaks that did not have a marked trail. The other was in determining the appropriate maximum size for day hiking groups.

With regard to the herd paths, the opening statement by the 46er representative said that a poll of the 46er membership overwhelmingly rejected marking the herd paths. After that representative no longer attended the meetings, there was concern that without

Pitchoff balanced rocks
NANCIE BATTAGLIA

some management action the herd paths would continue to deteriorate and proliferate as they had between Street and Nye. It was then that I proposed that with a minimum amount of clearing and some marking with cairns, hikers could be kept on what was considered the best route. Where herd paths had proliferated, brushing could close off undesirable routes. The Committee generally liked this approach, so I wrote an article for the 46er magazine *Adirondack Peeks* proposing this solution. The article generated a few favorable responses and no negative ones. The final plan thus initiated the current system of volunteer maintenance of "designated" herd paths.

As of 1990, the seemingly greatest concern for day hikers were the frequent busloads of 40-plus hikers (mostly from Canada) that swarmed up popular trails and often seemed to pretty much take over a summit. Additionally, domestic camp groups—often church-affiliated—would send groups of as many as 300 up Ampersand or St. Regis. Some on the committee wanted day groups to be as small as camping groups but I advocated for a limit that dispersed the busloads while still allowing camps and other youth groups to operate efficiently with their vans—then mostly 15-passenger vans. After several votes, the committee accepted my "van standard" of 15 for the maximum group size.

By July 1992, the CAC produced a 160-page book of recommendations for the DEC to consider. The DEC's first draft of a UMP went beyond the CAC's recommendations in proposing camping permits to actually limit the numbers that could camp in some of the popular areas such as Lake Colden. Also proposed were day use "trip tickets," both to ensure that every user registered and to provide better data on actual use. User groups including ADK objected to these additional restrictions while more preservationist groups such as the Adirondack Council wanted actual limits on day use as well as a guarantee that the non-conforming South Meadow Road would finally be closed. There were other contentious issues that delayed the actual implementation of the plan until 2000—ten years after the first meeting of the CAC. On the positive side, the work of the CAC and the final High Peaks UMP provided a "template" for the UMPs for the Dix Mountain and Giant Mountain wilderness areas that followed soon after 2000.

Looking to the future

Looking to the future, management and maintenance of the High Peaks is, in my view, not likely to change all that much. I say this despite the 2014-15 seeming surge in use and consequently the record 117 backcountry incidents recorded by the DEC during the 2015 summer hiking season. As I saw years ago at JBL, there are hikers who have no idea what it takes to prepare for hiking a mountain trail. Higher overall numbers naturally mean more hikers in the unprepared category. Unlike those I saw at JBL, however, this generation carries cell phones, making a call for help sometimes all too easy. Looking back, it appears that every 20-25 years, or roughly every new generation, brings a sudden increase in backcountry use. The 1970s increase was managed by a greater educational effort along with a few new regulations on use. The 1990s increase was managed by the implementation of the High Peaks UMP that added some regulations—particularly on the size of day groups—and an acceptance that trails, bridges and campsites be constructed and maintained to handle the increased number of users. The current increase will likely require a redoubled educational effort to try and make plain that one is responsible for getting oneself out of the woods along with what one needs to do to properly prepare.

Judging from past experience, I am confident that the High Peaks will "survive" this latest increase in use. The summits of Cascade, Algonquin, Marcy and Giant will be crowded on fair weekend days and parking will spill out onto the highways. No one can expect to find a solitude wilderness experience on those peaks on those days but there are still many options for those who do want that experience. Many other attractive places in the Adirondacks still have no trails at all and are visited by only a handful each year. As long as there is a choice that can be made, I believe we can continue to allow the current patterns of use to continue.

Adirondack Hermit Noah John Rondeau attending to his hermitage's flower garden, August 26, 1949
ALDOPH G. "DITT" DITTMAR—AUTHOR'S ADIRONDACK COLLECTION

Loving the Adirondacks to Death

By William J. "Jay" O'Hern

"It's all about the Adirondacks," William J. "Jay" O'Hern *explains. "My parents introduced me to the High Peaks 67 years ago. We camped in Lake Placid and the Central Adirondacks."*

"I'm definitely interested in the social history. It is not just about someone like Noah John Rondeau. I have met many other folks whose family were Adirondack natives. I feel privileged that they have shared cherished heritage information with me. I feel a real obligation to the families and to the history of the mountains. It's going to disappear if we don't record it."

And record it he does. His current thirteen titles can be viewed at ***www.adkwilds.com*** *and on* ***www.adirondackmountaintraders.com****. Upcoming releases are* Adirondack Logging, Adirondack Camp Stories, Adirondack Life Around the Indian Clearing in the Moose River Plains *and* Adirondack Vacationland: Through a Mountain Window.

Today Jay lives near Camden, NY, with his wife Bette and two cats. His house is often brimming with grandchildren. He continues to enjoy camping, hiking and paddling. Beyond work on Adirondack projects, Jay is available for book signings and programs.

ADIRONDACKS

Ragged, serrated peaks of mountains rise
In lofty grandeur 'gainst my northern skies
Mantled about with robes of living green
Crowned with gray stone, enduring and serene.

Low hills or rolling prairies may be fine;
Or beating sea and winds that taste of brine;
But forest aisles and rising slopes alone
Comfort the ache that calls me to come home.

—Julia Simmons, Rouses Point, 1948

It's 6 o'clock and one more leg of my trek is finally at an end. I rush to pitch my tent and start an evening campfire. I need to warm my aching knuckles once again.

I had been experiencing weather I could not explain; I just considered it an early October phenomenon that at several places along the footpath I would be struck by a waft of air that was not only cool but cold. That had continued throughout the day as I trekked along; generally it was warmish and then suddenly stony cold for a couple of minutes, and then comfortable again.

While hiking over the snaky trail, my attention was repeatedly drawn high and far off to the lofty mountain range beyond the river. The closing kaleidoscope of autumn colors called. It seemed I could hear, faintly carried on the breeze, the words of the valley's former and only resident—a hermit who used to declare as he outstretched his arms at the panoramic setting:

Handsome view fer sure. It all belongs to me.

Those words came from Noah John Rondeau.

In 1913, the year Noah chose to leave civilization by stepping into the wilderness refuge of the High Peaks of Essex County to follow the trails of the generations of hunter-trappers who preceded him, his only boundary was the horizon. "I just lived the way I wanted to," he said years later, when asked to explain his reason for going off to a mountain retreat, "and that's it." He was running free—living how he saw fit, but slowly and unwittingly, he developed a land ethic philosophy.

"Conservation is a state of harmony between men and land," wrote Aldo Leopold.

It is possible to believe Noah came to agree with Leopold. The open space gave him a place to stretch—to feel free and reward him the opportunity to replace his restlessness for a world that fit his dream.

Each year, from mid-September into early October, Noah John chose to pen his daily observations "At Open Air Studio." The painting studio was Cold River Hill, a high bluff overlooking the Santanoni Range, the site of my camp for the next several days.

You might say Rondeau was a High Peaks pioneer in a way, for he single-handedly established a hermitage that evolved into a way stop for hundreds of mountain climbers, anglers and hunters over the decades he occupied the hermitage positioned on a tiny wedge of private property in Cold River country. It was isolated—a long day's hike at a good pace from any habitation. Most forest travelers thought they had hit the jackpot when they dropped into "Cold River City—population one." There, the lone resident and his guests would sway in homemade rocking chairs as the pipes of autumn called to them. Few visitors found their way to the High Peaks hermit's doorstep in late fall. The same is true today, and yet I find the season spectacular.

During days of "Perfect autumn sunshine," a phrase Old Whiskers used, Noah spent his days in comparative hermit-luxury—loafing, doing stints of work interspersed with creative cooking, playing the fiddle, smoking, working on an oil painting of the mountains, and composing observations like: "You'll find spruce [trees] like a woman of the gay 1890s—wearing its skirts to the ground just because Deer don't eat Spruce." He worked on refining his hieroglyphic code, created poetic mountain "peeks" verses, arranged his scrapbook, target shot with bow and arrows, and tended the mouse trap line inside his Town Hall hut and enjoyed the simple pleasures of a backwoods life.

As I dined, I looked upstream where I saw that the flow narrowed before the bend in the river. Marshy areas along its edges added to the tranquil scene. I thought of the "Adirondack clears," an atmospheric condition Noah named. He explained it as the "hours when the air appears to depart and only the limited vision of our eyes prevents us from reading a newspaper a mile away."

Then he would point to Panther Peak to the south.

> *I had this notion in me, that I'd do something once and for all about the clears and sunsets. I got me some canvas and oils and began to put those visions on canvas, but the tubes of paint dried out before I could master the proper technique of transferring the images fittingly. Mind you, I wasn't an expert or anything, but I could produce a fair resemblance.*

I own a lithograph of that oil painting. The original had bear grease, drops of maple syrup and a layer of wood smoke that needed to be removed before reproducing prints. Noah's finished work was, and remains today, a charming, albeit primitive, rendering of his Cold River hermitage. In the left foreground is the "Big Dam," followed by piles of boulders and raging rapids to the right. Perched on a bluff above the rapids is Noah's "Town Hall." Dotting the hills and dells is the kaleidoscope of

One of several images Noah had taken when he produced postcards to sell.
TED HILLMAN—AUTHOR'S ADIRONDACK COLLECTION

Noah's oil on board painting titled "Cold River City, Population one". Noah presented the painting to a friend. It read, "To my fisherman friend Roy E. Lash (Cold River Citizen) Noah John Rondeau".
ADIRONDACK ARCHIVES, INC.—AUTHOR'S ADIRONDACK COLLECTION

autumn colors which greeted Noah every day. Scarlet maples, yellow birches, green pines and browning grasses generously overtake the landscape. In the distance, the Panther and Couchsachraga Peaks of the Santanoni Range rise majestically over the scene, while animal-shaped clouds dance across the blue-gray September sky. It remains an everlasting tribute to the joys of autumn and to the legendary Adirondack hermit.

The route to another pleasant view Noah claimed as his own takes one across the narrow river from Cold River Hill into a quiet valley where "Bellyache Swamp" gives no hint of the upland toil it takes to reach distant Couchsachraga Peak. There is a carpet of muck and several miles of heady, exciting bushwhacking that pound the human heart—and color everywhere is a delight beyond expression.

Fall offers a symphony of scarlet maples, russet beeches, and birches and tamaracks glowing yellow. Noah often guided Helen and Mary Colyer and Ruthy Prince without compass or map on summit ventures. He was familiar with the best routes to all six summits in the Seward and Santanoni Mountain ranges, but "Couchee" was his favorite mountaintop. Couchsachraga is a treed-over peak, with peek holes to survey seemingly all of Noah's country.

I am reminded of Noah John Rondeau's tongue-in-cheek remark when he pointed out his world as the robust mountaineers crawled through trees at the summit to a vantage point. "It all belongs to me. How much would you give me for this pleasant, handsome view?" Pointing to a distant summit, he'd say, "That mountain's for sale. Would you like to buy it?"

Duck Hole, 1986, when there was a walkway, a dam and a lean-to.
GARY KOCH

Well, of course it wasn't true. The land was not for sale nor would it ever be. The veteran hermit-guide was just fooling. *His* first-class views and the sensations of "uph'istedness," a term coined by Old Mountain Phelps, are there for all to experience.

The Adirondack Park is vast—some 6 million acres. Bigger than the national parks of Yellowstone, Glacier, the Great Smokies and the Grand Canyon combined. The public land is about 43% of that acreage and every last lesser peak, each deep wooded valley, and all the streams and bogs far below Couchee are public domain. It is all *ours*—millions of acres, yours 'n' mine, where we can camp, hunt, fish, and hike over hundreds of miles of forest trails, blazed for self-guiding. There are lean-tos and campgrounds, boat launches and trout streams, landmarks, mixed and boreal forests and alpine tundra.

Adirondack Country is a blend of mountains and forest, rivers and lakes. It is also woodland solitude, wild critters, fields, hills, and greening grass; bugs and singing birds, germinating seeds, rocks and tumbling trout streams that were once vital to spring log drives.

And people have put up some major fights to save these lands from spoilage. Of course, some wanted to protect the watershed, others wanted the hunting and fishing for themselves, but that wasn't all—not by a long shot. The visionaries were looking ahead; they wanted all that and more. The conservationists wanted it for the children of tomorrow and for those childrens' grandchildren—like mine.

The years have been good to the mountains and forest. Unbridled logging has stopped, waterways are protected, and large chunks of state land have been parceled into primitive wild forest, and designated as wilderness—decrees that are not always popular.

I'm willing to bet that if all those people who use the public land could sit on the edge of Couchee and see what Noah saw, they would feel just as he did and as I do. The view would crystalize into a reality the splendid dream of the forefathers of the Adirondack Park. They'd fight, not only to keep the public land intact by cooperating with the state departments; they'd support the laws and volunteer their time and contribute monies to make it bigger and better for their own children and grandchildren.

New York State has invested in a pretty big thing. I'd like to see my grandchildren and great-grandchildren get the same kind of dividends from our Adirondack Park land that I have, and so help me, I'll never have any part in destroying it—whether that means thoughtlessly dropping a lighted match, cutting trees where they shouldn't be cut, taking game out of season, polluting rivers and brooks, or favoring legislation that will make it possible for greedy men to invade and exploit lands controlled for the benefit of people like you and me.

Cold River with photographer's canoe and the Sewards in background, 1989
GARY KOCH

Back at Noah's snug undersized cabins and log wigwams on Cold River Hill's grassy meadow that served as his home until 1950, he could look out the tiny windows of his sleeping quarters and see the flower beds in the front, and over the river, past the far shore, he could see a good portion of the Santanoni Range span from the twist in the river to almost the summit of Panther Peak, and the massive southeast flank of Couchsachraga Peak, with cloud shadows chasing over it and fog shrouding its distant summit in the spring when it was warm and cold fronts met in the valley below. Couchee was his favorite mountain, and a view he never tired of—never the same, but always attractive, no matter what the weather conditions or the season.

Noah's lifestyle would not be considered forest-friendly today. Imagine 20,000 Noahs living in the park, often cutting live trees, poaching deer, illegally trapping bear, and taking far more fish than the daily legal limit because full stew pots are essential to survival!

Today's Adirondack enthusiasts primarily visit the area for its sheer natural beauty and recreation. Trails can become worn, lean-tos must be maintained, and traipsing all over a summit is discouraged in order to protect alpine vegetation. These are vital to the health and well-being of forest and mountains.

On my return trek to the Outside, I scrambled up one final peak—Mount Donaldson. There I paused and took in a deep breath and gazed out across the valley below where seas of fog can hide other seas of Adirondack peaks.

I felt no more alone than Noah ever did, even though he was often in the wild alone for months at a time. The sky and the water were with him. The mountains and trees, the insects, birds and animals were with him—albeit impersonally. He'd point out when asked, "See that nuthatch half-hidden in a tangle of leaves? The pink blossoms nearby? And those yellow buttercups? Chickadee birds sing short squeaky notes and squirrels scold. I'm hardly alone."

Watching minute snowflakes in late autumn drift over almost leafless wooded slopes below, and far beyond, I pictured this scene in winter, a blend of grays and evergreen and white with snow that softly veiled the earth, blending all in a winter tapestry, and Noah perhaps wincing from the cold winter winds. But regardless of the weather each season brought, he felt a purity of thought and of mind in the mountains that he experienced nowhere else. It is a magical, and some would say spiritual, experience many others have also felt in their own way.

Soon winter would set in among these Adirondack peaks, and by the time the bears were snug in their dens and crusted snow four feet deep, Noah would be expecting to hear ole St. Nick's reindeer prance too hard all over the Town Hall roof.

One thing Noah did for entertainment during winter was share how he spent his holidays in the wild—correspondence that often was mailed months after it were recorded. A number of the hermit's Christmas cards recorded events of the season. He'd report in a jocular voice: "Santa was a mite hungry. Ate up all the cookies, drank too much scotch, and slept in my bunk. I'll be ready for him next year, might even roast a raccoon marinated in my special sauce. But, next year Santa will have to obtain the proper permits. I just can't have people landing on my rooftop without first receiving the proper authority from the mayor."

Perhaps as Santa Claus passed high above the Adirondack High Peaks he too might have exclaimed, "It all belongs to me," as he dreamily flew over it all.

**

It is very much in the romantic tradition to picture yourself as a solitary figure atop a lonely mountain summit. I've been something of a connoisseur of mountain tops and a collector of climbing experiences. With continued public interest in New York's alpine ecosystem and the High Peaks Summit Stewardship Program, a partnership of the Adirondack Mountain Club, The Adirondack Chapter of The Nature Conservancy, and the New York State Department of Environmental Conservation, summit and trail protection is an achievable goal.

My hope is that future climbers will find the same enjoyment I have of climbing to see the sunrise, to share a remote mountain communing only with chipmunks, to climb a historic fire tower, or just drink in a fine view as they tip-toe along the blazed routes, knowing they are protecting rare, fragile plant communities found only on the highest mountains of the state.

Boreas Ponds, October 2015
NANCIE BATTAGLIA

Adirondack Park: Surviving and Thriving Through Common Ground and Compromise

By Joe Martens

Joe Martens *served as Governor Andrew Cuomo's Commissioner of the Department of Environmental Conservation from March 2011 to July 2015, guiding the Administration's efforts to protect and expand access to the state's open spaces, boost environmental funding programs after years of cuts, and launch numerous initiatives to protect drinking water, improve air quality and reduce greenhouse gasses. Following an exhaustive review, Commissioner Martens issued a Findings Statement concluding that high-volume hydraulic fracturing should not be allowed to go forward in New York State.*

From 1995-2010, Mr. Martens was successively Executive Vice President and President (1998) of the Open Space Institute, directing and overseeing land acquisition, historic preservation and farmland protection. Prior to that, he served Governor Mario Cuomo as Deputy Secretary for Energy and the Environment from 1992-94 and as Assistant Secretary from 1990-92. He was Chair of the Board of the Olympic Regional Development Authority, Chair of the Environmental Facilities Corporation and sat on the board of the Energy Research and Development Authority. He studied resource economics at the University of Massachusetts at Amherst and received an M.S. in Resource Management from the State University of New York, College of Environmental Science and Forestry at Syracuse University.

Much has been written about the Adirondacks, and deservedly so. It is vast (some 6 million acres), mountainous (46 peaks over 4,000' in elevation), water rich (3,000 lakes and ponds, and 30,000 miles of rivers and streams) and controversial—see *Contested Terrain* by Philip Terrie. From the creation of the Adirondack Park in 1892, to the creation of the Adirondack Park Agency (APA) in 1970, to skirmishes over newly-acquired state land, the Park had been a battleground for decades. Local government officials, Park environmental advocacy organizations, a variety of groups from railroad advocates to miners, state agencies like the APA and the New York State Department of Environmental Conservation (DEC), the tourism industry and year-round and seasonal residents are all interested parties. I had the good fortune as President of the Open Space Institute (2008-2010) and as DEC Commissioner (2011-2015) to play a significant role in bringing people together and setting a path that relies on cooperation and communication rather than open hostility.

Tahawus acquisition—a new approach

Historically, local government officials opposed state acquisition of land in the Park because it becomes part of the Forest Preserve and "Forever Wild" pursuant to Article XIV of the state constitution. Although the state pays taxes on lands it owns in the Park, the Forest Preserve land cannot be developed[1] and no timber can be harvested from it. Consequently, many local government officials argue that state ownership, in effect, limits property tax revenues, discourages private investment and attracts users (hikers, cross country skiers, etc.) who contribute little to the local economy. Putting aside the merits of their arguments, suffice to say that adding to the 2.6 million acres of state-owned land in the Park is typically not an easy sell.

In 2003, when the Open Space Institute (OSI) acquired a 10,000-acre property in the heart of the Adirondack Park known as the Tahawus Tract, it made a concerted effort to engage the community and win its support for the project and achieve a suite of objectives including conservation, historic preservation and community economic development. My colleague Dan Luciano and I worked with Town Supervisor George Canon and the Newcomb Town Board to custom design a project that would result in a major addition to the Forest Preserve in the heart of the High Peaks Wilderness Area, protect several historic structures on the property including an iron blast furnace built in 1854, a fire tower, a large corporate retreat and the remains of an abandoned mining town. In addition, at the Town's request, OSI avoided acquiring a 2,000-acre portion of the property that contained substantial mineral reserves.

After fully developing and vetting its plans with the Town and other interested parties, OSI secured subdivision approval from the APA to keep the historic resources on the site out of the Forest Preserve[2]. It then turned its attention to restoring and interpreting them so they could be understood and enjoyed by the public. The Tahawus project is a success story that opened a new chapter in Adirondack land conservation that fostered a cooperative relationship between non-profits like OSI, Adirondack local governments and involved state agencies.

---

1. The NYS Department of Environmental Conservation manages land within the Park and builds trails and other related infrastructure on state land including trailhead parking lots and campsites.
2. A law passed in 1984 discourages the state from acquiring historic resources in the Park to avoid conflicts with the "Forever Wild" provision of the state constitution.

Finch Pruyn acquisition—a game changer

Finch, Pruyn & Company was one of the largest and oldest industrial timberland owners in the Adirondack Park until 2007. It managed 161,000 acres of stunning, diverse forest lands that included 415 miles of rivers and streams, 300 lakes and ponds, 90 mountain peaks and 16,000 acres of wetlands. In 2007, Finch's Board of Directors voted to recommend to its shareholders that they accept a bid from Atlas Holdings and Blue Wolf Capital Management to purchase all of its assets. Atlas and Blue Wolf announced that they would continue to operate Finch's 600-employee mill in Glens Falls, under the newly formed Finch Paper Company. In a joint press release it was also announced that The Nature Conservancy concurrently acquired the Finch timberlands—all 161,000 acres—for $110 million. The breadth, scope and transaction price of the deal were immense. The Finch lands spanned six counties and 27 towns, with more than 80% of the lands within the five Adirondack towns (the "Five Towns") of Newcomb, North Hudson, Minerva, Indian Lake and Long Lake.

Perhaps even more impressive than the land was the process that followed the announcement. The Nature Conservancy (TNC), led by the Executive Director of its Adirondack Chapter, Mike Carr, which had a few years prior followed the Tahawus model to successfully work with seven towns in two counties in the northern part of the Park to protect 104,000 acres, followed the model for engagement again but this time on a much grander scale. Mike and his staff met with each of the towns involved as well as DEC officials and worked out a conservation plan that eventually garnered the support of all 27 towns and the state. TNC agreed to resell some 92,000 acres of the Finch lands and convey a conservation easement to DEC, limiting the use of this land to sustainable forestry, hunt club leasing and some public recreation, including new snowmobile trails. (The buyer was

Marcy, Colden and the McIntyre Range, January 2015
BRENDAN WILTSE

a Danish pension fund.) Furthermore, TNC agreed to sell 65,000 acres of the most environmentally sensitive and recreationally important lands to the state for inclusion into the Forest Preserve. Finally, TNC set aside more than 1,000 acres to three Adirondack towns for community purposes. The final agreement was the product of a thoughtful, deliberative process that would ensure a continued paper supply to the Glens Falls mill, protect jobs in the woods and enhance the Park's recreation and tourism economy by bringing into public ownership some of the most beautiful land in the state. It was the deal of a century—but the Great Recession of 2008 threatened to undo it.

Land acquisition moratorium

Faced with severe revenue shortfalls spawned by the financial crisis, in January of 2008 New York Governor Paterson proposed a two-year moratorium on land purchases funded by the state's Environmental Protection Fund (EPF). Even though a moratorium was never formally enacted, the state's land acquisition program all but ground to a halt and DEC was not in a position to acquire key Finch lands from TNC, which had borrowed the necessary funds to close this huge transaction. As a result of the state's hesitation, the teetering economy and an unfavorable ruling in a western New York real property tax case regarding the payment of taxes on state-owned land, a number of the towns that had already agreed to the deal were nervous enough to begin to oppose it even though the window had long passed for them to officially block the state from spending from the EPF on the project. And some statewide elected officials questioned whether it was prudent to buy more land when other essential state services were subject to budget cuts. Two nervous years and millions of dollars in carrying costs later, TNC was left wondering if the state would formally commit to moving forward with the carefully crafted deal or whether it needed to pursue an as yet undetermined "Plan B."

In the final days of 2010, TNC patience paid off when the state acquired the conservation easement protecting nearly 60 percent of the former Finch lands. However, the state was still in precarious fiscal condition when Governor Andrew Cuomo was sworn into office on January 1, 2011, and support for significant additions to the Forest Preserve was waning. New York faced a $10 billion deficit, economic recovery was not in sight and the fate of the remaining Finch lands remained in question.

Complex environmental issues

I began my tenure as Acting DEC Commissioner in early January 2011 shortly after Governor Cuomo took office, and the NYS Senate confirmed my appointment in March. Fortunately, I had an exceptional staff to help confront a host of controversial, complex and complicated environmental issues—high-volume hydraulic fracturing of natural gas, the looming expiration of the state's brownfield and Superfund programs, aging and failing environmental infrastructure, and, of course, the fate of the Finch lands in the Adirondack Park, to name a few.

Completing the acquisition of the Finch lands was not the only issue in the Park that needed resolution, and given the relatively short historical tenure of DEC Commissioners, time was of the essence. Several other issues had been brewing in the Park—one for more than thirty years, another for more than one hundred! The separate histories will be written on each of these issues, but in summary here my Adirondack agenda included securing passage of two constitutional amendments. The first one addressed a more than hundred-year-old dispute between the state and 200 landowners in the Town of Long Lake in an area known as "Township 40," regarding ownership of some 1,000 acres of land. The second one authorized a land swap that would expand the Jay Mountain Wilderness Area by more than 1,000 acres and allow a private mining operation, NYCO Minerals, to expand its mine on to 200 acres of Forest Preserve. I also hoped to look for a compromise on the future of the "Remsen to Lake Placid" rail line between trail advocates, who sought to convert the entire 119-mile rail corridor to a multi-use public trail, and rail advocates, who sought to keep the entire rail corridor intact and upgrade it so that two scenic railroads located at each end of the corridor could expand their operations over the entire corridor. I think it is fair to say that all four issues—the acquisition of the Finch lands, the two constitutional amendments and the fate of the Remsen to Lake Placid railroad—fall under the rubric of Terrie's book, *Contested Terrain*, and my team at DEC and I were determined to find common ground and break some longstanding stalemates.

Falling back on a formula that worked for the Tahawus project, we reached out to virtually everyone who had a stake in these issues and who we knew would engage in a constructive conversation, including statewide elected officials, town supervisors and environmental organizations. And since all issues in the Park have a way of becoming intertwined, we worked on these issues simultaneously, encouraging stakeholders to recognize that economic and environmental issues are two sides of the same coin.

DEC developed draft constitutional amendments for both NYCO and Township 40, met with virtually everyone who had an interest in them, and discussed its approach with state legislative leaders. The riddle to the longstanding Township 40 dilemma was cracked by DEC attorney Ken Hamm, who crafted an ingenious, understandable, low-cost process that would simultaneously settle claims and provide an overall benefit to the Forest Preserve.

Author (right) paddling the Upper Hudson with Mike Carr, Executive Director, TNC
NANCIE BATTAGLIA

The process required the state legislature to pass proposed constitutional amendments in two successive legislative sessions and a majority of the state's voters to approve them at the polls in November. Due to strong support for both amendments from elected officials from both within and outside the Park—and in the case of NYCO support from the business community, the Adirondack Council and the Adirondack Mountain Club—both proposals were approved overwhelmingly by the state legislature in 2012 and 2013. They were placed on the ballot, along with four other unrelated constitutional amendment proposals in November 2013. The Township 40 amendment was approved by nearly 73% of those who cast ballots and the NYCO amendment was approved more narrowly by 53%. Both of these amendments solved longstanding issues and reinforced the opinion that stakeholders who often hold opposing points of view will work together for the betterment of the Park and the people who care about it.

The Remsen to Lake Placid Railroad dates back to the 1890s and service along the line operated intermittently during the twentieth century. The state purchased the corridor in 1974 and leased it to a private operator in 1977. Following the 1980 Winter Olympics in Lake Placid, all activity ceased on the corridor until the early 1990s when the Adirondack Scenic Railroad started operating two tourist lines, one on the north end of the corridor between Lake Placid and Saranac Lake, and one on the south end of the corridor between Utica and Big Moose. One of the most hotly contested debates in the Park erupted several years ago when a loose-knit group of trail and snowmobile advocates suggested that the corridor would be more beneficial to the public if the tracks were removed and a 90-mile, multi-use trail created that could be used by hikers, cross-country skiers, bicyclists and snowmobilers. The debate grew as trail advocates became more organized and formed an organization known as ARTA (Adirondack Rail Trail Association) to take on proponents of the Adirondack Scenic Railroad. This battle, which was playing out in the press and town halls, needed a referee.

Great blue heron scouting the Ausable River
CARL HEILMAN II

Department of Transportation Commissioner Joan McDonald and I decided to enter the fray and in 2013 formally reopen a nearly 20-year-old Unit Management Plan for the travel corridor. Jointly we held numerous public meetings, hearings and took testimony from hundreds of people who cared about the future of this corridor. Everyone agreed on exactly one point—the corridor is a recreational and economic asset that is underutilized. Commissioner McDonald and I agreed that it was time to solicit input, lots of it, and take action. After nearly two years of input, we made a decidedly un-Solomon-like proposal to actually split the baby. In June 2015, DEC and DOT submitted a draft amendment to the Corridor Unit Management Plan that proposed removing the rails from Lake Placid to Tupper Lake, a 34-mile segment, and keeping the rails intact and bolstering rail service from Remsen to Tupper Lake, a distance of approximately 85 miles. We also found that the rail and trail, side-by-side, was infeasible.

Although neither side in this debate got everything they wanted, the compromise makes sense. A multi-use trail from Lake Placid to Tupper will provide a recreational outlet for the thousands of tourists who visit Lake Placid, bringing them to nearby towns that don't get the volume of visitors that Lake Placid enjoys. It will be inviting to people of all ages and abilities who want to experience a taste of the Adirondacks without the level of effort required in more remote areas. Similarly, extending the rail line north from Big Moose to Tupper will provide families and people of all ages with an intimate glimpse of remote and wild areas that they may not otherwise have the ability to get to. Tupper Lake, the epicenter and meeting place for the rail and trail, may be the biggest beneficiary of this proposal, bringing thousands of new visitors to a town that is eager to reignite its tourist economy.

Delivering on Finch—the last installment

On August 5, 2012, Governor Cuomo and I traveled to Lake Placid with some good news—the state would buy, over a five year span, 69,000[3] stunning acres including such iconic landscapes as the Essex Chain Lakes, Boreas Ponds, OK Slip Falls and miles of river frontage along remote stretches of the Upper Hudson River. During that announcement, we committed to working with the communities where the lands were located to ensure that they would realize economic benefits from increased tourism, and that to the extent practicable and within the confines of sound natural resources management, the lands would be managed to promote a variety of activities including snowmobiling, bicycling, hiking, paddling, and be accessible to people of all ages and abilities.

NANCIE BATTAGLIA

3. This total includes 65,000 acres that TNC bought from Finch Pruyn and 4,000 acres of land adjacent to the Finch lands purchased from other landowners.

DEC closed on the first installment of the five-year acquisition project, the 18,300-acre Essex Chain Lakes tract, in the final days of 2012, and followed with seven additional tracts, including OK Slip Falls, in April 2013. Three months later, the Adirondack Park was in the national limelight, thanks to media attention drawn by Governor Cuomo's first-ever Adirondack Challenge. The two-day event, designed to bolster economic activity as promised at the 2012 press conference in Lake Placid, included an invitational whitewater rafting race on the Indian River. State legislators, state agency staff, local elected officials and others joined the Governor for this event, and found themselves in rafts piloted by professional guides for a three-mile whitewater run through the state's newest Forest Preserve acquisition. As far as I know, Governor Cuomo is the first governor to make such a highly visible, direct link to newly protected lands and the communities that host them.

Along similar lines, Governor Cuomo in a 2013 press release also announced TNC's $500,000 grant to the state to support community connections and economic development linked to the former Finch lands in Newcomb, Minerva, North Hudson, Indian Lake, Long Lake and other towns. This money was disbursed in 2014 by TNC and DEC in grants to support equestrian staging areas, modernized lodging, campground improvements, expanded guide services and an Essex County IDA microenterprise start-up project.

Ultimately, the APA-proposed classification for the property included a large, new primitive area around the Essex Chain Lakes, expanded wilderness around the Upper Hudson and an expansion of wild forest areas and wild forest corridor that will provide for a snowmobile community connector trail between the towns of Indian Lake and Minerva. The Governor approved the APA-proposed classification package in February 2014, announcing that it accomplished the goals he hoped to see achieved for the property. Once again, neither the local government representatives nor the Park advocates were entirely happy with the outcome but the classification package is a successful compromise that protected the resource and provided opportunity for a wide variety of outdoor recreation.

As of this writing, the state has acquired 48,000 acres of the former Finch lands from TNC—24 parcels in all. Only the Boreas Ponds tract remains, and like the acquisitions that preceded it, the property is stunning and should be added to the public trust. But history has a way of repeating itself. Even before the state has acquired the tract, advocates have called for the Governor to commit to classifying the bulk of the property Wilderness. This, unfortunately, is rekindling some of the historic tensions that many of us hoped were a thing of the past.

I'm optimistic, however, that this chapter in Adirondack history will end with the crown jewel added to the Forest Preserve. Boreas Ponds, along with other former Finch lands, will draw visitors from around the world, and nearby towns will continue to improve visitor amenities and attract private investment to bolster the recreation and tourism industry. While there will always be differing views and competing interests in the Park, just like in other geographies, common ground will help the Park survive and thrive into the next century and beyond.

NANCIE BATTAGLIA

Adirondack Mountain Club: Invested in Wilderness

By John Million

John Million *is Deputy Executive Director of Adirondack Mountain Club. In this role, Million oversees all the daily operations of the programs, services and business units of ADK. He has been with ADK since 1999, first as North Country Facilities Director, then Operations Director, and in his current position since 2004.*

Before joining ADK, John had a successful career as a business executive in outdoor recreation and sporting goods retail management. He has worked for Recreational Equipment, Inc., Timberland and Champs Sports, among others, throughout the northeastern United States. He enjoys live music, Syracuse Orange basketball and all things outdoors. He and his wife Katie live near Mt. Van Hoevenberg with their cats Bear and Bark, and a chubby but sweet golden retriever named Kelly.

The Adirondack Mountain Club (ADK) stands for conservation, advocacy, recreation, education and stewardship. We are a non-profit grassroots organization of nearly 30,000 members and 27 locally active chapters, dedicated to the protection and responsible recreational use of all New York State public lands. We build and maintain trails; we advocate and educate; we offer wilderness hospitality and hiker information; and our facilities provide the base of operations for tens of thousands of outdoor enthusiasts each year. Our strength and most valuable resource is our members—volunteers extraordinaire—who never tire of giving back to the lands they love. They donate literally thousands of hours of their time each year in supporting our mission, programs and activities—performing trail work, shaping our policy positions, voicing their opinions at public hearings and supporting environmental causes. Just as important, their annual membership dues and gifts support a professionally staffed organization that is responsible for managing ADK assets and providing leadership for ADK initiatives from a sustainable, member-inspired perspective.

An essential conservation partner

By birthright, ADK is intimately connected with the Adirondack Park and the people who come to enjoy its wonders. By legacy, we own precious parcels of land and facilities in the majestic surroundings of the High Peaks Wilderness Area. By the dedication of our members and staff for nearly a century, we have earned our reputation as trusted stewards of the land. Together these attributes have made ADK an essential partner in, and credible advocate for, both responsible recreation and the protection and preservation of New York State's wilderness areas.

As recreational use of and impact on the very popular Eastern High Peaks has increased over time, New York State has been forced to implement more stringent land use regulations to protect the natural resource. As inherited gatekeeper to this wilderness, ADK has historically been the primary educator and administrator of these regulations at the main access point for these lands. In recent years, state resources for stewardship services such as forest rangers, assistant forest rangers and backcountry caretakers have become stressed, shifting even more of the burden of providing information and education to the public to our non-profit organization. This has occurred at the same time as the number of day hikers visiting the High Peaks has increased exponentially while the number spending overnights by backpacking has diminished.

Author backcountry skiing

We thrive in this role even as it strains our financial resources. Having the front-country visitor services that allow for a successful transition for urban visitors to learn about and be well prepared for a backcountry experience is vital for the safety and enjoyment of the users and for the protection and long-term sustainability of this wilderness. Meeting people as they arrive for their Adirondack experience, and ensuring that their recreational choices lead to a meaningful connection with the natural world, is the highest and best use of our facilities, and is at the core of our mission.

We also provide information services, maps and guidebooks for numerous civic agencies and training for local Visitor Bureau staff. In addition, we train New York State Department of Environmental Conservation (DEC) assistant forest rangers, backcountry interior caretakers and backcountry stewardship interns.

Wilderness hospitality

Our facilities include lodges, cabins, a campground and an information center where guests and visitors can learn about and interact with the surrounding wilderness. Hundreds of miles of marked wilderness trails and New York State's highest peaks are within easy reach of these facilities.

Heart Lake

Our Heart Lake Program Center is the primary access point to the High Peaks Wilderness Area. This 640-acre portal to the Adirondack Park's most popular public lands is the gateway for approximately 75,000 visitors annually and includes the busiest hiking trailhead in New York State. ADK maintains the High Peaks Information Center, which includes a small retail store, and a 200-car parking lot. Forty percent of the visitors who pass through the Heart Lake trailheads are making their first visit to the Adirondacks. The information and education provided by ADK staff at the Information Center is critical in ensuring a safer and more comfortable experience for these visitors. The small store in this facility carries essential items for backcountry travel and equipment to allow visitors to remain in compliance with land use regulations.

High Peaks Information Center
NANCIE BATTAGLIA

Adirondak Loj

Our best known facility is the venerable Adirondak Loj, which is the center for much of the programming and activity at Heart Lake. The current Loj, built in 1927, has space for 38 guests in a combination of private rooms, family bunk rooms and a co-ed loft. Delicious home-cooked meals, with homemade breads and soups, are served family style in the rustic

Adirondak Loj
NANCIE BATTAGLIA

dining room. The comfortable Great Room with its stone fireplace is perfect for recounting the day's adventures or just relaxing with a book from our Adirondack library.

The nearby Wilderness Campground has 54 total sites in a variety of configurations including tent sites, lean-tos and "canvas cabin" walled tents with bunks. There are also three traditional cabins at Heart Lake—the Wiezel Trails Cabin sleeps sixteen, Tyler Cabin sleeps six and the Campground Cabin sleeps four. Canoes, kayaks and stand up paddleboards are available for rent at the Loj, and the beachfront of Heart Lake is open for swimming to overnight guests. The most popular hike is the short but steep trip up Mt. Jo. While the trail is just a mile in length, the view from the summit provides a great perspective of the vast expanse of the High Peaks.

Johns Brook Lodge

Johns Brook Lodge (JBL) is a backcountry lodge located in the heart of the High Peaks, accessed via a 3.5-mile hike in from the Garden parking area in Keene Valley. The lodge sleeps 28 people in co-ed bunk rooms. During July and August, JBL is fully staffed by an accommodating "hutcrew" who provide three meals, including cooking and serving breakfast and dinner, and preparing and packing trail lunches. From mid-May to late June, and Labor Day to Columbus Day, the lodge operates under caretaker service. This means guests bring in and cook their own food and have full access to the JBL kitchen. Education programs and lectures are offered during the full service season.

The Johns Brook property also has two cabins available for the public that operate year round. Camp Peggy O'Brien is a spacious rustic cabin that sleeps twelve and Grace Camp is a cozy smaller cabin that sleeps six. There are three lean-tos on the property that can be reserved at any time of year and offer privacy and tranquility in what can otherwise be a busy backcountry.

The Johns Brook Valley offers a wide variety of hiking opportunities. The trip into the lodge alone can be a great hike for those just getting into hiking or backpacking. For those looking to hike the High Peaks, there are nine summits easily accessible from the lodge. JBL was opened in 1925 as ADK's first lodge, and it has been a backcountry oasis for High Peaks exploration ever since.

Johns Brook Lodge
NANCIE BATTAGLIA

Education and outreach

ADK's Education Department offers dozens of workshops for all interests and outreach programs for schools and youth groups. The Summer Naturalist Intern Program provides a wide variety of interpretive experiences, nature walks, lectures and talks, and maintains the popular ADK Nature Museum. The museum is a hands-on, fun stop for families to enjoy an interactive experience with the natural world surrounding Heart Lake. Skills workshops and guided hikes are held year round by ADK's knowledgeable staff of state licensed guides and instructors. ADK is also one of only a handful of nationally authorized providers of Leave No Trace Master Educator training courses.

The Three Seasons at Heart Lake School Outreach Program brings fourth graders from nine Adirondack public schools to Heart Lake for an experiential learning excursion. ADK educators go into the school classroom and teach a lesson that is followed up with a field trip to Heart Lake. But rather than a one-off trip, teachers lead the students through an accompanying classroom journal throughout the year and the process is repeated in the fall, winter and spring. Nearly 500 students will experience the changing of the seasons, animal adaptations, and develop some outdoor skills and an expanding appreciation for the great bounty of nature right in their own backyards. By targeting fourth grade students, ADK is assisting the local schools in meeting state mandated curriculum requirements and developing the next generation of conservationists and environmental advocates.

Field Programs

ADK and its members have been maintaining and building trails for over 90 years. In fact, one of ADK's first major projects was the construction of the approximately 133-mile long Northville-Placid Trail in 1923. Beginning with this major trail project, ADK volunteers and employees have spent countless hours creating the trails and lean-tos that hundreds of thousands of hikers have enjoyed. The major components of ADK Field Programs are the ADK Professional Trail Crew, ADK Supervised Volunteer Trails Program, Backcountry Stewardship Programs and the High Peaks Summit Stewardship Program.

Professional Trail Crew

ADK Professional Trail Crew is currently comprised of sixteen highly trained seasonal staff members who work on trails all over New York State. Most of the work is done through a contract with the state and ADK staff work closely with DEC personnel to determine the highest priority trail projects. Using hand tools and working both in teams and individually, the crew performs intensive trail reconstruction using primarily native materials. This crew is nationally recognized for their skilled techniques in creating sustainable backcountry trails through sound layout and long-lasting trail structures. Wes Lampman's chapter on page 247 provides a personal insight on trail work.

NANCIE BATTAGLIA

Marcy from Skylight
BRENDAN WILTSE

Supervised Volunteer Trails Program

The Supervised Volunteer Trails Program strives to provide all of its volunteers with a positive and rewarding experience while giving back to trails. Volunteer projects are inherently educational, allowing participants to not only learn the skills associated with trail work but also the natural history of the area and "Leave No Trace" backcountry ethics.

Backcountry Stewardship Programs

These programs provide opportunities and support for those who want to give back to the places they love with their time and labor. Among the opportunities are the Adopt a Lean-to Program, in which adopters visit their respective lean-tos at least twice a season to perform basic maintenance and clean-up duties, maintain registers and note major repairs needed. Under the Trail Steward Program, volunteers do the critical routine maintenance needed to keep trails sustainable. In addition to keeping the trails open by clearing brush and cutting blowdown, they also work to offset erosion by keeping drainages clear. The Adopt a Wildland Program allows volunteers to act as the eyes on the ground where DEC staff seldom gets to visit. With three million acres of public land within the Blue Line, there are many special places that do not always get the attention they need and deserve. Wildland adopters are people who are willing to take the time and effort to visit some of these less traveled areas and report back on their condition.

Led by Brendan Wiltse, teens sample for macroinvertebrates in the West Branch of the Ausable River under a partnership program with ADK and AsRA called Discovering the Ausable: An Aquatic Stewardship Program—SETH JONES

Summit Stewardship Program

The nationally acclaimed High Peaks Summit Stewardship Program protects New York State's alpine ecosystem through education, trail work and research. These fragile alpine plant communities are found only on the highest mountains of the state. Summit Stewards hike to the summits every day during the summer where they greet and speak with every visitor and educate hikers to enlist their help in protecting alpine plants from human trampling by staying on the solid rocks. Summit Stewards also do trail work to protect alpine plants, building scree walls and cairns to guide hikers and define the trail, and packing susceptible areas with rock to prevent soil erosion. They also complete research projects examining plant communities, recovery from trampling and rare species. The High Peaks Summit Stewardship Program is a partnership of ADK, The Adirondack Chapter of The Nature Conservancy and DEC. Julia Goren's chapter on page 59 recounts the challenges and joys of summit stewardship.

Conservation and advocacy

Fully invested in wilderness through direct actions in the field every day, we also pursue our mission through ADK's strong and respected voice. Our Conservation and Government Affairs staff lobby the State Legislature and Senate on matters of interest to ADK members. Among common issues we advocate for are public land acquisition and access, environmental protections for clean air and water, battling climate change's effects on fragile ecosystems, and ensuring that stewardship programs are funded to the highest sustainable levels.

Colette Piaseeki-Masters and her team climbing up Gothics during ADK's Johns Brook Valley Teen Adventure
SETH JONES

We champion nearly five million acres of publicly-owned lands across New York State, including the Adirondack and Catskill Forest Preserves, state parks, state forests and wildlife management areas. Our environmental advocacy program grew out of the need for responsible public policies to protect these lands and to ensure they remain accessible to the public for appropriate recreation. We believe ADK is truly the leading voice for the state's muscle-powered recreationists. As such, we represent the hikers, paddlers, skiers and other backcountry recreationists who enjoy exploring the state's vast wild lands and endeavor to educate those users on how to responsibly interact with their chosen environment. Neil Woodworth's chapter on page 189 details ADK's work in defense of the wilderness during the past three decades.

Our advocacy staff is knowledgeable about environmental law, public lands and state land management policies. State policymakers have frequently looked to ADK for our expertise and advice in developing sound environmental and public land policies. We use a balanced approach to weigh recreational access and resource protection, and recommend land classifications and recreational use plans appropriate to each public land parcel. Our Conservation and Advocacy office is located in Albany, NY.

External and internal publications

Our Publications program produces over thirty titles, including an award-winning annual calendar, the membership magazine *Adirondac*, and the most comprehensive and complete map and guidebook series for the Adirondacks and Catskills. We have partnered with National Geographic Maps to coordinate trail coverage and information between National Geographic's *Trails Illustrated* Adirondack, Catskill and Northville-Placid Trail Map Series, and ADK's own meticulously researched and edited guidebooks. ADK volunteer authors are constantly out on the trails, and submit updates regularly to provide hiking enthusiasts with the most consistently accurate and recent information. Our High Peaks trail guides and maps are essential gear for anyone exploring New York State's highest and wildest mountains.

Membership and administration

Our Member Services Center and administrative functions are headquartered in Lake George, NY. The Membership department caters to the upkeep and enhancement of ADK member benefits and supports the vibrant programming organized by local chapters. The Development team is responsible for fundraising and donor and grant management, while our business office supports all ADK programs and operations. The Adirondack-themed bookstore and information center in Lake George is often the first stop on travelers' adventures to the mountains.

NANCIE BATTAGLIA

Making a difference

As a member-supported organization, ADK has been making a difference on issues involving New York State's wilderness areas, parks and open spaces for nearly one hundred years. Looking ahead, we will remain on the front lines as a democracy of recreationists and conservationists. We will defend what we believe in with vigor and authority, while continuing to help visitors enjoy their outdoor experience and connect with wilderness on a personal level. Through the efforts of great staff and volunteers, we will inspire new generations of recreationists to take up the mantle of advocacy and stewardship of New York State's public lands.

A January morning from the summit of Big Slide
BRIAN HOODY

Taking and Giving: Mountain Feelings of a 46er

By Brian Hoody

A native of Webster, NY, **Brian Hoody** *spent his formative years under the guidance of his grandparents, roaming about the woods, hills and ponds of the northwestern Adirondacks (St. Regis Falls area). As a youth he climbed local peaks such as Azure, St. Regis and Baker, which eventually lead him into the High Peaks region.*

After several rounds of climbing the 46 High Peaks (#4410W), Brian still continues to return to the mountains that have given him so much over the years in the form of memories, friendships and respect. He is a longtime member of the Adirondack Mountain Club, as well as the Adirondack 46ers, where he has been a Correspondent, Director and is currently President. Brian has also taken part in the 46er volunteer Trail Crew since the late 1990s and, since 2007, he has maintained the herd path between South Dix and Grace Peak.

Brian shares his love of the Adirondack High Peaks in Notes From Above Treeline: Stories from the Adirondack Back Country *published in 2006, and* Tales from Above and Below the Treeline: Fact and Fiction from the Adirondack Back Country *in 2009 (**www.adkpublications.com**). He currently resides in Penfield, NY, with wife Karen, daughters Maeve and Ryne, as well as a series of cats and dogs.*

For many of us, climbing the 46 Adirondack High Peaks is a journey that never ends. That's because we never cease to marvel at all that the mountains, the wilderness and nature have to offer, no matter how many summits we cross off our list. We take and never seem to get enough. As the journey continues, many come to realize this very special place deserves something in return—that we must also give. In doing so we embrace a common cause to ensure this gift will keep on giving to future generations.

Our journeys are unique. Mine is already two decades in the making.

Part 1: Taking

My first High Peak, as for so many before me and probably after, was Algonquin. I made that first climb with my younger brother and a friend of his. The colors, what we ate, the cold, are all still vivid. The summit was astounding—beyond words. I can't describe the feeling. The amazing views of Colden, Iroquois. Mountains everywhere. The sky was streaked with blacks and grays, shafts of sunlight penetrated here and there. Unable to take the cold and the wind any longer, we took one last glance around and began our descent. For me, it was just the beginning. Over the next two decades, I would climb the 46 in all four seasons.

Fall on Cascade; the leaves were making their final stand with bright patches of yellow splashed around the landscape. We spent the better part of a quarter of an hour at the summit but the cold chased us down out of the always blowing wind.

The climbing up Colvin began almost immediately and really never ended. I really had a feeling of isolation on the trail. It was rough and passed through some extremely dense forest. I ran into a rainstorm halfway up and weathered the storm under some pines. The rain soon ended and the clouds had just begun to break up as I made the summit. The views of the lakes were breathtaking. The clouds raced right below the summit, sometimes allowing views, other times obscuring them in a thin blanket of white.

At the lowest point of the descent I found a small cool spring and refreshed my water supply. I was now ready to make my final assault on Rocky Peak Ridge. I gained my second wind after my water break and made good time out of the valley. I passed a group of older folks who must have been in their sixties or seventies and a hope was kindled inside of me that I too could one day grow old and still traverse the mountains I loved so dearly. The small trees and patches of meadow broke away quickly to reveal the gorgeous summit of Rocky Peak Ridge. There were views of Round, Noonmark, the scarred flanks of Giant, and the Great Range loomed in the distance. The alpine vegetation was just beginning to turn colors and fall was in the air.

We found a spring in the col between Dix and Hough and filled our water bottles up. We then began the final ascent of Hough. We arrived at the summit elated at our accomplishments, signed in (the canister) and took in some truly amazing views of Elk Lake. The late afternoon sun shimmered off the lake like sequins. Dix looked menacing and huge, just off to our right.

After a false hope, I began to ascend into a col that was over-run with stunted conifers, all seemingly with extremely sharp branches. I had passed by a large glacial erratic when the herd path finally began to improve somewhat. I came to a wet area and began my final ascent to the summit. I reached the summit of Marshall in the early afternoon; a large rock with no views. I had heard that if one looked about, that views could be found, so I signed in at the register—some of the comments where pretty rough; like "I don't know why I came back here again" was one that stuck out—and followed a herd path directly behind the canister to some truly wonderful views. I could make out part of the Great Range with Marcy tucked in there, the Seward Range and off in the distance, lake country shimmered in the haze.

The weather had changed to mostly cloudy, it was about thirty-five degrees and there appeared to be about the same amount of snow as there had been on Nye. I had heard tales about views off of Street, so we packed up and headed briefly back the way we had come and pushed our way to an amazing view of the MacIntyre Range. Clouds were streaming off of the Range and the snowy summits looked hostile and cold. I was glad that I was on Street and not on Algonquin, where the winds must have been whipping across the snow and ice.

The wind and snow intensified as we began to top off on Tabletop's long, flattened summit. I really could not believe how deep the snow was and how far above the trees we were. I cursed the clouds and snow for I knew behind their angry swirling mass lay wondrous views. We soon reached what we thought was the summit, and I was hoping that the canister was not buried beneath the snow. We decided to split into two parties and meet back at where we started out in ten minutes. About three minutes later I heard Ben shout that he had found the canister.

As I crested a rise on what I thought was the summit, I was treated to a fairly awesome view. Clouds were shooting below me through Ouluska Pass, with an occasional bank of clouds breaking away and passing over the summit of Seward. And there was Donaldson and then Emmons. Looking at the range from Seymour really put it into perspective. The whole range looked just immense to me and, with the clouds passing below through the pass, it made for an unforgettable sight.

Like most Adirondack peaks, there seemed to be about ten false summits but finally we began to level off, a strong, cold wind whipping the summit. Small patches of snow and ice still lingered. On a flat section directly below the summit, a small meadow allowed for views back to Couchsachraga, as well as several other old friends, like Seymour and the rest of the Seward Range. The sky was a piercing blue and the mountains had a fresh green look to them.

As I crested the summit, I began to realize why everyone loved Haystack so much. There was hardly any sign of civilization, save the mine near Tahawus. Mountains soared grandly everywhere. The sky was blue with occasional puffy white clouds. I quickly greeted the few people I saw on the summit and then went off on my own. There was a spot tucked away behind some rocks where the view of Marcy and Skylight was exceptionally breathtaking.

Cascade, January 2015
BRENDAN WILTSE

The lake shone in the pale rays of the ending day and we marveled over its beauty and remoteness. We headed up along the right shore of the lake and towards Four Corners. Along the way we passed the site of the old Lake Tear lean-to and soon thereafter reached Four Corners itself. I picked up my rock and then another. The second was for all the people I loved whom I knew would never carry a rock to the summit of Skylight themselves; but especially for my Grandfather, who had just recently passed away.

The sign at the junction stated .05 miles to the summit of Marcy. In less than one hour I would be a 46er. It was both a pleasant feeling and a sad one as well. I started up slowly, bringing up the rear. Soon after the junction we reached tree line. The views were spreading out behind us. Basin, Haystack, Tabletop. They were all there, seemingly urging me onwards to the highest point; to a conclusion of a part of my life. Four years. Some of my best times and memories were locked away in these hills.

Algonquin, this time in early October; the snow was falling steadily and the wind howled. We had to step carefully, for all of the rocks were covered over with ice. We met two Summit Stewards at the final approach to the summit. They said we were the first up for the day. I looked at my watch and noted that it was after one o'clock. I had planned on summiting around eleven. We made the summit, which was socked in by clouds, and sat down on a cold flat rock to eat some lunch. As we finished up the clouds suddenly began to break up and panoramas began to open up every which way—blue skies chasing away the gray—it was an amazing sight to behold.

A few stats for the two-day overnight trip to Big Slide Mountain. Number of inches of new snow—around twelve. Number of attempts to get up that final "hill" to the Garden parking lot—two. Number of cars dug out of the Garden after the trip was over—three. Number of cars dug out of the Rooster Comb parking lot after dropping off some fellow climbers—two. Early in the morning of day two as we approached the summit proper we were treated to one of the most incredible sights that I have ever had the privilege of witnessing in the mountains. The sun had just crested the horizon and in fact, had just risen between Giant Mountain and Lower Wolf Jaw Mountain. Below us clouds filled in all of the valleys and lowlands, leaving the bigger peaks thrusting up into the early morning sky. A soft pink-orangish glow filled the eastern sky, in stark contrast to the darkness that still lay to the northwest. Eventually the sun totally crested Giant and began to climb into the sky.

Just about to reach Algonquin summit
NANCIE BATTAGLIA

Although the view was awe-inspiring, Gordon and I only stayed on the summit of Macomb for a few minutes before the bone-chilling cold forced us to descend. The descent back towards West Mill Brook was quick to say the least. The deepening cold had made the snow slippery and glissading was easy, if not a bit tight in spots. We were back at our campsite in less than half the time that it had taken us to climb. We popped out of the conifers and into the birch forest, which looked as though someone had planted the trees purposefully, they were so well spaced out. Snow clung to the branches and trunks, and the soft evening glow made it look like something out of a postcard.

The snow was very deep and powdery, making for a tough ascent up to Boundary. Another tough section between Boundary and Boundary II, and I could see Iroquois looming in front of me. The wind was fairly screaming now. My jacket flapped wildly and my goggles kept fogging up. I attempted to ascend to the summit going the usual way but ice forced me over to the Indian Pass side, where I was able to make my way among the erratics and finally to the summit. I stayed briefly about the summit, hiding from the wind behind the summit cairn.

Nearing the summit of Basin the wind really started to pick up and the views that we had hoped to get were nonexistent. You could just make out Haystack and that was about it. We discussed briefly about heading down Chicken Coop brook but one look at the steep ice covered chute that lead toward Saddleback and we decided that we would head back the way that we came. One more quick look around the summit—somehow a sole shaft of sunlight found its way out of the clouds, which was a beautiful sight to behold.

After leaving the summit of Skylight and just as I was about to drop down below treeline something amazing happened. The clouds suddenly parted and snow-covered peaks began popping into view. The view of Haystack across Panther Gorge was one of the most rugged views I ever had the pleasure to witness in the Adirondacks. Gray was splayed out in front of me, with Lake Tear right below it, with Colden standing out behind it. Marcy's upper dome was still in the clouds but its lower flanks were in full view.

The wind was fairly blasting the ridge now, mounding up drifts along the ridge. Amazingly, I could still see the track in most places. The other thing that I noticed along the way to Emmons was the acute drop in temperature. It took a long time to reach Emmons but finally I was standing under the yellow disc. Again a very short break and I started back the way that I had come. This time the trek back to Donaldson was not so easy—the blowing snow had started to cover up the track in places, so that basically I had to break out sections that I had just broken through an hour earlier.

The woods and snow shone in the late daylight and it was quite a sight. When we got to the lumbered stretches the last of the daylight was fading out and I could see everyone ahead of me strung out along the path making their way along the final half mile. The last of the sunlight was snuffed out and we used our headlamps for the remainder of the journey. Cliff and Redfield slumbered behind us as night closed in.

My thoughts were a jumble of past trips and not believing that I was actually about to finish. I'd like to say that I strolled confidently up to the summit—but I could not tell exactly where the summit of Colden was, as the usual summit rock was buried under several feet of snow. I hit the highest points along the summit ridge and then it was over —46 winter peaks under my snowshoes. A few more minutes of staring off at Wright Peak where it all started 14 winters ago and then I took my leave of the summit.

Part 2: Giving

Inspired by so many Adirondack 46ers before me, I became an active Club member and volunteer, mainly doing trail work, lean-to adoption and working for the Historian's Office as a correspondent. Several years ago, I joined the 46er board of directors and was more recently appointed as Club president. My involvement with the Club has given me a true appreciation of the important contribution of 46ers individually and as an organization.

At the core of today's 46ers is the same goal that originally drew the Marshall brothers and their guide Herbert Clark to the Adirondacks—climbing the 46 High Peaks. However, the evolution of the 46er organization through the years features a continued movement away from being a social club to an environmental steward. In his chapter beginning on page 85, 46er Treasurer Phil Correll describes many of the Club's signature initiatives to protect the mountains and wilderness we love. With our membership growth, we are in a position to do even more in the years ahead—and that is our firm intention. In particular, the Club is devoting more resources and efforts towards trail work projects by 46er volunteers and

Above and next page: 46ers volunteers building a lean-to, Marcy Dam 2013
PETE HICKEY

by helping to finance larger trail improvement projects by the Adirondack Mountain Club (ADK) and the Adirondack Trail Improvement Society (ATIS). This direction was guided by Ed Ketchledge, Jim Goodwin and others in the 1970s, and taken up by their successors.

Recent history shows a steep rise in the number of people completing the 46 summits. Between 2012 and 2015, the club recorded 2,069 finishers, swelling our ranks. Like a lot of organizations, we struggle with the explosion of social media—where people post advice, route information and photos—in that it is challenging to reach these people and educate them in proper mountain etiquette, as well as current rules and regulations governing the High Peaks. Additionally, the Club also works with both the Adirondack 46er Conservation Trust as well as #507 Fund for further outreach opportunities.

Along with the growth in climbers comes increased pressure on the existing trail system, including the 20 peaks with herd paths—Wilderness Paths—which were not designed with any specific plan in mind other than that others had gone that way before. The 46ers contributed monetarily to the extensive bog bridging and trail work between Algonquin and Iroquois, as well as on the currently ongoing trail improvement project on Mount Colden—moving into Phase 3 and 4 in 2016—both of which were led by ADK. The 46ers have also supported various other trail projects with ADK and ATIS. A fully volunteer Trail Crew led by a series of Trailmasters (starting with Jim Goodwin as the first

Trailmaster in the 1970s) perform work on many of the herd paths, as well as some official trails under the guidance of the Department of Environmental Conservation (DEC)[1]. Current Trailmasters as of 2015 include Pete Hickey, Sam Eddy and Joe Bogardus. As the years passed the 46er Trail Crew gained experience and moved onto larger and more complex maintenance projects, centering around lean-to rehabilitation and rebuilds[2].

In 2013, the traditional correspondence system established by 46er matriarch Grace Hudowalski at the Club's inception was discontinued due to the large amount of finishers and the "mountain" of paperwork that came along with it. All aspiring 46ers had to report their climbs and write about their adventures in the High Peaks to the Historian's Office lead by Jane Nye, Anton Solomon, Mindaugas Jatulis and an army of volunteer correspondents. Hikers received a response and guidance from their assigned correspondent and, upon climbing all 46 peaks, they had to fill out finisher paperwork. The current Historian's Office is comprised of the husband/wife team of Siobhan-Carney Nesbitt and Lee Nesbitt. They currently have the formidable task of registering all incoming climbers, who are still required to fill out the traditional Mountain List and Questionnaire, which have been in use for decades. Aside from registering climbers, they also answer a multitude of questions that come in from climbers pursuing the 46, as well as maintain the current official 46er Facebook page. In 2015, an electronic version of the correspondence tradition was pioneered by the father/son team of Mark and Neil Simpson.

Another recent Club accomplishment worth mentioning was the renaming of East Dix—a High Peak located in the Dix Wilderness area, Town of North Hudson—to Grace Peak, in honor of Grace Hudowalski. The renaming effort, led primarily by Doug Arnold, was a long and at times difficult task but after 12 years, the United States Board of Geographic Names approved the renaming on June 12, 2014. In a true grassroots campaign, many individuals helped with the effort, including film maker Fred Schwobel whose documentary on Grace, entitled *The Mountains Will Wait for You* and narrated by Johnny Cash, helped to cement the final outcome.

PETE HICKEY

Future goals include educational outreach through the Outdoor Skills Workshop, educational materials available on www.adk46er.com, as well as direct contacts through the new correspondence program and the Club's social media pages. The trail crew will continue with ongoing maintenance of trails, hopefully expanding to include all herd paths at some point, as well as large, more complex projects, such as lean-to and bridge work.

The 46er organization has the critical mass and the motivation to realize its ambition as environmental steward. I salute all past and current 46er volunteers for their commitment to protecting our beloved mountains and encourage all new finishers to join us in giving back.

Note 1:
Trails and mileage estimates recorded by 46er Trail Masters: 50 total miles of herd paths and trails, as follows:

Herd path maintenance	Miles
Redfield	1.4
Marshall (Herbert Brook path)	1.7
Street/Nye	3.7
Esther	1.0
Tabletop	0.7
Various Dix herd paths	5.8
Total herd paths	**14.3**

Marked trails	Miles
Adirondak Loj to Summit Rock	6.0
Scotts Dam to Wallface Pond	2.8
Whiteface Wilmington trail	5.2
North Trail to Giant (maintain to lean-to)	5.7
Dix/Round Pond to junction	6.4
Elk Lake – trail junction	4.3
Hunter's Pass segment	3.0
Beckhorn segment	2.3
Total marked trails	**35.7**

Note 2:
Below is a non-comprehensive list of larger lean-to projects over the years as recorded in *Peeks* magazine, the club's publication:
July, 1986: The volunteer 46er Trail Crew rehabbed the Slide Brook Lean-to. Many of the older lean-tos had no floor and the base logs sat directly on the ground, which eventually caused rot. The season before, the group placed a stone foundation under the Boquet River lean-to and installed new plank flooring. The materials to rehab the Slide Brook lean-to were brought in by the DEC and left where the state trail entered the woods. Volunteers then began the task of carrying them in the .6 miles to Slide Brook. The "Deacon's Seat," the big log that forms the front base of the lean-to was rotten out and replaced. Once stabilized, the floor joists and planking were installed. The old roof was then removed and a new one nailed in place.
May, 1991: Bushnell Falls old #1 lean-to was razed, a new lean-to was built, the remains of the old Chicken Coop Brook lean-to were burned, both sites were cleaned up, and two privies were relocated.
August, 1991: Clear Pond Lean-to rehab included new base logs and new roofing. Similar rehab of Grizzle Ocean Lean-to.
August, 1993: Tubmill Marsh Lean-to rehab included a new roof, a new floor and replacement of all four base logs.
July, 1994: Extensive Uphill Lean-to rehab.
July, 1995: Boquet Lean-to rehab. Using a hydraulic jack under the base logs, first on one side, then on the other, the lean-to was raised and then large stones were hauled in to form a foundation. Then the crew installed floor joists and a solid plank floor was nailed in place. The roof was also patched.
August, 1995: Rock Pond Lean-to rehab. Raised with jacks, the rotted logs were pried off and new logs fitted into place. Slots were cut into the base log for the floor joists. The lean-to was lowered back down and then everything was nailed back into place.
July, 2003: Berrymill Pond Lean-to rehab. The lean-to was jacked up and rocks inserted under the corners. The fire ring in front of the lean-to was also rehabbed.
July, 2006: Avalanche Camp Lean-to rebuild. The 46ers funded parts of the lean-to rebuild, including the floor, roof, spikes and related items. The materials were then flown into the work site by the DEC. Day 1 of construction involved establishing the base of the lean-to, as well as the floor. Day 2 saw some erecting the log walls and the rest of the crew began demolition of the old structure. On the way out to Marcy Dam the crew carried sacks of asphalt shingles removed from the old lean-to for eventual pick up.
August, 2008: Grizzle Ocean Lean-to roof work. A new roof was installed after the DEC had stripped off the old one.

Highlights between 2009 and 2015:
The Slide Brook lean-to was dismantled and moved across Slide Brook and then reconstructed (Dix trail).
Extensive trail hardening on the Slide Brook trail to Dix.
Re-roofed a lean-to at Marcy Dam.
Installed extensive bog bridging on the Bradley Pond trail.
Several bridges built in Pharaoh Lake Wilderness.

Cranberry Lake, third largest lake in the Adirondack Park
CARL HEILMAN II

Conservation Calling

By Neil Woodworth

Neil Woodworth *is Executive Director and Counsel of the Adirondack Mountain Club (ADK). Woodworth is an environmental lawyer who has served in many official capacities in conservation affairs, including service on the Congressional Northern Forest Lands Council, the Empire State Task Force for Land and Water Conservation Funding, New York Open Space Advisory Committee, the New York Forest Preserve Advisory Committee, and the Governor's Task Force on the Adirondack Park Agency.*

He has worked on a variety of legal cases involving wilderness protection of the Adirondack and Catskill Forest Preserve, public navigation rights on rivers (Moose River case) and has represented ADK in lawsuits against the U.S. Environmental Protection Agency to successfully challenge attempts by the Bush/Cheney era EPA to weaken the New Source Review acid deposition and MACT mercury control prevention provisions of the Clean Air Act. Woodworth spent ten years as a trial and litigation lawyer before assuming his ADK duties in 1989. He is a graduate of Hobart College (1975) and Albany Law School of Union University (1978).

Growing up in Johnstown, NY, where the Mohawk Valley transitions into the foothills of the southern Adirondacks, I inherited a love of the outdoors from my mother, a descendent of Italian farmers and avid walker, and my father, a trout fisherman. Mom and Dad took my brother and me on many walks, and our trips into the Big Eddy of the West Branch of the Sacandaga River and climbing Kane Mountain fire tower and getting to know the fire tower observer are among the fondest memories of my youth. Scouting gave me the opportunity to acquire camping and cooking skills, and I later taught other scouts to backpack and camp as a teenage instructor at Woodworth Lake Scout Camp inside the southern boundary of the Adirondack Park. My introduction to the Adirondack High Peaks came in the early seventies through a high school coach, and I was hooked. At Hobart and William Smith Colleges, my wife-to-be Holly and I helped found the first Outing Club. The two of us backpacked from Keene Valley to the Upper Works in the summer of 1973 and I led my first winter backpack in the High Peaks later that winter. After graduating from Albany Law School and beginning my legal career, we joined the Albany Chapter of the Adirondack Mountain Club (ADK). Many of the chapter's hikes were in the High Peaks and we especially enjoyed the winter climbs[1]. It never occurred to me then that protecting New York State's Forest Preserve would be my calling and that I would devote almost my entire professional life to conservation advocacy.

As fate would have it, in 1980 I joined the Conservation Committee of ADK and, as the cliché goes, the rest is history. ADK was then led by widely respected conservationist David L. Newhouse, and the Conservation Committee included Adirondack luminaries Robert J. Ringlee, Eleanor F. Brown, James C. Dawson, Bruce Wadsworth and Barbara McMartin. Newhouse became ADK President in 1985 and I succeeded him as Conservation Committee Chair in the following year. Among my early actions was the hiring of Hope Donovan, formerly the conservation director for the New York League of Women Voters, as ADK's first paid lobbyist. Hope and forest ecologist Edwin H. Ketchledge, representing ADK, testified before the U.S. Senate Environmental and Public Works Subcommittee in 1986, on the vulnerability of Adirondack forests to the effects of acid deposition. Our first Conservation Director was Bob Linck, and he and I worked with the volunteers of the Conservation Committee to create a comprehensive list of key properties for acquisition by the state for inclusion in the Forest Preserve. With Bob leaving in 1988 and Hope Donovan indicating that she would be retiring soon, the stage was set for ADK to hire me in 1989 as full time Conservation Director and Legal Counsel[2]. The following year I also became ADK's lobbyist in Albany.

Author

---

1. I am an Adirondack 46er (#2036).

2. John "Jack" P. Freeman joined me in 1993 as Associate Conservation Director. Jack is well known for his fire tower restoration work.

One of my first responsibilities as legal counsel was to defend ADK against a $52 million lawsuit brought by two Pennsylvania men who were poorly prepared to ascend Mount Marcy in March. They had alleged that ADK had a duty to rescue them and that we had misled them on the posted weather at the High Peaks Information Center. We successfully contested this claim and did not pay a dime. In the 1990s, two other very important legal cases received my full attention. One was a lawsuit by the Balsam Lake Anglers Club to deny the state and ADK the right to build hiking trails on Forest Preserve lands on the basis that removing any trees was prohibited by the "forever wild" clause of the state constitution. The state and ADK won the case by demonstrating to the trial and appellate courts that the precedent setting 1930 McDonald case permitted the cutting of an "immaterial" amount of trees to provide trails to enable the public to use the Forest Preserve. In 1991, ADK intervened in a court case where the Adirondack League Club sued paddlers who canoed on the South Branch of the Moose River through League Club lands after launching from state lands and exiting on state lands[3].This case went all the way to the state's highest court, the Court of Appeals. We won at every level and the Court of Appeals' decision interpreted New York riparian laws to be that a waterway could be determined to be navigable in fact and thus open for public use if it was suitable for recreational travel by boats, canoes and kayaks. The decision also granted paddlers the right to portage on private property around an occasional rapid or waterfall.

Years later, then Attorney General Eliot Spitzer invited ADK to participate in three lawsuits that were designed to enforce the acid rain and mercury reduction provisions of the Clean Air Act. I drafted our ADK legal papers to show the federal courts the damage that acid rain and mercury from burning soft coal without air pollution control devices was doing to the Adirondacks. Again, ADK and the state prevailed at every level with two of the cases ultimately decided by the U.S. Supreme Court. Our most recent litigation was a lawsuit against the New York State Department of Environmental Conservation (DEC) and the Adirondack Park Agency for asserting that the lakes and ponds of the Forest Preserve were not subject to classification as were other parts of the Forest Preserve. DEC was trying to permit floatplane use of Lows Lake after the surrounding shoreline land was classified

---

3. As in the Balsam Lake Case, Glens Falls attorney John Caffry was my co-counsel on the case and donated his services to ADK in the Moose River case.

Winter dawn from Cascade
CARL HEILMAN II

as Wilderness. ADK took the position that water was just as much a part of the Forest Preserve as the mountains, wetlands and forests. State Supreme Court agreed with ADK on this part of the law. Floatplanes were banned from Lows Lake and Bog River because the state had a duty to classify the waters as Wilderness under the Adirondack Park State Land Master Plan and the "Forever Wild" Clause in the state constitution.

During my tenure, ADK has also devoted considerable effort to lobbying for state purchase of additional lands in the Adirondacks and statewide. In 1990, the state had no money for buying Forest Preserve or state parks, an Environmental Quality Bond Act failed to get statewide voter approval by less than a football stadium's capacity. ADK worked hard on legislation to replace the failed Bond Act. In 1993, we and our conservation allies were able to secure passage of the Environmental Protection Fund (EPF), which then and now is funded primarily by the real estate transfer tax. The EPF finally gave the state funds for buying land and easements. The EPF also provided a critical source of funding for taking care of these lands. This EPF land stewardship money could not be used to pay for state employees at DEC, but it could be used to help ADK fund our professional and volunteer trail crews and the Summit Stewardship Program. Since the EPF was enacted, an important part of my budget lobbying has been focused on securing sufficient funding for the land stewardship account.

Bird watching near Wilmington
NANCIE BATTAGLIA

In 1996, Governor George Pataki proposed a $1.7 billion Clean Water Clean Air Bond Act, which was handily approved by the voters. This Bond Act provided $150 million for land acquisition and conservation easements. EPF and Bond Act monies could not have come at a better time. For years, ADK had lobbied the state to buy the William C. Whitney tract, a paddler's dream with its interconnected lakes, ponds, and streams. The Whitney family sold 15,000 acres including Little Tupper Lake, the largest privately owned lake in the Adirondacks, for $21 million. Around this time, Champion International invited me to participate in a small study group to determine what portions of its 144,000 acres would be valuable to the state for Forest Preserve and conservation easements[4]. Within the month of the conclusion of our study process, the company offered to sell all of its timberlands to the state. Besides 110,000 acres of conservation easements, the state was able to purchase some 39,000 acres of Forest Preserve including ADK's canoe priorities on over seventy miles of the St. Regis, Oswegatchie and Grass Rivers. Not long after the consummation of the Champion purchase, the largest Adirondack forest landowner, International Paper Company, asked me to participate in a study group similar to the Champion study. This gave me the opportunity to canoe and hike much of their holdings and I prepared a report for DEC of the lands which would provide the best hiking and paddling opportunities. When the state bought the land, most of my priorities were opened to the public by inclusion in the Forest Preserve for many forms of outdoor recreation.

Bluebead lily between Basin and Saddleback
CBR

Between the Court of Appeals' decision in the Moose River case, and the great purchases of lakes and rivers from Whitney, Champion and International Paper, ADK was able to restore to public use many of the popular 19th century Adirondack canoe voyages described by author Paul Jamieson. No work is more important for ADK's advocacy team than ensuring that the land stewardship category of the EPF includes funding for DEC support of the Summit Stewards and for support of ADK's professional trail crew for work on the hiking trails of the Adirondacks and Catskills[5].

In 1996, I was appointed Deputy Executive Director for Public Affairs and ADK opened its Albany advocacy office. During that time period we were very involved in discussions over the future management of the High Peaks Wilderness Area (HPWA) and adoption

---

4. Beginning in 1991, I was appointed to represent New York's conservation groups on the Northern Forest Lands Council, which studied the northern forests from New York's Tug Hill to Maine's great timber holdings.

5. ADK's advocacy staff now includes Cathy Pedler, Conservation and Government Affairs Director, and Paul Gallery, Conservation Coordinator.

Above tree line on Wright
NANCIE BATTAGLIA

of the final unit management plan (UMP)[6]. ADK supported a total ban on open fires in the entire Eastern High Peaks, the prohibition of glass containers, mandatory use of designated campsites in the South Meadows to Flowed Lands corridor, and the reduction of the maximum number of persons per campsite to eight. We also endorsed a maximum day use limit of 15 persons per party everywhere in the HPWA. Outside of the designated camping zone in the Eastern High Peaks, we supported campers being allowed to select their own place to camp so long as the camping was beyond 150 feet of any road, trail, spring, stream, or water body unless at a DEC marked campsite. ADK later supported the requirement that campers be required to use approved bear canisters for food storage.

ADK did not support a campsite or lean-to reservation system in 1996. There was no DEC inventory of such locations and we believed that the aforesaid rules and regulations should be tried first before rationing systems were applied. We were also concerned about DEC having enough staff to properly and equitably administer such a system. For many of the same reasons, ADK did not support a day use rationing type permit system. Instead, DEC proposed a self-issuing travel permit system to gather information that might later support imposition of a rationing permit system for day users. After only two years, DEC abandoned the self-issued travel permit experiment and to the best of my knowledge, the collected permits were placed in storage without any evaluation or analysis of the information collected.

---

6. I was spending a lot of time in the High Peaks climbing the 46 High Peaks with my son and daughter. My perception was that backcountry camping was having the greatest impact on the HPWA, especially in the very popular Marcy Dam, Lake Colden Flowed Lands travel corridor. I represented ADK in the stakeholder discussions preceding the issuance of the final HPWA UMP.

In 2004, ADK's volunteer leadership asked me to become Executive Director as well as retaining key responsibilities as lobbyist and lawyer. A dozen years later, I am incredibly proud of what we have accomplished at ADK. Edwin Ketchledge's vision of rehabilitating summits by protecting alpine plants from trampling, seeding, and fertilizing exposed summit soils has been implemented under the Summit Stewardship Program, a cooperative effort of ADK, the Adirondack Chapter of The Nature Conservancy and DEC. Our Education Program teaches hiking and mountaineering skills and Leave No Trace principles to the over 70,000 annual visitors to our Adirondak Loj, Heart Lake Property and Johns Brook Lodge. Our professional and volunteer trails programs have rehabilitated many degraded trails throughout the Adirondacks and Catskills, but especially in the High Peaks where we are finally getting an opportunity to replace the original "straight up the fall line" trails with switch-backed, properly drained trails. Our publications program continues to produce high quality books and maps. None better than Tony Goodwin's guidebook *High Peaks Trails* and new map *Trails of the Adirondack High Peaks* (2015).

In conservation and advocacy, we helped convince Governor Andrew Cuomo to allocate $300 million for the EPF in his 2016-17 state budget. This almost doubles the size of the 2015 EPF appropriation and we expect additional state funding to help us augment some of our programs, notably trail improvement and summit stewarding. The state will also be able to purchase the valuable Boreas Ponds Tract and the much dreamed about Follensby Pond Tract. ADK is currently working on a proposal to add some 35,000 acres to the High Peaks Wilderness. ADK and its allies must convince Governor Cuomo, DEC, and APA that the Boreas Pond Tract should be classified as Wilderness. The addition of the MacIntyre East and West tracts as well as the Casey Brook Tract will create a continuous addition of the High Peaks Wilderness from the Santanoni Range east to the Dix Wilderness, allowing that Wilderness Area to be added to the HPWA, bringing the size of the HPWA to just over 280,000 acres.

Ketch on Skylight, 1988

With these great opportunities at hand, and our dedicated ADK staff and volunteers ready to defend our cause, the next decade promises to be very exciting.

American beavers
LARRY MASTER

The Ausable River Association: Voice of the River

By Kelley Tucker

Kelley Tucker *has worked in the non-profit conservation field for over 20 years protecting freshwater, conserving birds and their habitats, facilitating the reintroduction of endangered whooping cranes and Mexican wolves, and using science and policy to limit the registration and use of pesticides toxic to wildlife. She has served as Vice President of Programs for the International Crane Foundation, founded and directed the American Bird Conservancy's Pesticides and Birds program, and been a consultant to the John D. and Catherine T. MacArthur Foundation and the Manomet Center for Conservation Sciences. Kelley is currently Executive Director of the Ausable River Association, a non-profit organization dedicated to monitoring the health of the Ausable River and working collaboratively to protect and restore it. A licensed private pilot and former raptor rehabilitator, Kelley holds degrees in economics and political science from Rice University, and did doctoral work at the University of Chicago in social anthropology with field sites in Tunisia and Saudi Arabia. She lives in the Adirondack Park with her husband, the writer and photographer Stephen Longmire.*

Few communities care for a river so much that they come together to create a non-profit organization dedicated to protecting and restoring it. That's what happened 20 years ago in the Adirondack Mountains. Ausable River valley residents, aided by municipal leaders, county planners, and the National Park Service conducted a planning study so that local stakeholders would be better able to conserve and manage the natural and cultural values of the river. The Ausable River Association (AsRA) was born.

AsRA's mission is to identify, conserve and restore the Ausable River watershed's natural and recreational resources, for their ecological value and for the benefit of human communities.

There is much to cherish and protect. The river's magnificent scenery, ecological diversity and clear waters make it a jewel of the Adirondack region. Coursing down from the High Peaks, plunging over waterfalls and through steep bedrock gorges, and then meandering through valley lowlands, the river creates extensive wildlife habitat, hardy forests, fertile valleys and stunning landscapes before it empties into Lake Champlain.

The watershed covers 512 square miles, includes 94 miles of river channel, 27 High Peaks and is fed by more than 70 streams, including the Ausable's two major tributaries, the Chubb River and Black Brook. The headwaters of the river's East and West Branches begin on opposite shoulders of Mount Marcy (also the source of the Hudson River, flowing south instead of north). They join at Au Sable Forks, merging to form the Ausable's Main Stem. Seven towns, eight hamlets and one incorporated village lie within the watershed, which covers portions of two counties. These diverse human communities owe their economic vitality—past and present—to the river's health and resilience. Today, the watershed is a destination for world-class trout fishing, wilderness hiking, rock climbing, paddling and many winter sports, including downhill, backcountry and cross-county skiing.

Ausable River
LARRY MASTER

For over 200 years people have relied on the river as an economic resource, even as they have cherished its wild beauty and recreational value. But reliance on the river has taken its toll. A history of logging for much of the 19th and 20th centuries had profound effects on the river, which was used as a highway to convey logs to mills downstream. (This is why the Ausable is considered a navigable river—paddlers know better, except at high water.) Logging to smelt iron ore in one century, and to produce paper in the next, cleared streambanks of trees, built dams to control water flow, straightened channels and removed

Great blue heron
LARRY MASTER

Boreal chickadee (above), Dark-eye junco
LARRY MASTER

boulders to facilitate the annual spring log drives that continued into the 1920s. Paper mills along the Main Stem used the river for waste disposal until the 1970s. Because early settlements relied on water power, homes, businesses and roads were built alongside the river, often blocking its access to the floodplain.

With the demise of the local paper industry in the 1970s, new challenges to the Ausable River's health became apparent. Today, water quality tests show increasing levels of chloride from winter road deicing and phosphorus spikes from aging septic systems. Miles of river channel, destabilized after being manipulated to serve short-term human needs, are incised with deeply eroded banks. Erosion leads to increased sediment pollution, which can smother delicate aquatic ecosystems. Terrestrial and aquatic invasive species threaten water quality and biodiversity. Poignantly, the desire to drive alongside and live within viewing distance of the river—to see mergansers hunting for minnows, trout rising, deer drinking, early winter fog lifting—keeps its floodplain overdeveloped, aggravating the damage that occurs during flooding, for which the river itself is too often blamed. Infrastructure alongside the river and its tributaries—roads, poorly placed bridge abutments, undersized culverts—constrict water flow, block streams from their floodplains, and intensify road and property damage in flood conditions.

The Flume Falls, West Branch Ausable River, Wilmington
BRENDAN WILTSE

While healthier and ecologically more intact than many of its counterparts in the Adirondack Park and the northeastern United States, the Ausable River's future hangs in the balance.

Fortunately, the Ausable has attracted a broad community of supporters. Anglers from far and wide, especially fly anglers, revere the Ausable for its challenging waters, the opportunity to catch stocked brown and rainbow trout on the West Branch, and the challenge of luring native brook trout in East Branch tributaries. The river's scenic beauty and the many opportunities it offers to enjoy the outdoors, ensured by the protections of the Adirondack Park and supported by a thriving local outdoor industry, have

River otter
LARRY MASTER

made it a destination throughout the year. For residents, its waters are a barometer of the seasons, rising in spring and autumn, falling in summer to reveal bedrock and boulders, freezing over in winter—but always flowing underneath the thick ice that protects myriad aquatic species. The river connects human communities, winding through hamlets, alongside roads and fields, supporting diverse wildlife, enriching our spirits, and testing our love in times of flood.

This community of residents, visitors and admirers continues to rally to protect the river and to rely on the Ausable River Association to be its voice. Like any conservation organization working to protect a specific landscape, AsRA's emphasis is local. We work in the backyards of our supporters and critics, focusing on issues that make a tangible difference.

The health and diversity of our native brook and lake trout populations informs many of our efforts. These sentinel species are losing ground throughout their ranges, retreating to higher elevation streams and lakes as waters warm. While climate change poses increasing challenges for these charismatic fish, AsRA's efforts to preserve them in the Ausable watershed must focus on restoring hydrological integrity to damaged stream segments, replanting riparian buffers, curtailing pollution from road salt and aging septic systems, and reducing sediment pollution from stormwater and compromised streambanks. Meanwhile, we advocate rethinking the stocking of the East Branch and its tributaries with non-native fish, such as brown trout, that can outcompete native trout.

AsRA's strength is our willingness to work in partnership and share our success, providing models for other local communities. We work cooperatively with landowners, researchers, outdoor enthusiasts, municipalities, government agencies, and other non-profits to conserve and restore the valued resources of the Ausable watershed. AsRA's staff provides scientific and technical expertise, undertakes restoration efforts that rebuild stream channel function and aquatic habitat, disseminates knowledge to inform river stewardship, and fosters collaboration and data sharing across the watershed and beyond.

Fly fishing, Ausable River
NANCIE BATTAGLIA

If all politics is local, real improvement in environmental policy and practice begins at home—with a watershed and a community that loves it. The solutions AsRA seeks are practical. They include protecting the ecological diversity of the Ausable River watershed, for its own sake and for the sake of the people who live, work and play here. Join us.

Framed by the Sentinel Range, the Ausable River's West Branch
LARRY MASTER

The Living Part of the Earth

By Kelley Tucker

Kelley Tucker's biography is on page 198

Bald eagle along the Saranac Lakes
NANCIE BATTAGLIA

My work as a conservationist began with a desire to protect birds. Much like water, they ignore human boundaries, forcing conservation to operate at a landscape or watershed scale. A career in conservation can lead to migrations of one's own. Mine bounded back and forth between urban and rural, east and Midwest: Chicago, Minnesota, Washington D.C., Wisconsin and far eastern Long Island in New York. A desire to find a home on our terms led my husband and me to the Adirondack Park—a place where conservation and ecological protection is writ large, contested and balanced, won and lost, in everyday life—the perfect place for someone dedicated to the wild.

Buffalo Ridge

North of Pipestone, Minnesota, not far from Lake Benton, a series of knolls rises above the softly rolling landscape, running northwest to southeast. This is farming country, once a sea of prairie, now boxed in by roads built on section lines, treeless except for thin lines of windbreaks and small clustered edges where tractors can't roam. To an eye constantly searching for the next river valley, the line of knolls, forming a ridge, seemed notable. Or so I told myself on a bright June day in 1998.

I had been chasing Swainson's hawks. Magnificent birds with the wingspan of red-tailed hawks but much smaller feet—better for catching mice or grasshoppers than rabbits. The Swainson's hawks were returning from their winter homes in Argentina. I was working as a field biologist on a University of Minnesota (UMN) study tracking their nesting success on this the easternmost edge of their summer range. Just two years before, roughly 8% of the Swainson's hawk population had been killed in Argentina, victims of monocrotophos, a pesticide banned in the U.S. but used by Argentine farmers trying to control grasshoppers. The birds, comfortable foraging on the ground, were exposed to the extremely toxic pesticide dermally and by inhalation, and they also gorged on the dying grasshoppers. An estimated 20,000 Swainson's were lost. The UMN study, in its third year, was intended to determine the status of Swainson's hawks in the state in the wake of this environmental disaster.

As I followed the hawks' return, their mating, nest building, nest loss, chick rearing, heart-wrenching predation, and, in a few stirring cases, successful fledging, they led me and my old Ford pickup to the ridge over and over. Plotting new nest sites on a large map, I realized they traced the running height of land, favoring the southern side to the northern—likely in response to prevailing winds.

In 1998, the Internet was not the resource it is now. No quick check of a GIS map or Wikipedia search would help me answer the question forming in my head. Instead, a request for USGS topographic maps and visits to the early morning farmer coffee klatch in Pipestone led me to the discovery of what my eye had captured. The ridge I was visiting daily was the Buffalo Ridge, my farmer friends told me. The Buffalo Ridge, the topo maps told me, was the spine of my Midwestern homeland—the drainage dividing the watersheds of the two Great Rivers, the Mississippi and the Missouri.

The Buffalo Ridge begins in eastern South Dakota, extends through southwestern Minnesota, into the northwest corner of Iowa. At 1,995 feet, its high point is the highest land for hundreds of flat miles. Armed with this knowledge, and the blessing of the landowner, I was soon standing on the highest point in Pipestone County. The Kelleyometer—my husband's teasing label for my ability to sense proximity to major river valleys and my tendency to wax poetic about them on long highway drives—was definitely registering. It was thrilling to recognize these sloped farmland edges as starting points for the migration of water into the two longest rivers in North America. Something I knew in my bones was made plain to me that day: every inch of the earth belongs to a watershed, moving freshwater downslope to meet rivers, lakes, swamps, and, eventually, oceans.

Small and essential

We forget that the water cycle and the life cycle are one. —Jacques Cousteau

Top: Boreas flowing south, above: Boquet flowing north
ADK ARCHIVES

When precipitation falls, some soaks into the ground, some evaporates, but most tends to run along the surface. Droplets join one another and eventually form rills, rills become gullies, and gullies lead to channels that, when sustained over time, are the small streams that form identifiable headwaters. These join other streams and increase in size until we call them rivers. These, inevitably, flow into oceans. Groundwater is never far from this process. Precipitation that enters the ground replenishes aquifers, and water reemerges naturally to recharge existing streams or wetlands. Year-round streams do not rely on rainwater or snowmelt but draw in varying degrees from groundwater resources for their base flows.

Even with the earth providing wall-to-wall catch basins that efficiently move every drop, freshwater is scarce. While 71% of the earth's surface is covered by water, most of it is saline. Only 2.5% of all water on the planet is freshwater (Shiklomanov, 1993). Of that estimated 2.5%, the majority (68.7%) is held in glaciers and ice caps, cooling the earth's oceans and climate, but not readily available. Groundwater makes up 30.1% of all freshwater. Non-saline rivers, lakes, and swamps—surface water—make up a little more than a quarter of 1%; 0.296% of all freshwater on the planet. All told, surface and ground freshwater—the water that directly sustains plant, animal, and human life—makes up less than 1% of the earth's water.

The Opalescent along the trail to Marcy above Lake Colden
CBR

Streams and rivers are the most visible form of freshwater. Dominant features of our landscapes and watersheds, the source of lakes and swamps, they provide drinking water, food, transportation and recreation—for humans and wildlife. Healthy rivers with a full complement of native plants and trees along their banks help cool the earth and are essential habitat for a multitude of plant and animal species. Their beauty inspires us. The capacity of rivers to change even as they retain their identity has inspired writers, philosophers, artists and scientists. Their power, wearing down bedrock and carving channels, is awesome, enriching to their floodplains (that's why so much farmland is streamside), and can be devastating to the constructions of beavers, birds and people.

I attribute my love of rivers to my birth at the confluence of the Mississippi and the Missouri Rivers. I grew up exploring a child's world of semi-rural backyard streams, following the paths of songbirds, discovering frogs, snakes and pockets of landscape with a memory of being forest. I was mesmerized by the ebb and flow of water in our furtive neighborhood stream. No more than three-feet wide at its broadest, and often starved for water, it was a back alley for wildlife increasingly hemmed in by creeping suburbanization. The little nameless stream made its way several tortured miles westward, dodging developments and roads. It joined a fellow furtive stream, Fee Fee Creek, and they travelled north merging with other small streams eventually to meet the Missouri River. The quarter-mile breadth of the river easily swallowed their combined flows. Thirty miles downstream from this confluence, the Missouri would meet the Mississippi in a channel a mile wide.

Moose River
NANCIE BATTAGLIA

Adirondack High Peaks

No one ever steps in the same river twice, for it's not the same river and he's not the same person.
—Heraclitus

More than a decade after my sojourn along the Buffalo Ridge, I'm hiking along the Great Range, overlooking the vast and magnificent watershed of the Ausable River. Steeply cascading streams, rills, waterfalls and wetlands are everywhere. The water is clear and cold, heavy with boulders and cobbles, rich with aquatic life—including genetically diverse populations of brook trout. Many channels are dominated by bedrock—hard anorthosite and assorted igneous and metamorphic rock thrust up 65 million years ago by a cataclysmic uplift that created the geomorphic dome that defines the High Peaks region. Shaded by lush forest, these waters have created extensive wildlife habitat for a range of species: fisher, black bear, bobcat, snowshoe hare, ermine; palm warblers, Bicknell's thrush, rusty blackbirds, black-backed woodpecker, spruce grouse and saw-whet owls; spotted salamanders, American toads and more. Balsam, quaking aspen, black spruce, hemlock, alpine sweetgrass, diapensia and other trees and plants of the northern boreal forest are found along the higher elevations of the Ausable's two branches, and an incredible diversity of hardwoods, pine and spruce flourish in its valleys. It is a wilderness paradise, a rural home, a recreational destination—defined by water and shared by people.

The contours of the watershed visible below the Great Range peaks are more explicit than the rolling hills and flatlands of the upper Midwest. Views south reveal a pronounced valley with two long lakes connected by a stream—steep, wild country. The Ausable lakes and their stillwater source receive surface water from Mount Marcy and the rest of Great Range, Allen, Nippletop and Dial, Blake and Colvin, and mark the beginning of the Ausable River's East Branch. To the north lies Johns Brook valley, fed by the northwest side of the Great Range and the southeast faces of Tabletop, Howard, Yard and Big Slide mountains. These two subwatersheds, augmented by tributaries flowing off Giant Mountain, join in Keene Valley. They are the headwaters of my home river—the East Branch of the Ausable. The headwaters of the West Branch flow off the north and east faces of Algonquin Peak, into a broad basin fed by tributaries of Marcy and Indian Pass brooks. South Meadow and Klondike brooks add their flows, not far from Heart Lake, as this branch of the river flows north to Lake Placid.

River of sand

The river is everywhere at once, at the source and at the mouth, at the waterfall, at the ferry, at the rapids, in the sea, in the mountains, everywhere at once, and ... there is only the present time for it, not the shadow of the past, not the shadow of the future. —Hermann Hesse

A swift, mid-sized stream brook descends from the Sentinel Range pools and steps briskly through my back yard. I own a few hundred feet of it. After leaving my care, it flows on to pay tribute to the Ausable's East Branch. I know every inch of my little section but must relearn it every year. Everything moves, except for well-rooted trees and boulders weighing more than half a ton—though Tropical Storm Irene took some of those when she turned the brook into a raging river. Hard anorthosite lies at key points under the rushing water; cobbles and small boulders pave the bed, sandy sediment barely filling the cracks and seams.

The midsized boulder that used to allow me dry passage across a three-foot pool tumbled downstream last spring in a flood of snow melt and rain. A few minnows scatter as I step in. A flash of color—a small brook trout, crayfish or frog? Under the cobble I pick up, I find the cases of caddis flies to be. I try to put it back the way I found it.

I've followed the cries of a broad-winged hawk upstream. The large female offered me a quick glance before she flew off, the remains of a milk snake in her talons. Winter walks have shown me an annoyed fisher, numerous wild turkeys, the prints of bobcat, fox and snowshoe hare. Eastern coyotes decided the largest center boulder was an excellent spot to howl last spring. Songbirds visit throughout the warmer season, making me guess their names. The mergansers stay on the river but the kingfishers love the challenge of dodging ferns, willow, low hanging hemlock, ash and birch branches in search of a minnow meal. Downstream, the slope of the stream steepens after flowing over a channel-wide slab of impenetrable bedrock, then rushing toward the river.

The Ausable is one of 14 major rivers that descend from the Adirondack dome, but only it and the south-flowing Hudson have their headwaters on Marcy and Algonquin, the highest of the High Peaks. Lake Placid, Mirror and Fern lakes, the Ausable and Cascade lakes, Chapel, Connery and Taylor ponds, and dozens more bodies of water are all part of the watershed, which also covers portions of two counties and includes over 20,000 residents, living primarily in settlements downstream of its protected headwaters.

The Ausable's two branches meet in the hamlet of Au Sable Forks. From there, the Main Stem meanders through gently sloping lowlands before tumbling through the spectacular sandstone gorge of Ausable Chasm, finally entering Lake Champlain just 100 feet above sea level. This rapid descent from its 5,000-foot headwaters to the lake makes the Ausable the second steepest river in New York State, after its shorter neighbor, the Boquet. At its mouth, it forms a sandy delta that led early French explorers to call it the "sandy river," or "river of sand." From Lake Champlain, its waters drain into the Richelieu River, joining the Saint Lawrence as it flows northeast into the Atlantic Ocean.

For most of the time since the glaciers receded 12,000 years ago, the Ausable was the dominant land-shaping force in the region, determining, by the sheer force of water, the nature of its watershed. With settlement of the region in the late 1700s, the river's power was put to work fueling industries that cleared its banks of trees, deforested large swaths of its headwaters, built dams to control water flow, straightened channels and removed boulders to facilitate spring log drives—annual events until the 1920s. For another half century, the river continued to serve as a highway, disposing of the waste from pulp papermaking.

Rivers are resilient but the effects of this early industry scarred the Ausable. The ecological legacy remains—miles of river channel are incised and over-wide with deeply eroded banks, leading to increased sediment pollution, which can smother delicate aquatic ecosystems and damage transportation infrastructure. And new challenges from development, winter road deicing, aging infrastructure and invasive species make active protection and restoration of the Ausable a priority.

Loon at Stillwater Inlet Lake
MIKE MCLEAN

The math of a stream

The river is the architect of its own edifice. —Luna Leopold

In their natural state, unimpeded, streams are stable and self-regulating. Their width, curving pattern, slope and roughness are mathematically precise, defined by water volume and by the size and amount of sediment they carry. All rivers move sediment; the gradual erosion of channels is a natural process that benefits the stream and its riparian ecosystem. Erosion, in this case, is a dynamic process critical to the creation of diverse habitats for aquatic life, birds, plants and more. With an increase in water velocity, channel slope, width, depth, discharge, or the size or amount of sediment, a stable river will adjust its form and structure (Leopold et al., 1964). Stable streams in equilibrium minimize flood damage, maintain water quality and provide habitat critical for diverse healthy ecosystems. Of course it is easiest to find

The source of the Hudson River, named by Colvin: Lake Tear of The Clouds, Marcy in background
NANCIE BATTAGLIA

such conditions on rivers that flow wild, with minimal human intervention but streams flowing through populated landscapes can be managed, and restored, in ways that keeps them stable and in equilibrium.

I'm standing in the West Branch of the Ausable. Ten times wider than my backyard brook and on a much less urgent grade, it moves sinuously, its water swirling, looking heavy and patient. I wade toward the main channel to catalog and measure, knee then chest deep. Starting at the crest of a broad riffle, where the water is shallow, concentrating the force of its flow to shove my feet downstream, I measure the depth of the water and the elevation of the streambed. Moving along the channel with a surveyor's rod and receiver, I catch the light of a laser positioned on the bank, measuring each shift from riffle to run to pool to glide and on to the next riffle. Hours later, I have recorded the data that will describe the slope of this reach of river: its channel bed, water surface and banks. I'll know the locations, length and depths of its pools and riffles, and the width of its meander. Measured cross-sections of these same features will detail the width and shape of the channel and the height of the flow that just fills the banks before spilling over into the floodplain. Carefully measured substrate—sand, gravel, cobble and boulder—will provide an accurate sense of the rate of discharge and the volume of water that moves through the channel.

This data, once collated and scrutinized, will guide the ongoing implementation of stream restoration efforts along this section of the river. The goal is to give the river a head start in its effort to rebuild a stable channel—to provide the key pieces of the equation so the river can gradually find its equilibrium. Solutions to other equations for river health begin with: reducing chloride inputs from road salt and phosphorus inputs from aging septic systems, managing stormwater flows, eradicating invasive species and restoring lush riparian buffers, and rethinking old road infrastructure—replacing undersized culverts that squeeze forest streams into narrow plastic pipes, curtailing the passage of fish and increasing flood risks. Last, but far from least, is the task of inviting people, young and old, to experience streams first-hand, to learn the contours of a watershed, to pause, watch and dream with a stream and the creatures it harbors.

The life of a stream

A river seems a magic thing. A magic, moving, living part of the very earth itself.
—Laura Gilpin

The facts of streams and their watersheds can be mesmerizing or numbing in their complexity. What you need to know is most easily found in the stream itself. Streams are the sum of their parts, no more, no less. Their magic lies not just in their beauty but also in their perpetual liveliness, their ability to sustain life, provide home and habitat, and in their desire to be in balance. They shift as needed to accommodate changing conditions. When damaged by the human hand or natural catastrophe, if given time and space, a river will heal itself. The river is alive.

Ausable River
BRENDAN WILTSE

References

Igor Shiklomanov, "World fresh water resources," in Peter H. Gleick, ed., *Water in Crisis: A Guide to the World's Fresh Water Resources* (New York: Oxford University Press, 1993).

Luna Leopold, *A View of the River* (Cambridge, MA: Harvard University Press, 1964).

New York State Forest Rangers marched proudly in Lake Placid, NY, on September 15, 1985, in a parade commemorating the 100th anniversary of both the Forest Preserve and the creation of the state's ranger service. The parade was but one of many events held throughout the Adirondack Park marking the centennial.
NANCIE BATTAGLIA

The Great North Woods

By Edwin H. Ketchledge

Edwin H. Ketchledge, *Ph.D., was a sought-after speaker before and after his retirement. This speech, which he titled* The Great North Woods, *was first delivered in April 1985 at the New York State Forest Preserve Centennial Symposium at Union College, Schenectady, NY. He gave the same talk, with minor changes, in September of the same year in Lake Placid, NY, at an event sponsored by the New York State Department of Environmental Conservation (DEC) celebrating the same milestone. The speech is reproduced from Ketch's original manuscript without alterations to his punctuation, numbering and underlining.*

We thank Tom Martin, Regional Supervisor of Natural Resources, and Sean Reynolds, Forester, for finding the speech in DEC archives and Ketch's family for allowing its publication.

My assignment with you this morning is to discuss the nature of "The Great North Woods", as the Adirondacks were called some 150 years ago, and to try to interpret the human perspective embraced in those three simple words: GREAT. NORTH. WOODS.

I happen to believe that the expression tells us as much about the people of the times as it does about the landscape they were viewing. I also confess at the start that I personally interpret the "Great North Woods" more as a "process" than a "product"; more as a shifting mosaic of forests from place to place than as a continuous and stable and uniform system. In this context, the Great North Woods may be interpreted as a time-series of varying vignettes, each reflecting the environmental-vegetational complex as it existed at particular points in time over the centuries and millennia.

I would like, therefore, to re-cast my assignment into three sequential questions:

I. What <u>was</u> the Great North Woods as first encountered by the early European settlers?
II. What <u>became</u> of the Great North Woods as people settled into the region and became the new environmental force changing the landscape?
III. And where is the Great North Woods today, <u>both</u> as a physical reality and more importantly as our natural heritage?

First Question. What <u>was</u> the Great North Woods which greeted our forefathers and at once generated such conflicting and polar perspectives as atavistic awe and reverence on the one hand and economic challenge on the other. Let's try for a few minutes to put aside our individual histories and experiences and forget briefly our own background with and understanding of the modern region, and assume an attitude of virginal innocence. Let's wipe the slate clean, turn back the clock to the late 1700s, and make believe we are the very first pioneers entering the region. What do we see?

We'll stop here a moment for our own orientation and review the fundamental nature of this forest region <u>as it was</u> seen by those first settlers. To that end and for purposes of argument, I will now evoke my supernatural powers, transform this auditorium into a time machine, and transport us all back to the beginning of the Pleistocene glacial period, about 1,600,000 years ago. We will hover over the central Adirondacks and from our viewing platform turn on the time-advance forward, fast rate, and see what unfolds as history proceeds below us.

Ketch lecturing in the woods
NANCIE BATTAGLIA

We first see that the climate is quite warm, the forests are green, made up mostly of deciduous leaved tree species, all of which we can recognize if we beam down to the ground. Indeed, we feel quite at home. This would be a great place to settle. Deep, rich soils; mild seasons; a veritable Garden of Eden.

But quickly things change in our time scope. Suddenly, the winds shift strongly out of the north, and the temperature collapses. Winters last longer, as our time lapse races forward. Quickly, there are no summers! Winter continues unending. Snows no longer melt; instead ice builds up. In a few minutes, a wall of ice advances from the north. Before we know it, the ice is two miles deep and covers the whole world as seen from high above the future "Adirondacks". Then before our eyes we see the ice suddenly melts and disappears leaving in its wake a silenced landscape of bare rock, and glacial debris. All is chaos. Our "Eden" has been wiped out by continental glaciers. But quickly forests and wildlife again spread into the area, from ice-free refuges in the south, and in minutes the forest community is restored, less vigorous admittedly because of the loss of the ancient soil, but with all the species we know once more present.

The respite lasts only a few minutes, for here come the glaciers again, a second time overriding and destroying the newly restored vegetation. What a tragedy! All evidence of prior forests is destroyed a second time. The whole process is like a monotonous record because sixteen times the glaciers advance, and last nearly 100,000 years, then retreat for less than 10,000 years, only to re-advance once more. In our startlement we realize: all is change, nothing persists. The "Adirondacks", which emerge from time to time in a history dominated by glaciers, are each a temporary expression of long term processes characterized by continuous change. The "Adirondacks" of a given century or millennium is an approximation of a series of "Adirondacks" (plural) over time.

Phil Correl and Alex Radmanovich enjoying Seymour's wooded summit—CBR

For our immediate purpose here, we must slow down our time machine as we reach the peak of the last glaciation a mere 16,000 years ago. At a slow rate, now we see the glaciers melting again, until at 13,000 years ago they melt fast and by 11,000 years disappear. Within a few hundred years the forest species are returning, first the cold-hardy Black Spruce and Balsam Fir, then the Jack Pine followed by White and Red, then the Hemlock, and lastly the heavy-seeded and slower migrating hardwoods. At 7,000 years before present we see a thermal maximum has been reached and forests have briefly advanced way northward into Canada, but are starting to retreat as the climates again start shifting back

NANCIE BATTAGLIA

to the pre-glacial conditions of historical times. Off to the east if we can see far enough, Bjarni Herjolfsson and Leif Eriksson are exploring the Newfoundland coastline.

Let's beam down to the surface for just a moment and scan this primeval landscape, about to be invaded by strange new creatures. We would find really <u>three</u> kinds of "Great North Woods", differing in appearance and composition across the "Adirondack" region.

1. Wetland coniferous forests dominate all the low ground and watershed drainages between the rolling hills. These are deep, dark, dense forests of Black Spruce and Balsam Fir and Tamarack and White-cedar, all tolerant of the boggy soils developing on these saturated sites, too inhospitable for most demanding hardwood species; just some Red Maples and Yellow Birch sticking up here and there. The understory is just as dense, as these wet sites are lush habitats for a host of hardy, northern shrubs and semi-woody plants. It is tough going here, for all but the moose. We note that although the wetland forests make up only about 15% of the regional landscape, their long meandering arms engulf all the lowlands, surround most of the mountains, enmesh the whole region with a grid of impenetrable coniferous forests and bogs, no place for human beings seeking farm sites.

2. Similarly, we find another zone of coniferous forest covering all the high and steeper slopes, anywhere from about 2,000' elevation all the way up to the mountain tops. We note that Red Spruce here is the dominant, long-lived tree but that on the highest slopes where the glacial debris was washed away right after glacial retreat, only the hardy Balsam Fir now grows, producing its own organic soil from its own remains. Where a tree has blown over—a frequent occurrence on these windswept

Tony Goodwin, Frank Krueger and Bunny Goodwin on a Tahawus ski adventure
NANCIE BATTAGLIA

highlands—Paper Birch gains temporary control over the site. These forests, perhaps 10% of what we see, will prove of little obstacle or interest to the settlers approaching just over the horizon. They will bypass this high country; after all, only a fool would want to climb a mountain!

3. But look at that other 75% mixed forests on the gentle slopes and terraces where soils are best. Great places for Sugar Maple and Yellow Birch and American Beech. Yet Red Spruce is here in good numbers too—rarely less than a third of the trees. Hemlock also. And big White Pine where the canopy was opened sometime in the recent past. This is better country here, for both beast and that other creature, man, getting closer. He will find these forests more to his liking, which fact will in short time prove to be a new kind of disaster to the landscape heretofore responding only to natural environmental changes.

So—a fresh world is what the first explorers found in the Adirondacks; a young landscape newly covered by forests adjusting to a constantly changing climate, growing on young infertile soils; a landscape slowly recovering from a glacial disaster; a forest of three dozen tree species competing to gain a new root-hold; a whole mountain system unmarked by two-legged animals. A pristine world free as yet of the second most disastrous force to strike the region, so-called Homo sapiens.

This was the Great North Woods that awaited the colonists, a transition forest responding each day to a shifting environment, an ecosystem technically "in balance", actually a flux of many species all marching to their own particular tune but producing what we now call, generally, the WILDERNESS, or locally, the Great North Woods. The lesson we read here is that the Great North Woods is a healthy, energetic, dynamic system that can't be held down for long. Create a change, and the vegetation will re-occupy it. The forests are resilient. They can be displaced for a period of time, but not even the continental glaciers can destroy them. From our time-ship, as time runs out, we see that the forests below, new though they are, look beautiful, undisturbed, natural, you might say ancient since in composition and form they extend backward in time to the start of the Cretaceous Period, 130,000,000 years ago when the species first evolved. This perfection—I use the word deliberately—is what the first pioneers below inherited when in the course of events, they arrived on the scene in our last time-lapse frame, at about 1780 AD.

Black bear crossing Ausable Club Road, 2015
NANCIE BATTAGLIA

What <u>was</u> the Great North Woods? It was—divorced from the simplistic quick answer about appearance—really three things to the human arrivals on the scene, to the settlers seeking their destiny on a virginal landscape:

1. A foreboding Vastness, a dark landscape at once threatening and challenging and mysterious. The use of the word "Great" conveys this meaning: big; large; endless to the pioneer without roads; difficult to penetrate by rapid-plagued waterways; inaccessible overland; requiring days to explore with pack and impassable by wagon. Simply an unexplored forest without end.

Henderson lean-to
NANCIE BATTAGLIA

2. A fearful Emptiness, totally devoid of human beings, other than an occasional "aboriginal" after game. Not a single structure or vestige of civilized man. Not a fellow human within days of travel. As uninterrupted as the ocean their forefathers had recently crossed. As separate and isolated from civilization as the unknown continent far to the west. Simply as barren of people and the comforts of civilized life as was Europe 8,000 years earlier. An emptiness to tantalize the imagination of the restless explorer but certainly unworthy of serious attention by the struggling farmer.

3. An apprehensive Wildness, a strangeness, a northern forested land unsuitable for human endeavors, a barbarous country of wild animals best left alone by industrious homesteaders seeking productive home sites. Poorly drained and therefore boggy soils. Impassable streams and rivers. A piece of Upper Canada misplaced to the south, habituated only by wild animals or "wild men". A wild land where nature ran wild, a land uncontrolled and unmanaged, a landscape to be feared. A wilderness.

Enjoying one of many new DEC designated campsites within the Essex Chain of Lakes
NANCIE BATTAGLIA

This, I believe, was the perception of the "Great North Woods" as seen by the earlier pioneers who only skirted the flanks of the Adirondacks so long as some acres were yet to be claimed elsewhere in the civilized portions of the State.

Certainly this harsh judgment was to be ameliorated as the truth of the region became known, later in the 19th century, but I believe earlier perceptions of the Great North Woods were conditioned by this initial perception of Vastness, of Emptiness, and of Wildness. As I read history, it wasn't until well into the second half of the last century that the public began to appreciate these three conditions as <u>quality</u> characteristics, to be respected and preserved as part of our wildland heritage. I hold that it was these three fundamental philosophical images that in time evolved into the groundswell of public concern for intact forests, for pure water, for unspoiled wildland, in short, for the Forest Preserve we commemorate today.

II. And what became of The Great North Woods? We all know the story; some of you in this audience have told it often and with greater clarity than could I. Here I want only to make a few observations and extract a few relevant generalities from that history. I would note:

1. The dichotomy we see today between the conservation ethic of wise use and the preservation ethic of resource protection stem jointly from the gradual disappearance of the Great North Woods, which process actually began for strictly utilitarian reasons (mature White Pine for ship masts, for example) late in the 18th century and reached its climax in the 1894 constitution.

Newcomb's Lake Harris
BRIAN SUTHERLAND

2. The evolving public concern for watershed protection was inversely related to the decreasing size of the Great North Woods throughout the 19th century. The harvesting of timber, which in those times was typically destructive, had the effect of changing the public attitude of "wilderness to be conquered" to one of "landscape resources to be preserved". Post-logging erosion and flash-flooding on devastated lands was the first signal to the public that something had gone wrong. The price of exploitation was too high.

3. Two parallel alternatives emerged in the public conscience during the 19th century:
   a. manage and restore the private lands better and,
   b. preserve some of the wildlands from any disturbance at all.

The near-polarization we often see today between "Preservation" and "Conservation" is an artificial distinction because the two concepts have not only a common ancestry, they have a shared purpose of serving both living people and people yet to live.

4. The appearance of "public recreation" in forest environments was a new social phenomenon. As the forest resource was exploited, and people moved more freely thru the region, popular perceptions began to change, and hereafter Vastness, Emptiness and Wildness were perceived as a disappearing heritage to be preserved.

5. The "cost" of eventually positioning the remnants of the Great North Woods under constitutional protection as an inviolate Forest Preserve was, historically speaking, acceptable because it reversed a philosophy of exploitation dominant in its time and bespoke the public conscience.

With a heavier presence in the northern Adirondack Park, moose now number in the 800s, a spectacular comeback.
NANCIE BATTAGLIA

6. The Great North Woods of the late 17th century is now gone: Vastness is now replaced by scattered parcels of forest land, all but a few acres accessible in a day's hike. Emptiness is a thing of the past; people are everywhere. Wildness on the other hand is slowly returning because we have set aside lands where no development at all will be permitted (Wilderness areas in the State Land Master Plan) or only minimal development to control and minimize more concentrated human impact (Wild Forest Land).

We have lost a vast resource, to our collective regret, but we have gained a new insight into the human condition and human conscience. Without the pain of losing the latest iteration of the Great North Woods, by which I mean pre-colonial wilderness, we could not have learned the meaning of our wilderness heritage, nor created the constitutional promise of its eventual return on dedicated portions of the landscape. What I am trying to say here is that we have transmuted a temporal physical resource into a permanent principle of government. The Great North Woods has become a guiding concept incorporated in our very constitution. By creating the Forest Preserve, we have set aside a portion of the landscape free again to respond as it will to the natural forces as it did for ages prior to man's appearance on the scene. We have guaranteed that these forests therein will in time return to a wilderness condition equivalent to the Great North Woods of our forefathers.

III. Which leads me to my third question: Where is the Great North Woods today?

I have above indicated that the Great North Woods is now, as a physical reality, essentially gone. But I want to qualify that overly broad statement in three ways:

1. The Great North Woods has not been destroyed. Natural forces cannot long be arrested; you appreciate I am sure. So long as we let nature take its course—as we are trying to do on Forest Preserve land—a new natural balance will prevail. After all, the species are all there, none have been destroyed by the clearing, logging, burning. The forests have been set back, but not destroyed. In our climate, forests are inevitable. Even after a wild-fire, in fifty years a high canopy of pioneering aspens and birches rises over a site and within the decades the shade tolerant climax species slowly return. Admittedly, some sites have been degraded, some on steeper slopes eroded to bedrock, yet plant succession is everywhere underway on every acre of wild land not otherwise developed for campsites and the like. Nature cannot be stopped. The forests are returning. Within a hundred fifty to two hundred years, all the character species are back, at least in low number and mature size. It only takes another generation or two for the original balance and combinations—floristic composition we call it—to return. After three hundred years, on most sites only an expert ecologist can interpret the landscape with sufficient skill to read forest history. The destruction you see today on Forest Preserve land once logged and burned and now covered with crummy popple[1] and sparse trees, will in due time be mature timber reminiscent of yesteryear. Your great, great grandchildren will not know the difference. I frankly find that a comforting, reassuring thought. The future is inevitable. So is the forest. Only written history will record the earlier damage to the Forest Preserve.

Northern blue flag iris
NANCIE BATTAGLIA

Yellow violets
NANCIE BATTAGLIA

The Forest Preserve is our promise to future generations that they will have a Great North Woods in fact as well as in history and heritage.

2. The Great North Woods still exists, in new form, in the minds and perception of a whole generation of people. To people grown accustomed to an urban environment, a walk in a park is a return to nature, a hike in the woods a wild land adventure and an overnight camping trip a wilderness experience. These reactions to a natural world evoke the same awe as did the Vastness and

1. Crummy popple is not a scientific name but a local expression. Popple is a catch-all name for aspen of all species, and has been in local use in the Adirondacks for many years.

Emptiness and Wildness to their great grandfathers. The meaning to each individual is the same, perhaps only the intensity may differ. I don't want to trivialize the true meaning of wilderness as perceived by the initiated, nor do I want to be insensitive to the expanding perceptions of a less sophisticated novice whose inner reward may be just as intense, and if I may say, as worthwhile.

3. And lastly, with some hesitation I would be so bold to claim that the Great North Woods does still exist BUT, because of cultural and psychological acclimatization is available to few of you in this room. Vastness, Emptiness and Wildness are still out there, granted on a lesser scale, but still out there but you are tied to your daily circumstances and may never experience it.

What I mean to say, as gently but firmly as possible, is simply that few of you avail yourself of the wilderness experience in the Great North Woods on its terms. You don't accept the challenge. The wilderness is out there, but you aren't! You are locked into your comforts and, more unfortunately, your mind-sets of theoretical wilderness, while the real Great North Woods awaits you.

Barred owl
NANCIE BATTAGLIA

Let me ask you, rhetorically please, when was the last time you put your pack on your back and went out into the Great North Woods in the Forest Preserve and spent 2-3-4—5 days alone, off the trails, by map and compass, exploring from one lake to another or one mountain to another, alone, camping out wherever evening found you, deliberately off-course, staying away from places where you might run into people, relaxing, taking some pictures, identifying some plants or insects, carefree, as if you were the only one that week in the Five Ponds Wilderness Area or in the Cold River country?

There is no reason whatsoever that prevents you from doing the same on skis in January. You are even more alone then, on your own, your fate in your own hands, no-one around to bother you. All the world is asleep. You can ski across a lake in the moonlight, knowing that you are the only person left in that part of the Adirondacks wilderness.

At that moment, you know there is still a Great North Woods, full of Vastness and Emptiness and Wildness. As much as you can handle, and it is yours! You and your creator.

Chapel Pond and Giant's Washbowl
CARL HEILMAN II

Being There

By Carl Heilman II

Carl Heilman II *is an internationally published photographer and author who has been photographing the Adirondacks since 1975. He started climbing the High Peaks on a pair of handcrafted snowshoes in the 1970s and continues to explore and photograph the mountains and lakes, while pursuing his passion for portraying the unique beauty of the Adirondack Park—and sharing his decades of experience with others in his photography workshops and tours, coffee table books and how-to photography books.*

Information on Carl's photography workshops, fine art prints, calendars, books, and puzzles, is online at ***www.carlheilman.com****.*

ALL PHOTOGRAPHS IN THIS CHAPTER ARE CARL'S.

We spend so much of our lives "doing," and so little time "being."

During the first three years of living on my own in the Adirondacks, I spent much of my time just living life and *being*. I was in my late teens and early twenties, out in the mountains every weekend hiking and camping, enjoying the freedom of the hills, captivated by nature's wonders. As decades have passed by, the demands and pressures of daily life necessitate a *doing* schedule, so I eagerly look forward to every chance I have to spend time in the woods with a camera just *being* again. But even in the woods it's easy to get caught up in conversation, working with the camera, or getting to the destination—*doing* rather than *being*.

I recall a hike several years ago up Bald Mountain, where I planned to photograph the sun rising above the sea of fog that filled the valley floor, blanketing the expanse of lakes from Old Forge to beyond the hamlet of Inlet. When I reached the top, however, both summit and fire tower were cloaked in a thick mist that was being blown over the summit by a steady breeze.

This situation required me to make a decision—hang around to see if conditions might change or head back down. While pushing my way to the top, I had been thinking of how I would set the camera to handle the light and conditions. I had been hiking *through* my surroundings without actually being aware of them. Although disappointed in the summit conditions I consciously chose to make the best of the moment, to let go of my active desire of *doing*, and transition to a state of *being*.

Round Mountain from Giant Ridge Trail, Dix and Nippletop in the background

Late fall on Giant, Rocky Peak Ridge summit in the distance

Northwest Bay Brook

I stood quietly in a small, calm hollow below the tower, closed my eyes, and let my other senses tune in to nature's more subtle beauty. A gentle breeze brushed my cheeks and hands and whispered through the nearby pines—a gentle accompaniment to the magic chorus of morning song birds. I sought to relax the furrows between my eyebrows and on my forehead, and release any tension I was holding in other parts of my body. Being alone and relaxing helped me tune into my surroundings, moving into a state of *being*. I became aware of slight changes in the wind and how they affected the gentle sensations across my skin. The intensity and direction affected the sound in the pines, spruce and balsam, and I noticed birds were calling from different directions. These sensations became my whole experience at the time, and I became a part of nature rather than a passerby.

Colden and Marcy from Algonquin

Looking southwest at Giant's Washbowl from Ridge Trail, mid-October

After a while I opened my eyes, and enjoyed the soft misty look of the pines and rocks at the summit. I felt refreshed, relaxed and in tune with the details of nature around me. I soon noticed the small flowers and other features of the landscape I hadn't seen before. Setting up my camera, I went into a photography meditation, a state of *being* where I feel no other distractions, and completely lose track of time.

Nature is much more than recreation, beauty and photos; being in nature can be a spiritual experience. Nature provides sustenance for all the wild creatures, as well as our own existence, and it also helps our mental well-being. While safety rules suggest a minimum group size for being in the mountains and wilderness, the best way to fully experience nature is spending time alone, hiking, relaxing and tuning in.

Sunset over Tupper Lake from the causeway

At some point we all ponder our existence, consider our mortality, contemplate the meaning of life, and what gives life meaning. Climbing and being in the mountains fuels my inspirations, connects me to my spirituality. It has taught me lessons for my approach to life, and helped create the person I am now. For me, the mountains are not a place to be, a goal to achieve, or a diversion; being in the mountains is a way of life, and who I am.

Over the decades I have spent climbing mountains in the Adirondack wilderness, I've had many unique and wonderful experiences—by myself, and shared with others. I've photographed and shared the visual experience with others, and worked hard to put myself in the right place at the right time to capture these moments. And though I've seen so much wonder over the years, I am still in awe of the magical beauty of nature—and especially the wild character I have found here among the Adirondack lakes, bogs, mountains and rugged High Peaks.

Photographing and climbing the mountains isn't my hobby; it's been a passion since I climbed my first High Peak on a pair of homemade snowshoes decades ago. When I'm climbing in the mountains and wandering through the wilderness I feel fulfilled and content, and know this is where I am meant to be as often as possible—in nature, wild and free.

The artist statement I composed some years ago for my photography business sums up my personal approach and inspiration. My goal is to recreate the feelings of place... to portray how special and unique a place is, and to evoke the sensations of being there at the time the photograph was created. I am inspired by the grandeur of the natural world, and seek out spiritual times in the wilderness when light becomes magical, and we are transformed by the simple power of beauty.

The ATIS team that built the new 1600' boardwalk on the Elk Lake Marcy Trail, 2015: back row, L to R, Victoria Challingsworth (DEC), Jared Smith, Eli Bickford, Erik Jacobson; middle row, Carly Dominick-Sobol, Jim Larson, Carly Poremba, Jesse Tang-Kong; seated/kneeling, Chaz Langston (DEC), Kellie Waksmunski, Zach Seaton, Katie Woltner.
CBR

The Adirondack Trail Improvement Society: 118 Years and Counting

By Karen Doman

Karen Doman *has been coming to the Adirondacks since 1974 and, although a self-proclaimed "beach girl," has succumbed to the lure of the mountains, lakes and streams of this very special place. All three of her sons participated in the ATIS programs and Karen and her husband Bruce are active in the Adult Program where, as she says, "you meet the nicest people." She is currently serving as one of ATIS' vice-presidents. After supporting her three sons and a daughter-in-law in earning 46er status, Karen recently accomplished the feat herself, finishing on Whiteface in 2015. But, she says, "That was never my goal. Somehow these mountains just crept up on me—or me on them. And my experiences in the Adirondacks encouraged me to expand my hiking horizons to the Whites, the Rockies, New Zealand... even the Dolomites!"*

While climbing Noonmark Mountain in Keene Valley via a trail that had not been maintained for years, three distinguished companions—Felix Adler, S. Burns Weston and William A. White—repeatedly met with serious blowdown. Legend has it that, well into the hike, a frustrated Dr. Adler told his companions, "My friends, we must at once establish an Adirondack trail improvement society"—and they did.

The Adirondack Trail Improvement Society (ATIS) was founded September 14, 1897. The first officers of the new organization were:

- President: William A. White (who held that position for 20 years);
- Treasurer: John H. Maghee (over the years his daughter Adelaide Maghee Marble and grandson John Marble also held the post); and
- Secretary: S. Burns Weston.

Established for a single purpose, ATIS broadened its mission over the years to include education and outings for children and adults. The organization's structure also evolved as Vice Presidents, Board of Directors and Advisory Council were added. For many years all aspects of its work were overseen by volunteer officers and Board or Advisory Committee members. But by 1986 it had become clear that someone was needed to give more time and attention to the burgeoning programs, and Tony Goodwin was hired for the position of Executive Director.

Treasurer John Marble (1937-2001) inspired the creation of the ATIS adult program

ATIS is a non-profit, tax-exempt organization, which has no formal dues. Most funds are raised from fully tax-deductible donations. From its beginning ATIS has enjoyed a close relationship with the Adirondack Mountain Reserve (AMR), more commonly known as the Ausable Club, and the two organizations have many members in common. Even so, they have always been—and remain—completely separate entities.

For the first decades of its existence, the primary function of ATIS was the improvement of existing trails on the property of the AMR and on adjacent lands of the State of New York[1]. At first the new organization hired local guides to do the actual work but through the years this changed. By the 1940s, ATIS was hiring students to clear blowdown, clip and mow brush, and build or maintain ladders and bridges during their summer vacations. Currently, the ATIS Trail Crew maintains some 115 miles of trails and this now includes hardening select trails to withstand today's high level of use. Executive Director Tony Goodwin logs well over 100 miles on the trails each season and is not above doing some of the clearing and maintenance himself.

---

1. ATIS markers were a common sight throughout the Adirondack High Peaks since they were used on all trails maintained by the organization, even on state land. Since 2006, ATIS markers are only visible on easement trails on AMR lands. Trail sections maintained by ATIS on state land now bear the familiar "Foot Trail" markers issued by the Department of Environmental Conservation.

The Adirondack Mountain Reserve

In 1886, as the land surrounding the Ausable Lakes was threatened with major lumbering operations, frequent visitor William G. Neilson persuaded his friend W. Charles Alderson to buy the land in question. By December 1886, the transaction was completed and title to the land was in Neilson's and Alderson's names.

The purchase included Lake Arnold, most of the Upper Bouquet Valley, Indian Falls, many of the High Peaks including the summit of Mount Marcy, Upper and Lower Ausable Lakes and lands extending to the flanks of Dix Mountain. By May 1887, the duo had put together a holding company of 29 members and The Adirondack Mountain Reserve (AMR) was incorporated on October 8 of the same year. Only two years later, eighteen additional stockholders joined. Descendants of many of the original stockholders are members today.

The State Forest Preserve had just been created in 1885 and the Adirondack Park was not established until 1892. In 1893, the AMR was the 11th largest private landowner in the Adirondacks. It had 55 members and comprised 28,625 acres. During the following decades, as sales and purchases took place simultaneously, a size of 40,000 acres is generally cited.

The size of the AMR landholding was reduced to 16,300 acres following a series of land sales to New York State between 1921 and 1932. In addition to Mount Marcy, the various parcels sold included Indian Falls, Johns Brook, some of the slopes of Tabletop, the Northern slopes of the Great Range from Little Haystack to the summit of Lower Wolf Jaw, part of Nippletop, the Bouquet River watershed, Chapel Pond, and part of the western slopes of Giant Mountain.

In 1978, the state purchased an additional 9,000 acres, including the slopes of the last 11 High Peaks that remained in private hands—Haystack, Basin, Saddleback, Sawteeth, Gothics, Armstrong, Upper and Lower Wolf Jaw, Blake, Colvin, Dial, Bear Den and Noonmark. The boundary between state and AMR lands was generally established at an elevation of 2,500 feet.

The 1978 deal included more than the peaks. The state also purchased an easement on the AMR's remaining 7,000 acres, excluding a 50-acre parcel near the club's golf course. Since the AMR always allowed the public to hike over its land to the peaks, the agreement merely put a longstanding tradition into writing. The state permitted the club to restrict some trails around the Upper Ausable Lake to members. Non-members are not allowed on the lakes or near the camps on Upper Ausable Lake. Nor are they permitted to bushwhack, hunt, fish, build fires, camp overnight or bring pets on AMR land.

1996 ATIS Trail Crew
SANDY SCOTT

After nearly 40 years of confining its mission to trail work, in the mid-1930s the organization introduced an educational phase by offering scheduled hikes on area trails led by sisters Peggy and Alice (Jo) Johannsen, its first so-called "trail hostesses." Both were daughters of the legendary Herman Smith "Jackrabbit" Johannsen (1875-1987).

Early schedules included weekly hikes for adults, hikes for those of all ages, and hikes for family groups, and were of varying degrees of difficulty. This facet of the organization's activities gradually grew into today's Junior Program, which now has a staff of Senior Trail Counselors, Junior Counselors and Counselors-in-Training. Together they lead hikes, paddles and campouts at varying levels of difficulty for children from 6 to 16. The Junior Program's most recent addition is a nature education program for children as young as 4.

In 1965, ATIS added a second educational program—High Peaks Camp for Boys—a two-week residential camp offering wilderness adventure and challenge to a small group of boys 11-15 years old. Thanks to the generous cooperation of the AMR, it was (and still is) based at the Upper Ausable Lake. The curriculum includes instruction in canoeing and camp skills, followed by four-day canoeing and backpacking trips to give participants an opportunity to practice lessons learned. It was an immediate success, and in 1972 it became coeducational. A leadership camp was added in 2013.

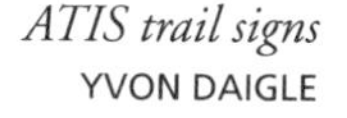

ATIS trail signs
YVON DAIGLE

In the mid-1980s, former ATIS Treasurer John Marble (who spent 63 of his 64 summers in the hamlet of St. Huberts near Keene Valley) proclaimed, "The kids shouldn't have *all* the fun!" This led to the creation of the adult program. Years later, thanks to cooperation with the Hurricane and Keene Valley chapters of Adirondack Mountain Club, a combined schedule made it possible to offer at least one and sometimes two trips every day of the ATIS July/August season. These outings continue today and include hikes ranging from death marches to gentle woodland strolls; paddles; bird watching; museum visits... and anything else a volunteer wants to lead and thinks others would enjoy. In recognition of John's contribution, after his untimely death a trail was cut to an overlook on the scenic trail leading from Sawteeth to the Lower Ausable Lake. Marble Point was dedicated in August 2004.

Over the years, ATIS has implemented its mission in expanding ways, and many cherished traditions have come into being. Best known of these are probably Monday night games of Capture the Flag, enthusiastically played by campers and counselors alike on the Ausable Club's golf course. Another is ghost stories told by the campfire at High Peaks Camp and overnights at Alderdice Lean-to and the Upper Ausable Lake. Jim Goodwin's[2] telling of *Ghost of the Indian Princess* was a favorite but nothing could top Jimmy's recitation from memory of *The Ballad of Yukon Jake/The Hermit of Shark Tooth Shoal.* Another long-standing tradition is the presentation of the annual ATIS Award, given to the camper judged best overall participant for the year. Long-time resident and internationally known artist Harold Weston[3] carved early awards and, in 1948, the original ATIS logo.

After nearly one hundred and twenty years, many descendants of original members are still part of ATIS. Indeed, many lifelong friendships—even a few marriages!—have gotten their start during ATIS outings.

Membership is open to anyone who is in sympathy with its stated purpose: "...in any and every lawful way and by any and every lawful means, to cultivate an appreciation of the natural beauty of the Adirondack Mountains."

ATIS hopes to continue to pursue that mission for many more years, by providing safe and scenic trails for hikers, introducing many more young people to the beauty and wonders of nature, and making it enjoyable for those of all ages to enjoy a very special place.

---

2. Jim Goodwin (1910-2011) led his first trip up Mount Marcy at age 12. For much of his life, from fall through the spring, he taught at Kingswood School in West Hartford, Conn. In the summers, he stayed in Keene Valley, eventually moving there full-time in 2002 to live in the cabin he had built in 1940. Goodwin cut new trails and maintained existing ones, while also guiding many aspiring 46-ers up and down the peaks. The trails he cut include Porter Mountain from Keene Valley in 1924, Big Slide from the Brothers in 1951, Hedgehog in 1953, Ridge Trail to Giant in 1955 and the Pyramid Gothics Trail in 1966. His long association with ATIS, as both director and trail maintainer, led to the new 1998 trail to Rooster Comb being named in his honor. His sixty-four-year commitment with ATIS includes two stints as president (1975-1980 and 1983-1987).

   Goodwin is also considered a pioneering rock and ice climber, and is credited with many first ascents in the Adirondacks. He made the first winter ascent of Mount Colden's Trap Dike in 1935, of Gothics in 1927, and became Adirondack 46er #24 in 1940.

3. Harold Weston (1894-1972), the son of S. Burns Weston, is a famous painter and a well-known author for *Freedom in the Wilds* published by ATIS in 1971.

"Please register, it could save your life." – DEC
YVON DAIGLE

Department of Environmental Conservation: Protecting Natural Resources and People

By David Winchell

David Winchell *is a Citizen Participation Specialist for the Bureau of Public Outreach in the DEC Region 5 which oversees the High Peaks Wilderness Area. He has worked for DEC since 1987 and lived and worked in the Adirondacks for the past 27 years. David initiated and maintains the DEC High Peaks Bulletin, which is updated and distributed weekly through the listserv DEC DELIVERS. He also initiated and maintains the Adirondack Trail Information web pages, which are also updated weekly. Visit the DEC web site* ***www.dec.ny.gov*** *to sign up to receive the High Peaks Bulletin or view the High Peaks Trail Information web page.*

The New York State Department of Environmental Conservation (DEC) is directed by Environmental Conservation Law to "exercise care, custody and control" of the Forest Preserve as defined by Article XIV of the state constitution. The Adirondack High Peaks Wilderness Area, which is part of the constitutionally protected Forest Preserve, is owned and managed by the State of New York. The dedicated DEC staff work hard to protect the natural resources of the High Peaks Wilderness Area and the people who recreate there.

The Adirondack Park State Land Master Plan provides the guidance by which DEC manages the High Peaks Wilderness Area and the other Forest Preserve lands in the Adirondacks. The Master Plan identifies its "unifying theme" as "...the protection and preservation of the natural resources of the state lands within the Park be paramount. Human use and enjoyment of those lands should be permitted and encouraged, so long as the resources in their physical and biological aspects are not degraded."

The Master Plan also defines a wilderness area as "...an area where the earth and its community of life are untrammeled by man—where man himself is a visitor who does not remain."

These are the primary tenets used by DEC Foresters to develop and implement the management plan for the High Peaks Wilderness Area and other Forest Preserve units within the Adirondack Park. The management plan assesses the natural and physical resources and identifies opportunities for public use which are consistent with wilderness guidelines while considering the ability of the resources and ecosystems to accommodate the use. The 1999 High Peaks Wilderness Complex Unit Management Plan directs DEC's management of the High Peaks Wilderness Area.

Up Gothics' cornice, February 2009
AR

The public's use of the High Peaks Wilderness Area is mainly guided by the State Land Use Regulations, including the special regulations for the area, which protect the natural resources and prevent user conflicts.

DEC Forest Rangers are the uniformed police officers who patrol the High Peaks Wilderness Area ensuring hikers, campers and climbers are properly prepared, and have knowledge of and comply with regulations and practices to minimize the impacts on the natural resources of the area.

Forest Ranger Chris Kostoss, center, talking to Peg Dennin, left, and Peter Davis, right
NANCIE BATTAGLIA

Forest Rangers are considered the successor of the Forest Wardens who were established under the 1885 law which created the Forest Preserve. Like their predecessors, Forest Rangers are charged with protecting the natural resources of the Forest Preserve and the people who recreate in it.

They are responsible for searching for lost and overdue hikers and rescuing injured or stricken people. On average, Forest Rangers respond to 57 search or rescue incidents each year in the High Peaks.

DEC Assistant Forest Rangers, Backcountry Stewards and Interior Caretakers assist the Forest Rangers in public education, search and rescue efforts, and stewardship of the wilderness.

DEC trail crews, Student Conservation Association Adirondack Program, Adirondack Mountain Club's Professional Trail Crew, DEC staff identified above, and volunteers all work together under the direction of the DEC Forester to maintain the trails, campsites, lean-tos and other recreational infrastructure in the wilderness.

The volunteers from Adirondack Mountain Club, the Adirondack 46ers, Lean2 Rescue, and other organizations and individuals are indispensable in the efforts to maintain and improve the wilderness recreational infrastructure and ensure a high quality experience for visitors, and protecting natural resources of the wilderness.

Four Corners, 1982
PETE BIESEMEYER

Forest Ranger Lieutenant Charlie Platt talking to hiker Kelly Paganelly
NANCIE BATTAGLIA

DEC also manages the fish and wildlife populations present in the High Peaks. DEC Fisheries biologists and technicians survey the various waters of the area to determine water quality—particularly pH levels, biological components and the type, number and size of fish present. Based on this information fish management decisions are made to determine fishing regulations and/or the species, strain and stocking rates of fish.

Waters in the High Peaks are mainly cold water trout fisheries. Many waters in the higher elevations no longer contain any fish life due to acid precipitation. The pH level in some of these waters is improving and in the future DEC hopes to re-establish trout in those waters where levels are high enough to sustain fish.

One water body in the High Peaks has served as a brood stock for the New York State endangered round whitefish. The round whitefish was once plentiful but saw a significant decrease in numbers due mainly to overfishing. DEC has created a program to re-establish round whitefish in suitable waters throughout the Adirondacks. This could not happen without the round whitefish found in the High Peaks Wilderness.

DEC Wildlife Biologists work in the High Peaks to monitor wildlife populations and minimize human-wildlife conflicts. Black bears in the High Peaks Wilderness had long ago become very adept at obtaining food from campers.

Avalanche Lake
BRENDAN WILTSE

Forest Ranger Dell Jeffery about to attend to a fire emergency

Forest Ranger Scott VanLaer

State Police helicopters provide vital assistance to DEC search and rescue efforts

Forest Ranger Kevin Burns in helicopter

DEC ARCHIVES

Forest Ranger Jim Giglinto on patrol, Marcy 2015

Forest Ranger Logan Quinn

Forest Ranger Ben Baldwin

DEC ARCHIVES

Forest Rangers Dell Jeffery and Art Perryman on the Hudson River

NANCIE BATTAGLIA

In the early part of this century, wildlife staff captured, collared and monitored bears, hazed nuisance bears and, with others, worked to educate campers on proper food management. This work led to the requirement for all campers to store food, toiletries and garbage in bear-resistant canisters, which resulted in a 75% decrease in the number of instances in which bears obtain food from campers. In the majority of such incidents, the camper was not using or was incorrectly using a bear canister.

Wildlife biologists have also studied fishers and martens, two members of the weasel family. The vast majority of the state's marten population is found in the High Peaks. The fisher population had been limited to the Adirondacks for many years but it has now spread across much of the state.

Rangers battling fire on the shoulder of Noonmark, September 1999
NANCIE BATTAGLIA

A 2001 forest fire on Hamlin between the towns of Jay and Wilmington.
NANCIE BATTAGLIA

Fisher and martens are sought by trappers during the legally established trapping season. Hunters pursue bear and white-tail deer in the High Peaks Wilderness Area but mainly in the western section. DEC Environmental Conservation Police patrol the area checking the licenses of hunters and trappers and their compliance with laws and regulations.

A bit of history

DEC and its predecessors have always had responsibility for the Forest Preserve lands. When the NYS Legislature established the Forest Preserve in 1885 it also created a three-person Forest Commission, which was responsible for the "care, custody, control and superintendence of the forest preserve." The Forest Commission became the Fisheries, Game and Forest Commission in 1895 when the Forest Preserve received protection in the state constitution.

This Commission and several other small Commissions were combined in 1911 to create the Conservation Commission, which became the Conservation Department in 1926. Finally, the current Department of Environmental Conservation was formed in 1970. All have been assigned the "care, custody, and control" of the Forest Preserve.

ADK Professional Trail Crew member Adam Gullo building a rock staircase on Blue Mountain Trail
ADK ARCHIVES

Memories of ADK-TFC and Wilderness Thoughts

By Wes Lampman

Wes Lampman *grew up in Ballston Spa, NY, exploring the foothills of the Adirondacks and the countryside around his family's home. He attended Paul Smiths College where he earned a degree in Forestry. Wes is currently the North Country Operations Director for the Adirondack Mountain Club, responsible for the success of the mission-based programs and facilities at Heart Lake and Johns Brook Lodge.*

ALL PHOTOGRAPHS IN THIS CHAPTER FROM ADK ARCHIVES

In the summer of 1993, I was accepted into the Adirondack Mountain Club's (ADK) Professional Trail Crew (TFC – Trail Fixing Crew). Unbeknownst to me at the time, this would be the beginning of what has turned out to be a lifelong fascination with trail building and maintenance, forever changing the way I understand a path through the woods. My six-season-long trail crew experience also uncovered something buried deep in my psyche—that living, playing and working in the wild is fundamental to my existence.

Lucky for me, my newfound career landed me in the Adirondack Park, a place that I had become enchanted with as a boy while on camping trips with my family. I consider myself fortunate that throughout my life there has always been a trail to follow, connecting me to the great mysteries of the natural world and transporting me to a place where I can muse on nothing in particular. Trails are also a conduit to challenge myself, pushing the limits of my mental and physical facilities. Trails take me to a destination, either a physical one like a summit or lake, or to the place in my mind where meditation and mindfulness flow perfectly.

I would imagine that my experience resonates with many people and that they, too, would probably choose to spend more time exploring the outdoors but live in such a way or in a location that does not offer the opportunity for trail outings. Increasing visitation numbers at the trailheads and summits of the Adirondack High Peaks region indicate that more and more people are searching for these experiences, with the number of hiker contacts made by High Peak Summit Stewards growing significantly—from 12,022 in 2005 to 23,804 in 2013 and 31,440 in 2015—and that represents only a handful of Adirondack summits.

Bucking a spruce log into stringers for the Slide Mountain Brook foot bridge in Johns Brook valley

If we only concentrated on maintaining the trails that already exist in the Adirondacks, it might be manageable to accommodate the growing number of visitors. But we want more trails. In fact, we demand more trails that specifically suit our individual needs and recreational pursuits. New trails do have the benefit of being designed properly and laid out so as to blend with the surrounding topography, requiring less maintenance and trail structures such as rock staircases and water bars. New trails are also "purpose built," meaning that they are designed to accommodate a specific type of recreational activity. In spite of these obvious benefits, I have come to realize over the past twenty-plus years that decisions on building new trails—and even fixing those already built—in the Adirondacks are never simple. We have heated disagreements about where they should be and what kind of trail should go where. Trails cost a lot of money, both to build and maintain—sometimes hundreds of thousands of dollars. Trails can be dangerous, hard to follow, and sometimes disappear altogether due to lack of maintenance or natural disasters. The combination of these obstacles and the ever increasing number of trail recreationists present many complex riddles for public land planners and trail designers to solve—what is an appropriate trail, how many are needed, how to properly manage and maintain the trail without infringing upon the wild character of the place, and how best to educate user groups before they enter the backcountry?

Algonquin Trail rock staircase under construction

My first week in the woods with the ADK-TFC was on the L. Morgan Porter Trail, which is located on the northeastern ridge of Mount Colden. It was the first week of a two-week-long project, so our pack frames were fully laden with tools, food, camping gear and other essentials. Starting at the Wiezel Trails Cabin located at Heart Lake, I quickly realized that this was going to be the heaviest pack that I had ever shouldered and that I was in for a hike like no other I had experienced. The goal was to make a spike camp above Lake Arnold at around 3800 feet in elevation, approximately six miles into the High Peaks Wilderness Area. The entire crew of five made it without incident, and once we set-up camp and ate lunch we followed our crew leader Sam (4th season) up the trail where he proceeded to introduce us to the trail project that we would each be laboring on for the rest of the week. I was asked to build a rock water bar, with the incentive that if I completed that satisfactorily, I could construct a rock staircase that was needed above the water bar to stabilize the steep, eroding trail. I could not have been happier; I was eighteen, the sun was out, I was in the mountains, and trail crew was my job for the summer. I recall digging and prying that first rock out of the mountainside, the complex problems that each stone presented to me, trying to imagine the last time those boulders were disturbed. The low, trembling thud each rock made as I rolled it down the trail towards the project site is still a vivid memory as is the loud crack and ensuing scent of burning gunpowder as stones collided into one another. It was an intoxicating feeling. To think that I was capable of such a thing—rearranging the mountain to create a better, more sustainable trail—caused my confidence to soar.

The rock water bar and staircase are still there, and should last at least another twenty years as long as the drainage ditches that protect them are maintained. These trail structures, along with others that were installed by my fellow crew members, will forever be a part of what defines the wilderness character of this section of trail for each hiker that passes over it. Just as other sections of trail resemble a deeply cut ravine with exposed soil and roots from the natural process of erosion or others still where you sink up to your knees in mud and water, this is wilderness too. But, given the option, my opinion is that a hardened, maintained trail that can be safely navigated and protects the natural resource is the right choice in all circumstances and does not degrade the wild experience or wilderness aesthetic.

Where do we draw the line? If a section of trail is rebuilt using pressure treated lumber or with steel that was flown in via helicopter (as opposed to using logs that were harvested on site or not having a bridge to span a wide river requiring a dangerous ford) does this diminish or eliminate the possibility of having a wilderness experience? For some, this may be the case. It would be a difficult question for me if I was referring to someplace other than the Adirondack Park, where one need only to step off the trail and bushwhack a short distance to experience a true sense of solitude amongst the vastness of the surrounding forest.

Author building a cairn on Marcy

I would hazard a guess that most people who visit the Adirondacks do not stray from the existing trail corridors or herd paths, which I consider to be easily followed trails, albeit unmarked. We expect that people will follow the trail routes found in reputable guidebooks and on maps to see where they can go in the Adirondack backcountry and plan accordingly. This is a contract of sorts—a promise to visitors that these trails are open and ready for use. We have an obligation to maintain and build new trails in the Adirondacks to the highest standard possible. Not only to protect the resource, which always should come first, but to exceed every visitor's expectation so they see that we are doing an excellent job as stewards of the land. And, so people can safely access the backcountry to appreciate and experience a truly wild place. Building the next generation of constituents that support the Forest Preserve is one positive outcome, but more important, it allows people of all walks of life to have a wilderness experience. This will become even more essential in the coming decades as our natural resources and open green spaces become scarcer and the human population much larger.

To me, the Adirondack High Peaks epitomize wilderness. The rugged landscape, dense forest cover and the unforgiving trails combined make up a place that shouts, "Humans are welcome but as visitors only." Nowhere is this best represented than in the alpine zone, a place where extremes are the norm. It is a rare occurrence for the ADK trail crew to work in the alpine zone. During my time on the crew, I was fortunate to have had the opportunity on four different occasions. The most memorable was working on the summits of Mount Marcy and Mount Skylight for a week. It was during my third season, and I shared our spike camp near the Opalescent River with just two other crew members, Amy (3rd season) and John (4th season). We quickly fell into the rhythm of making the daily walk up the Feldspar Trail, past Lake Tear of the Clouds to Four Corners, and then to either Marcy or Skylight.

The majority of the week was spent on Marcy, since at that time there were not many rock cairns in place from Schofield Cobble up to the summit. Spending approximately eight hours each day above tree line changed me forever. It is a separate world unto itself. The contrast of the yellow-green lichen against the exposed bedrock, the windswept krummholtz and the multitude of alpine plant communities made a kaleidoscope that I never grew tired of seeing. Or the clouds—so many different shapes and sizes, sometimes obscuring the surrounding peaks and then just as quickly moving to reveal another unique vista that would make me smile even wider. The wind was constant, sometimes almost violent, other times comforting, making me feel like I would always need it to keep me standing upright. It became my soundtrack, along with the grinding and clinking of rocks while I struggled to dry-set one stone at a time.

If you are reading this, then that probably means that you have purchased this book. Thank you! Give yourself a pat on the back for helping to secure the future of the Adirondack High Peaks Summit Stewardship Program.

When you are out and about on your next outdoor adventure, always remember to:
- Stay in the center of the trail, especially through muddy/wet sections.
- Stay on hardened surfaces such as bedrock, stepping stones or bridges, never on the vegetation when on or near the summits.
- Carry it in, Carry it out! Never leave anything behind, and pick up any refuse that you find.
- Be respectful of wildlife, keep your distance and do not disturb or harass.
- Be cheerful and kind to all fellow travelers you meet on the trail.

Heart Lake, Adirondak Loj
NANCIE BATTAGLIA

Adirondack Park Agency: Balancing Wilderness Protection with Human Activity

By Terry Martino

Terry Martino *was appointed Executive Director of the Adirondack Park Agency in July 2009. Prior to her work at the Agency she worked as Executive Director of the Adirondack North Country Association. For three decades, Terry has successfully managed organizations which balance community development and environmental protection. She has had the fortunate pleasure to raise two children in one of the world's most special places—the Adirondack Park. Terry holds a Master's Degree from The New School and a Bachelor's Degree from Carleton University. She has a Certification in Positive Psychology through a program with Dr. Tal Ben-Shahar, and is a certified Let Your Yoga Dance instructor.*

Magical and majestic, with the largest intact temperate deciduous forest in the world and communities that connect the past to the present and future, the Adirondack Park is a place like no other. It is a region where common ground is supported amidst divergent views on environmental protection and community development. It is a place where the Adirondack Park Agency, established by the State Legislature, is charged with the complex task of balancing natural resource protection with economic development. And after a four-decade plus legacy of administering two foundational land use plans—the Adirondack Park Land Use and Development Plan and the Adirondack Park State Land Master Plan—the Agency continues to have a pivotal role into the 21st century.

A "park" like no other

In the United States, if one mentions the term "park" it usually refers to a plot of land, publicly owned, set aside for protection of natural resources, historic features or for recreational use. On a grand scale, Yellowstone or Yosemite National Park may come to mind, or maybe Central Park in New York City. More commonly, parks are places like a public swimming pool or the local playground where people go with their children to picnic, bike or ride swings. Within these places everyone is just a visitor.

The Adirondack Park, considered by many as the crown jewel of the State of New York, is unlike any traditional park in several ways. First, the Park is 6 million acres in size, almost as big as the state of Vermont. Second, it is a mixture of public and private land. Third, because of this regional scale, land use and development on private land is regulated by a state agency.

The Adirondack State Forest Preserve, born in controversy, is undeniably the heart of the Park. In 1885, the state legislature set aside lands amid concerns for the water and timber resources. Given the vastness and isolated nature of the Adirondacks at the time, it became apparent more protection was necessary to prevent natural resource destruction. So, in 1894 the people of the State of New York amended their Constitution with the "Forever Wild" clause. Article XIV states, "*The lands of the state, now owned or hereafter acquired, constituting the forest preserve as now fixed by law, shall be forever kept as wild forest lands. They shall not be leased, sold or exchanged, or be taken by any corporation, public or private, nor shall the timber thereon be sold, removed or destroyed.*" This historic action may be unique worldwide.

Today, the Adirondack Park is the largest publicly protected region in the contiguous United States—greater in size than Yellowstone, Everglades, Glacier and Grand Canyon national parks combined. It is home to the state's highest peaks which ascend precipitously to heights exceeding 5,000 feet. These ancient mountains cast long shadows over the largest old-growth forest east of the Mississippi. Thousands of miles of rivers and streams flow freely and over 10,000 waterbodies large enough to be mapped on a USGS quad sheet exist inside its boundaries, commonly referred to as the "Blue Line." Approximately 15 percent of the Park is comprised of wetlands including boreal peat lands, flood plain forests and deep water marsh and emergent marsh systems.

These protected mountains, woods and waters provide a sanctuary for wildlife. Many species, which were once extirpated due to over-hunting and habitat loss, have returned. Moose now roam where black bear and whitetail deer are prevalent. Beavers alter landscapes through ceaseless dam building. Fishers quietly slither through the deepest woods. The howl of coyotes reverberates across river valleys. The Park is also a haven to species of special concern like the Bicknell Thrush, which summer in age-old fir waves, and the Spruce Grouse, whose southern range extends into the coniferous boreal forests of the northwest corner of the Park.

If the Forest Preserve is the heart of the Park then its lifeblood is the people who for generations have lived full-time or seasonally in the 101 towns and villages that are dispersed within the Blue Line. More than 130,000 people reside year-round. The summer population swells by an additional 50,000 and over 10 million tourists visit annually. This elaborate mix of private and state land is the underpinning of the Adirondack Park. It crafts a way of life one is hard-pressed to replicate anywhere else.

People are drawn to the quaint Olympic Village of Lake Placid, the All-America City of Saranac Lake, and the Home of the High Peaks—the Town of Keene. Outdoor adventures begin from the Adirondack Base Camp of Old Forge, the All Season Vacationland of Speculator, or the Heart of the Adirondacks—the Town of Newcomb. Agriculture is thriving along the Adirondack Coast towns in the Champlain Valley. Wilt Industries in Lake Pleasant, Creative Stage Lighting in Chestertown and General Composites in Willsboro are examples of innovative manufacturing companies operating inside the Blue Line. The forest products industry continues to harvest timber throughout the Park. International Paper's most profitable North American paper mill employs hundreds of people in Ticonderoga.

Within a day's drive of nearly 85 million people, the Adirondack Park offers a unique blend of wilderness solitude, outdoor recreation and small town quality of life. However, maintaining the fragile balance between wilderness preservation and human activity—between environment and economy—is a complex responsibility—one entrusted to the Adirondack Park Agency.

Balancing environment and economy

The New York State Legislature adopted the Adirondack Park Agency Act (APA Act) in 1971. A direct result of Governor Nelson Rockefeller's Temporary Study Commission on the Future of the Adirondacks, the Agency was charged with preparing a comprehensive plan for the Park. It was given not only authority for public lands planning but also powers to control private land use as well. The first action was the preparation of the Adirondack Park State Land Master Plan in 1972. The Agency then completed the Adirondack Park Private Land Use and Development Plan in 1973.

NANCIE BATTAGLIA

The Adirondack Park State Land Master Plan established a classification system for the public lands and formalized a unit management planning process. The Agency was directed

Hikers take a break
NANCIE BATTAGLIA

to share oversight of public lands with its sister agency, the Department of Environmental Conservation (DEC). The Agency is responsible for state land classification, long-range planning and the establishment of management guidelines. The DEC is responsible for the overall care, custody and control of the Forest Preserve and is responsible for preparing and implementing unit management plans. The Agency determines if the proposed plans conform to the Master Plan.

The Adirondack Park Land Use and Development Plan applies to private land use and development in the Park. On a regional scale, the plan maps all private lands into six land use classifications: Hamlet, Moderate Intensity Use, Low Intensity Use, Rural Use, Resource Management and Industrial Use. The Agency has limited jurisdiction in Hamlet and Moderate Intensity Use areas, increasing responsibility in Low Intensity and Rural Use areas, and extensive oversight of Resource Management lands.

Agency jurisdiction, building density guidelines and project review standards are defined through the APA Act and the accompanying land use plan. The plan directs high-density growth into areas adjacent to existing developments where public infrastructure is present and onto lands with lesser resource concerns. Residential and commercial construction is discouraged in critical environmental areas, on lands adjacent to Forest Preserve or in areas where the primary use is forestry or agriculture.

The Agency is guided by eleven Members with an Agency Chair appointed by the Governor. The Governor appoints eight members who are subject to confirmation by the Senate. The Agency also includes three ex-officio members: the Commissioner of the Department of Economic Development, the Secretary of State, and the Commissioner of the Department of Environmental Conservation. Agency Members are involved in policy decisions, permit approvals and unit management plan conformance determinations. The Agency Members represent a careful balance of local, regional and statewide interests.

Agency Members have a significant responsibility for the protection of the Park while simultaneously addressing the needs of the region's economy. Through the APA Act, the Agency is charged "to insure optimum overall conservation, development and use of the unique scenic, aesthetic, wildlife, recreational, open space, historic, ecological and natural resources of the Adirondack Park." Agency meetings are conducted on a monthly basis. The public is invited to attend monthly meetings in Ray Brook, observe via the live webcast or view the archived sessions at the Agency's website www.apa.ny.gov. Agency staff support board deliberations with presentations and are present to respond to technical questions.

The Agency and staff share in the responsibility for the decisions that affect the Adirondack Park. Agency staff, all of whom reside in the Park, respect the legacy of the Park's history and work professionally, are fully committed to upholding the Agency's legislative mandates.

Under Governor Andrew Cuomo's directive to all State Agencies to improve services to citizens, Agency staff restructured administrative processes. The Agency increased coordination between divisions resulting in timely decisions based on science and fully in accordance with the law. Enhancements to permit templates streamlined the application process for the general public. Guidance documents in support of development considerations listed in the APA Act were published. These documents clarify what is expected from applicants in regards to project design. By providing clear and predictable guidance, the overall burden on the general public is minimized while an environmentally rigorous review process still remains in place.

Pitcher plant
CBR

Based on 40-plus years of work, the Agency is consistent and efficient in responding to jurisdictional questions, development proposals and enforcement matters. Agency staff maintain a great track record answering more than 4,000 annual phone inquiries. Over

300 permits are issued annually. Hundreds of site visits are performed. On a daily basis, staff provide professional services including engineering, economic and financial feasibility analysis, local government workshops, site plan design, wetland delineations, soil testing, invasive species management and habitat analysis. The introduction of geographic information system technology significantly improved the Agency's regional planning capabilities as well as increased staff productivity and efficiency.

Staff interactions with applicants are important opportunities to explain the importance of environmental protection and well-designed projects. Wetlands mitigate floods, filter impurities and serve as critical wildlife habitat. Shoreline guidelines protect the scenic value of the Park's waterfronts and ensure waterbodies retain excellent water quality. Avoiding steep slopes minimizes stormwater impacts. Sustainable forestry results in long-term healthy forests. Blending development into the landscape retains the scenic appeal of the Adirondacks, which is the foundation of a vibrant tourism economy.

From controversy to a model for conservation

If declaring the public lands "Forever Wild" in 1894 was the first major controversy in the Adirondacks, the creation of the Agency was the second. Born ironically as a result of near universal opposition to an Adirondack National Park proposal, the Agency quickly faced fierce resistance. Self-reliant and independent, many Adirondackers resented what they felt was an intrusion on their private property rights. Developers were eager to profit from a growing boom for second homes and outdoor recreational facilities in wild settings. On the other side were concerned citizens and advocacy groups worried that with the completion of the Adirondack Northway (Interstate 87), and with very few local zoning ordinances in place, the unique qualities of the Park would be significantly diminished by chaotic commercial and residential development.

From left: Terry Martino, Bennett (son), Allison deFranco (daughter) and John Martino (husband) at Mount Van Hoevenberg cross-country center, Lake Placid Olympic Sports Complex

During its early decades there were many attempts to eliminate the Agency. Some came in the form of legal challenges regarding the constitutionality, administration and implementation of the APA Act. The Agency successfully defended against these lawsuits. The New York State Senate once voted to repeal the APA Act; however, the Assembly did not take up the measure. There were numerous public protests including overt hostile actions. An Agency member's barn was burned to the ground. During a project site visit a state vehicle carrying three staff members was struck by bullets. An arsonist was caught attempting to set the Agency's headquarters in Ray Brook ablaze. And on a lighter note, a truckload of manure was dumped at the Agency's front door. Through it all, often on pure determination, the Agency survived.

Building on a grand legacy

Now with the support of Governor Cuomo, the future of the Adirondack Park is bright. More than at any other time in the history of the Agency, people from around the Park work together to solve complex problems. There is a strong sense of unity, which can be attributed to a growing mutual respect for differing points of view. Young people are involved in planning for our future through yearly events such as the Youth Climate Summit. Common ground is now an accepted approach and opportunity.

Under Governor Cuomo the Forest Preserve grew with the acquisition of 69,000 magnificent acres of former Finch Pruyn lands from The Nature Conservancy. This was the largest single addition to the Forest Preserve in more than a century. The linkage of these wild lands to Park communities contributes significantly to the region's economy, its people, businesses and quality of life. The three Regional Economic Development Councils representing the Adirondack Park successfully secured over 1 billion dollars in grant and loan funds in support of transformational economic development projects. Adirondack communities devastated by superstorm Irene rebuilt stronger and more resilient infrastructure with the support of the New York Rising program. And with unprecedented action to combat the spread of invasive species, including the establishment of boat washing stations, Adirondack communities lead the way in this critical fight.

Today the Adirondack Park continues to be a model for conservation. International delegations annually visit the Park as part of educational exchange programs. They study the public and private land use plans and engage representatives from all sectors to ascertain how our regional land use plans work. Their common goal is to discover the best way to establish protected areas in their countries in which people remain and communities thrive.

It has been a tremendous honor to serve as the Adirondack Park Agency Executive Director since 2009. As an organization, the Agency is a fascinating integration of staff and Agency Members who all love the Park. Together we make complex decisions on a daily and monthly basis. We also take great pride in our responsiveness to an equally engaged public. I have come to expect, but do not take for granted, that year after year the Agency, one of the smallest in New York State, raises the bar to accomplish great things in pursuit of its mission.

The implementation of the APA Act was and remains an exciting challenge. Our commitment to the Adirondack Park is a responsibility we share with all community leaders, residents and visitors. As we continue to focus on achievement, we grow stronger through the appreciation of this special place.

Summer lodging guests of the Bartlett family resting on Hurricane summit, circa 1910
COURTESY OF TIMOTHY BARTLETT

Adirondack History Brought to Life in Elizabethtown

By Margaret Bartley

Margaret Bartley's biography is on page 124

John Wesley Otis (1847-1919) was a Keene native who, after serving in the Civil War and working as a mountain guide, was hired by the Adirondack Mountain Reserve as its first Game Warden. This was a difficult job for a man who had to enforce hunting and fishing restrictions on his friends and neighbors. Today he is mostly known for being the first person to climb Mount Marcy, a feat achieved on March 18, 1893 in the company of Benjamin Pond while stationed at Inlet Camp, which is located at the southern end of Upper Ausable Lake.

COURTESY OF ADIRONDACK HISTORY MUSEUM IN ELIZABETHTOWN

It takes some agility and balance to climb the 45 weathered steps to the top of the fire tower that looms over the Adirondack History Museum in Elizabethtown. But the view is well worth the effort. At the top of the staircase, in a 7 x 7 cramped cab, firewatchers spent long days looking for telltale wisps of smoke that signaled wildfire danger. Today, the tower provides visitors a panoramic view of Adirondack topography, including many High Peaks.

The most easily recognized local peak is Hurricane Mountain, located due west, because of its own much beloved fire tower. The Hurricane fire tower is a visual landmark on a line of mountains that run like a spine from Poke-O-Moonshine in the north—with its own glistening tower—to Giant Mountain and Rocky Peak Ridge in the middle of Elizabethtown. To the South is the Dix Range, with five mountains over 4,000 feet (Macomb, South Dix, Grace Peak, Hough and Dix). The structure was on its way to being demolished when many concerned citizens and organizations rose up to preserve it, notably a group of Elizabethtown residents led by Gretna Longware. This tower was once the workplace of Wes Hurley, a local firewatcher who even built his home at the foot of Hurricane Mountain Lane to make his "commute" to work easier.

The Adirondack History Museum's fire tower, which also provides magnificent views of the scenic Boquet River Valley, was actually assembled from the salvageable parts of two other Adirondack fire towers after the state dismantled and removed them from their mountaintops. The tower was rebuilt with the pieces and installed beside the Museum in 1979.

Operated by the Essex County Historical Society, the Museum has been a fixture in Elizabethtown since 1954. The building was once the Town's Union Free School, and was erected in 1916 after a fire destroyed the earlier wooden schoolhouse. For the next 38 years the three-story masonry building housed grades 1 through 12, serving the children of Elizabethtown and Lewis. But the post-war baby boom increased the number of children and a new school building was eventually constructed two blocks away. The School Board turned the old building over to the historical society with the condition that is be used for educational purposes.

In keeping with the mandate to educate, as well as preserve and promote the history of Essex County, the Museum has created a special educational program using the fire tower as its focus. "Up in the tower, we have a replica of what's called a fire finder," said Keene Valley's David Thomas-Train, an educator at the museum. "It's a map of the surroundings, with a pointer that observers would use to situate the smoke of fires. Then they would get on the radio and talk to their colleagues in at least two other fire towers who would also pinpoint the location. And then they'd call the firefighters into action."

Adirondack History Museum in Elizabethtown
OWEN GIBBS

The Adirondack History Museum offered six Adirondack Fire Tower Programs for students and families in 2015, which included a lesson at the museum followed by a guided hike to the Poke-O-Moonshine tower. "Fire towers are one of the emblematic sights in the Adirondacks, and this program offers insight into the history of these structures and the important role they played in fire protection and local history," said Museum Director Aurora McCaffrey.

There is much more to the Adirondack History Museum than this program and its fire tower. Researchers and genealogists from all over the country contact the Museum's Brewster Library for information and photos about their ancestors, many of whom were Adirondack natives. Melissa Otis's family came to the Adirondacks from Ireland in 1843. They first lived near the Cascade lakes then moved to the western slope of Hurricane Mountain, before finally buying land in Elizabethtown. Melissa recently completed a PhD dissertation on Adirondack Native Americans, which focused on the Abenaki, who for centuries had summer encampments in the High Peaks. She spent days doing research in the Brewster Library, and a copy of her work is now on file for others to read.

In 2015, the descendants of later immigrants to the Adirondacks were able to learn more about their ancestors in a new museum exhibit titled *Essex County Immigration, Faces and Stories*. The Museum built the exhibit around artifacts borrowed from descendants of Italian, French, Polish, Spanish, Chinese and Irish immigrants. The Museum also owns a unique collection of employee information cards from the Witherbee-Sherman Mining Company in Moriah, which tell the personal histories and data of several thousand immigrants miners from the late 19th and early 20th centuries.

A recent exhibit titled *Grace Hudowalski and the Mountains We Climb* portrays the history of hiking and the Adirondack 46ers. Another popular museum exhibit called *Worked - Wild* shows the interaction and impact humans have had on the Adirondack wilderness over the past 200 years.

A trip to the Adirondacks is not complete without a visit to the Museum and its treasure trove of local history. It is open seven days a week, from Memorial Day in May until Columbus Day in October. The Brewster Library is open year round for researchers.

George Bacon Wood photo collection

George Bacon Wood Jr. was a 19th century landscape artist who fell in love with the Adirondacks. Like many of the Hudson River artists, Wood came north from his hometown of Germantown, Pennsylvania, anxious to experience and to capture the beauty of Northern wilderness. He arrived just after the Civil War and became a regular visitor both in summer and winter. In the 1870s he brought his wife and children, and rented a house in Elizabethtown. Along with his paints and easel, he also brought a large frame camera to record a true likeness of the Adirondacks. Wood not only sold prints of his photos, he also produced an extensive collection of glass lanternslides, and put on shows where he told of his forays into the High Peaks. In the early 1970s, Wood's granddaughter donated over 120 of these slides, as well as several dozen large frame negatives, to the Essex County Historical Society. This rare and beautiful collection was graciously digitally copied by PelicanPR of Montreal, and several of the images are reproduced here.

Lake Henderson outlet
1886 - GEORGE BACON WOOD

Gothic View Camp, Upper Ausable Lake
Camp Colden
1886 - GEORGE BACON WOOD

Avalanche Lake
Gothic View Camp, Upper Ausable Lake
1886 - GEORGE BACON WOOD

Keene Valley
Panther Gorge Camp
1886 - GEORGE BACON WOOD

View from Marcy
Verplanck Colvin signal station on Marcy summit
Ausable Lake Road
1886 - GEORGE BACON WOOD

Keene Pass, today's Route 9N, with Knob Lock on the left and Hurricane shoulder to the right
Boom Box / Privy Hale's camp, Upper Ausable Lake
1886 - GEORGE BACON WOOD

Lapland rosebay on Algonquin
BRENDAN WILTSE

Adirondack Foundation: Sustaining the Economic, Social, Environmental and Cultural Health of the Adirondacks

By Cali Brooks

Cali Brooks *is the CEO of Adirondack Foundation (www.generousact.org). Together with a staff of five—Andrea Grout, Chris Morris, Beth Benson, Melissa Eisinger and Matt Brandi—they make up the dynamic Adirondack Foundation team. All have deep roots in the Adirondacks and the nonprofit world. Our staff value statement tells the story: working at Adirondack Foundation should be a privilege, a responsibility and a pleasure. These underlie and inspire everything we do. Fundamentally, we are committed to the highest integrity and excellence in all matters, so that our donors and the communities we serve can rely on us to be professional, fiscally responsible, transparent, and to add value by cultivating, sharing and making use of a deep knowledge of the Adirondacks and philanthropy. Cali, husband Galen Crane, daughter Maisie, and two guinea pigs live in Lake Placid, NY.*

In 1997, Fred Brown and Meredith Prime, board members of Lake Placid Education Foundation (LPEF), saw the need for an organization to encourage giving and philanthropy in the Adirondack region. Their LPEF board colleagues agreed, and together they decided to support the founding and formative years of a community foundation—Adirondack Community Trust (ACT). In 2013, ACT changed its name to Adirondack Foundation to better reflect its charitable character.

The Adirondack Foundation's mission is to lead and inspire the growth of generosity and community investment in a vibrant future for the Adirondacks. The Foundation seeks to be recognized as the pre-eminent provider of ideas, financial support and other resources for people and institutions that sustain the economic, social, environmental and cultural health of the Adirondacks.

Community foundations are tax-exempt public charities that guide philanthropy. Individuals, families, businesses and nonprofits work with community foundations to create permanent charitable funds that help meet the challenges of changing times. Community foundations invest and administer these funds so that they grow and become permanent charitable resources. In addition to investing and administering charitable funds, community foundations provide leadership, expertise and capital to address social issues and serve as a resource for nonprofit, civic, government and philanthropic organizations.

Today, there are more than 1,600 community foundations around the world serving as stewards of charitable giving and providing strategic advice and guidance about philanthropy.

From $3.5 million to $47 million in assets

In early 2001, Adirondack Foundation held just over $3.5 million in assets. By 2015, this had grown to over $47 million, allowing the Foundation to award over $2.5 million in grants annually to nonprofits and community organizations, in addition to a wide range of services and leadership in the community. These assets are contributed by generous people, families and community groups and cared for by the Foundation so that they can continue to support the donors' charitable goals well into the future. None of this growth, granting and good work in the community would be possible without the philanthropy of the Foundation's donors.

Adirondack Foundation approaches this work with 6 core values:
Responsible stewardship of the resources entrusted to it.
Leadership that mentors and encourages leadership in others.
Community enhancement—supporting Adirondack communities' ability to become economically sustainable while protecting the unique values of the region.
Generosity—encouraging generosity in both experienced and new givers, building the momentum and impact of philanthropy across the Adirondacks.
Collaboration to achieve greater results than anyone could achieve acting alone.
Legacy building—helping generous people invest in the future.

The core of the Foundation is donor service. We work with donors to craft charitable funds to reflect their values, interests and concerns. The administration of the funds falls to the staff of Adirondack Foundation, so donors can focus on the joy of grant making. The charitable resources entrusted to the Foundation are pooled and invested in a diversified portfolio—giving the Foundation access to options normally reserved for large investors. Funds grow gradually, even as the donors make grants to the causes that are dear to them.

Funds set up by donors

The funds which donors set up with Adirondack Foundation directly support causes that are important to them. In an area as unique and exquisite as the Adirondacks, many donors set up environmental funds to actively support important conservation work. The #507 Fund supports the Adirondack High Peaks Summit Stewardship Program, which protects New York's alpine ecosystem through education, trail work and research. In eighteen months this fund received over seventy seven thousand dollars in donations, establishing itself as a permanent stream of support for the cause.

The ADK Wilderness Legal Defense Fund was established by Adirondack Mountain Club to fund legal actions and research in order to protect the forest preserve and other wild lands of New York. The Clarence Petty Internship Fund supports young, emerging environmental leaders to work with the Adirondack Council in conservation, government relations, education or outreach to ensure the ecological integrity and wild character of the Adirondack Park.

Services, tools and seminars for community groups

Unlike most corporate donor-advised funds, community foundations are uniquely positioned to play a role as a catalyst for a wide range of exciting work. Adirondack Foundation takes this role seriously. Since its inception in 1997, the Foundation has committed significant time and resources to being a leader in the community, providing a range of services, tools and seminars for community groups.

Nonprofit Leadership Seminars are offered for board members and staff on topics including donor cultivation and solicitation, marketing, board roles and responsibilities, and board transformation. Adirondack Foundation helped found, and continues to administer, the Adirondack Nonprofit Network (ANN), which is comprised of a diverse range of over 40 nonprofits who build professional relationships among peers, identify proactive approaches, and have an honest conversation about redundancies and collaborations. Adirondack Foundation developed a free crowdfunding website called Adirondack Gives that hosts fund-

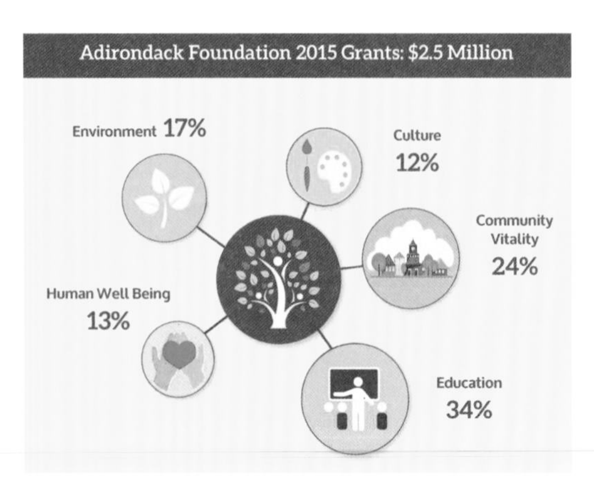

On Skylight
NANCIE BATTAGLIA

raising projects for the region's nonprofits, schools and municipalities. Finally, we help nonprofits manage their permanent funds, which create an annual stream of income for the organizations.

As a leader in the community, the Foundation also strives to address unmet needs in the Adirondack region. This requires identifying current and emerging issues and developing resources to address them in three key areas—education, particularly birth to three; capacity building of the nonprofit sector, economic development and health, particularly aging and the elderly population. This aspiration is realized in our Generous Acts Fund. This fund is unique in that it is administered by the foundation itself and allows us to make targeted grants as needs arise in the community. There are also specific focused initiatives, with the most recent launched in 2015 called the Adirondack Birth to Three Alliance.

The science of early childhood development makes a compelling case that focusing resources on each child's first 1,000 days can have a profound impact on their life and the entire community. Adirondack Foundation has joined with a group of partners dedicated to helping every single child get the best possible shot at success. At this writing, a network of more than 30 organizations is forming among state agencies, nonprofits, local funders and others devoted to serving children ages 0 to 3 and their families. To supplement this effort, the Foundation has also launched Small Grants for Small Children to support daycare providers seeking additional training, QUALITYstarsNY accreditation or equipment to enhance their programs.

From support for families with young children and building recreational assets for people of all ages to helping people live healthy, fulfilling lives and making the Adirondacks a more welcoming and inclusive place, Adirondack Foundation partners with generous people and nonprofits to build the power of philanthropy to benefit communities in the Adirondacks and beyond.

McIntyre Range from Old Orchard Trail, Heaven Hill Trails
SETH JONES

For most of Adirondack Foundation's history, Cali Brooks has been at the helm, first as executive director and more recently as president and chief executive officer. After working with nonprofits in Southeast Asia, Central America and in the U.S., Brooks returned to New York to join the staff of the HKH Foundation, where she conducted a survey to assess the economic, social, cultural and environmental strengths of the Adirondack region. She then joined the Public Affairs Office of the New York State Department of Environmental Conservation and co-founded the Wildlife Conservation Society's Adirondack Communities and Conservation Program. Brooks has served on the North Country Regional Economic Development Council, the Upstate Revitalization Initiative, the New York Attorney General's Leadership Committee for Nonprofit Revitalization, and the North Country Health Systems Redesign Commission.

Adirondack Foundation's office is located at the historic and picturesque Heaven Hill Farm. Once the home of Henry and Mildred Uihlein, the property was left to the Uihlein Foundation, which makes the historic farm available for use, without charge, for community groups.

Adirondack Foundation in a nutshell:

180 charitable funds managed for individuals and families
60 permanent funds managed for Adirondack charities
Generous Acts, the fund that makes grants to enhance communities across the Adirondacks
AdirondackGives.org our crowdfunding site where donors can find and give to projects they care about
$48 million assets under our stewardship
$29 million grants made since 1997
$2 million+ grants made annually (average)
$800,000+ grants made after Hurricane Irene (2011)
635 charities receiving grants in 2014
6 Adirondack residents employed
16 Adirondack residents on Governing Board
22 Adirondack communities represented on Board and Advisory Council

Haystack summit ridge
YVON DAIGLE

The Adirondack Council and the High Peaks Wilderness

By John Sheehan

John Sheehan *has been the voice of the Adirondack Council since 1990. As Director of Communications, he works works with the media to explain the unique nature of the Adirondack Park and to help the public understand the Council's efforts to sustain its clean air, wilderness, wildlife, clean water and vibrant communities. John is the principal author of the Council's annual* State of the Park Report *and assists with the editing of its publications. He has also overseen the production of two films about the Council's work—*The Adirondack Council *(1992) and* ACID RAIN: A Continuing National Tragedy *(1998).*

John is a frequent guest lecturer at several New York colleges and universities and regularly addresses civic and not-for-profit organizations, chambers of commerce, scientific societies and community forums.

Prior to joining the Council, John was managing editor of The Malone Evening Telegram, *a daily newspaper, after serving as an environmental and political journalist. Born in Troy, NY, he is a graduate of Catholic Central High School and the State University at Albany (B.A., Class of 1985)*

Wilderness is at the heart of the Adirondack Council's mission and vision for the Adirondack Park. It is our main point of orientation in a confusing and complicated world—our "true north." From the first moment our organization existed, it has had a special affection for the High Peaks Wilderness Area. Protecting it is one of our most solemn responsibilities and greatest honors.

The High Peaks Wilderness is special. It is the place many people picture when they think of the Adirondacks. It is the most popular wilderness by far in terms of annual visitors. It is breathtakingly beautiful and it needs special protection.

The Adirondack Council has played a major role in securing and shaping its future. We helped protect it from legal challenges that would have opened it to destructive, motorized recreation. We won significant victories against acid rain and smog, which have harmed its forests, wildlife and people. We worked to protect it from overuse and overcrowding. Now, as our fifth decade of fighting for the High Peaks begins, we are urging the state to expand it by 40 percent—further enhancing its cachet as a national treasure.

Back in the 1960s, conservationist Laurence Rockefeller wanted to turn the High Peaks into the Adirondack Mountains National Park. Instead, his brother Nelson, who just happened to be the Governor of New York, created the Adirondack Park Agency. Nelson and the Legislature also created the State Land Master Plan that established the Adirondack wilderness system. One of the first to be created was the High Peaks Wilderness Area (HPWA). If our expansion plan succeeds, the HPWA would grow to rival some of the nation's largest and most popular national parks.

Hogback lean-to, January 1979
R. SENGSTACKEN

A rare and beautiful thing

Wilderness is very rare in the heavily populated northeastern United States. Very few motor-free areas exist outside of the Adirondack Park. In most other places, public highways and existing communities prevent the creation of new ones. But here, there is more than a million acres, spread over a six-million-acre park. Better yet, there are still undeveloped lands surrounding the HPWA—room for the wilderness to grow and thrive. This part of the Park remains a quiet refuge for people who seek peace and solitude. It shelters wildlife that cannot survive alongside civilization and traffic. Its beauty continues to inspire artists and dreamers. But it can be bigger and better.

Many of the lands acquired by the state around the HPWA during the early 21st century had been off-limits to the public since the middle of the 19th century. This makes our quest to add some of them to the HPWA a once-in-a-lifetime opportunity. The expanded

Marcy summit
NANCIE BATTAGLIA

wilderness would be 280,000 acres. That's roughly the size of Rocky Mountain National Park in Colorado, and twice the size of Zion National Park in Utah.

When complete, a person could step into the woods at what is now—in 2016—the eastern edge of the Dix Mountain Wilderness, at Exit 29 of the Northway, and walk for 32 miles—nearly all the way to Tupper Lake—without crossing a road or private property. That would be a triumphant journey. During the Adirondack Council's first years as an organization, it looked like the wilderness might not last very long.

Our beginnings

When it was founded in 1975, the Adirondack Council's first board of directors hailed from local and regional groups such as the Association for the Protection of the Adirondacks, the Adirondack Committee of the Eastern New York Chapter of The Nature Conservancy, the Adirondack Foundation[1], the Adirondack Mountain Club and the Hawkeye Conservationists. They also came from The Wilderness Society, Natural Resources Defense Council, the Audubon Society and Sierra Club. This new council of

1. The *Adirondack Foundation* referred to here was a private foundation that ceased to exist more than two decades ago. Its founder gave the current Adirondack Foundation permission to use the name.

organizations grew and took on a life of its own, eventually becoming independent of the other groups in the 1990s.

From the beginning, the Council has sought to bring the greatest concerns facing the Adirondack Park and Adirondack wilderness areas to the attention of officials in Albany and Washington, D.C. Wilderness is always part of our pitch. The Council works with a broad range of Adirondack elected officials, fellow conservationists, community leaders and residents to better understand the Park's needs. We have fostered productive relationships with all six governors who have served New York since 1975. We have helped each to find ways to protect water, wildlife, wilderness and communities.

Our mission is to ensure the ecological integrity and wild character of the Adirondack Park. Our long-range vision for the Park consists of large, core wilderness area surrounded by farms and working forests and augmented by vibrant communities. We pursue this vision by keeping watch over the state agencies and officials who manage the Park's priceless natural assets. We also seek assistance for the Park from local and federal officials, whose actions can enhance or hinder the state's success. Every year, we publish a *State of the Park Report* to remind the public of how well all public officials fared in their duties toward the Park. There is an archive of those reports dating back to 1986 on our web site at www.adirondackcouncil.org.

One of our most important duties is to help the Department of Environmental Conservation (DEC) and the Attorney General to protect the integrity of the "forever wild" Forest Preserve and Article 14, Section 1 of the NYS Constitution, known as the Forever Wild clause. The clause protects the Forest Preserve against lease, sale, development and logging. We have helped defend the state against lawsuits aimed at weakening the clause. We have helped the Adirondack Park Agency (APA) hold on to its authority to classify state lands as wilderness, so it can protect them from the noise, pollution and invasive species spread by motorized recreation.

The APA's authority over the public's Forest Preserve comes from the State Land Master Plan. The master plan is the state's blueprint for managing all public lands in the Adirondack Park, ranging all the way from the parking lots under the state office buildings, to state-run ski centers, to motor-free wilderness. It was by no means clear in 1975 that the State Land Master Plan, or the APA, or Adirondack wilderness areas, would survive for long. Legal challenges were only part of the danger.

Pressure on the APA

Back in 1975, the DEC was only five years old. The APA was three. Both were under enormous pressure. The public was concerned with a growing population and easier access to the High Peaks, brought by a new superhighway between New York City and Montreal. When the Adirondack Northway (I-87) was completed in 1967, it delivered thousands of cars a day to new places at higher rates of speed. No longer did people need to spend all day navigating through every city and village on U.S. Route 9 to reach the High Peaks from the south. They could have breakfast in Manhattan and be in the mountains in time for lunch. Albany was now only two hours away.

Hoffman and the High Peaks from Schroon Lake
CARL HEILMAN II

Exit 30 dropped traffic on the doorstep of the Town of Keene. Until then, Keene had been losing residents steadily for almost a century. In 1960, only 726 people remained—its lowest total since 1820. But by 1970, just three years after the Northway opened, its population had risen by 5 percent. It would jump another 20 percent by 1980, reaching 1,105 by the 2010 census. In summer, the population is much higher.

Some of the pressure was political. Who were these people appointed by the governor? What plans did they have for the Forest Preserve? Many local officials felt the Legislature had diminished their authority by creating the APA. Many argued against wilderness, preferring motorized recreation. Some of the pressure was personal. People who used, sold or rented expensive recreational vehicles sought the right to use them anywhere they wanted on the Forest Preserve.

Conservationists were worried about the impact of this on wildlife and water quality. Some wildlife is easily disturbed by loud noises. Some is too slow to get off the road or off the trail in time to avoid being hit. In the High Peaks region, before the APA was created, both opponents of motorized access and advocates pressed the DEC to support their side.

Wilderness a new idea

The APA's State Land Master Plan would define some limits. It introduced the concept of wilderness areas to the Park. Prior to the master plan, all Adirondack Forest Preserve was "forever wild," protected by the NYS Constitution. But none was officially, permanently off-limits to motorized access.

The whole idea of a state-created and state-managed wilderness area was new. Other states were not doing this. The federal government had done it out west but the state

governments often had to be brought along kicking and screaming. Here, we were volunteering to create wilderness with no help from the feds. It felt good to know we lived in a state that recognized a priceless gem when it saw one, and did something to protect it. It still feels good.

Better yet, the master plan stated clearly that the Forest Preserve consisted of the state's most sensitive and valuable forests and waters. It said the state's first obligation would always be to conserve those assets. Recreation would be encouraged but only in ways and in places where it could do no harm to the environment. It was a bold, refreshing statement. Because the Legislature approved it, it was not mere policy—it carried the force of state law.

It did not come a moment too soon. Motors were everywhere. There were already thousands of miles of roads in the Park. Jeeps and trucks were getting more proficient at climbing rough terrain. Floatplanes were piercing the silence of the most remote crannies. Four-wheeled, all-terrain vehicles were not yet common but utility vehicles were in use throughout the Forest Preserve. There were already more than 800 miles of snowmobile trails. Sadly, not everyone agreed. Opponents of Adirondack wilderness immediately started to protest and sue the state.

If the master plan had been repealed or struck down by the courts in those early years, the High Peaks Wilderness would not exist today. None of the current 1.2 million acres of Adirondack Wilderness would exist. The only significant areas of protected wilderness on the East Coast of the United States today would be a few thousand acres around the Allagash River in Maine and the Florida Everglades—with practically nothing in between.

When advocates for float planes and recreational vehicles started suing, they would often accuse their opponents of discrimination against people with disabilities. The courts didn't buy it. The rulings preserved the APA's right to protect the High Peaks Wilderness Area from public motorized and mechanized access. Despite many challenges, the APA has prevailed in both state and federal courts.

This only underscores the wisdom and importance of APA's and DEC's policies that allow people with disabilities to gain special access to the Forest Preserve. This includes use of motorized wheelchairs and other conveyances made specifically for the disabled, which may be operated in wilderness areas where the terrain can accommodate them. A sizeable collection of non-wilderness roads has been designated by the state for use by people with disabled-access permits, who may ride an ATV on those roads. Still, the parade of these lawsuits continued into the 21st century, as people have tried to gain permission to fly floatplanes, use motorboats, drive logging trucks and use all-terrain vehicles in wilderness areas. There is no end to the pressure in sight.

Throughout the 1980s and 90s, our government relations team lobbied the Legislature and halted a series of bills that would have eliminated the APA's authority to protect wilderness. In those conflicts, the Council worked with Legislators from across the state to stop bad bills. We also kept the public informed about legislative or administrative attempts to weaken the Forever Wild clause, or to create loopholes that would render wilderness protection rules meaningless. The Council remains vigilant against legal and legislative attempts to wipe out or weaken wilderness.

Threats from the sky

One of the most persistent threats to the High Peaks is the air pollution that causes acid rain and smog. The Adirondack Council has been a national leader in fighting it. One of our earliest major accomplishments came in 1984 when the Legislature passed the nation's first law controlling acid rain. The High Peaks had suffered some of the worst damage in America from acid rain. To solve the problem, New York had to do something about its own power plants first, and then ask for help from the rest of the country. It was a daunting task. Many of New York's own power plants burned coal and lacked basic emissions controls. The Council played a pivotal role in changing both of those conditions.

The Park's tallest mountains were especially hard hit by air pollution. Because of their elevation and location, they received a two-fisted beating. They were afflicted by damaging levels of acidic precipitation, plus a constant bath of acidic cloud water passing over them. Cloud water can be 20 to 100 times more acidic than acid rain or snow. This was rapidly changing the soil chemistry on the High Peaks. The summits' naturally thin soils were steadily being depleted of their remaining calcium and other alkaline nutrients. When the acid interacts with the minerals, they create a third, more neutral substance. But the calcium and other minerals are needed by plants, insects and animals. Calcium is a basic building block for most life.

Lower Wolf Jaw
BRENDAN WILTSE

Once the calcium is used up, damage accelerates. Acid rain causes a chemical reaction that leaches harmful metals such as aluminum and mercury from the soil. It breaks down harmless compounds and transforms their components into harmful ones. Aluminum released by acid rain kills trees by destroying their roots, robbing them of water and nutrients. Acid converts harmless inorganic mercury into an organic form that contaminates the entire food chain, causing organ damage and birth defects in people, fish and other wildlife. Normally hearty high-elevation red spruce and balsam fir forests were dying off at an alarming rate. This harmed the habitat and food supply of extremely rare songbirds such as Bicknell's thrushes and Swainson's thrushes. Both make their nests and breed only in high-elevation trees.

Alarmingly, there was another problem at the tops of the mountains. It was only discovered when acid rain researchers added ground-level ozone (smog) monitors to their equipment arrays at high elevations in the Park. Most people think of smog as a localized, big city problem caused by automobile traffic. New York and Los Angeles certainly have such problems. But high-elevation smog can travel hundreds of miles, just like acid rain.

Pollution from the smokestacks and tailpipes of the Midwest drifts east every day. Much of it passes far above the heads of New York residents, eventually falling to earth somewhere else. But at an elevation of 4,000 feet above sea level, ozone enveloped the tops of the High Peaks. Rather than inhaling the sweet, healthy mountain air everyone was accustomed to in the Adirondacks, on some days, climbers were breathing smog that could be worse than Manhattan at rush hour.

Our publication *Beside the Stilled Waters* was the first attempt to explain acid rain to the general public in terms that did not require someone with an advanced degree in chemistry to understand them. We made sure all of Congress received a copy and spread them to the news media as well. After getting a state law enacted in 1985, it took another five years for the Council and its allies to persuade Congress to pass a bi-partisan acid rain law. The Clean Air Act Amendments of 1990 really helped. They resulted in deep cuts in sulfur- and nitrogen-based air pollution from power plants.

Snowshoe hare
BRENDAN WILTSE

Since then, the Council has helped secure additional measures to combat acid rain with its 1997 publication and short film of the same title: *ACID RAIN: A Continuing National Tragedy*. We also recruited entertainers such as Bonnie Raitt, Natalie Merchant and the Bacon Brothers (Michael and Kevin) to make television and radio commercials about the need to stop acid rain. We worked with several New York attorneys general to bring lawsuits against Midwest polluters, forcing them into settlements that required deep and immediate pollution cuts. We sought the creation of the U.S. Environmental Protection Agency's Clean Air Interstate Rule, the subsequent Cross-State Air Pollution Rule. Those were designed to stop smog but helped curb acid rain too.

The results have been dramatic. The amount of sulfur-based pollution falling on the Adirondack Park has decreased by more than 90 percent. Nitrogen-based pollution is down by more than 70 percent. Many areas of the Park—the High Peaks chief among them—are recovering their chemical balance, which is the first step to biological recovery of their native plants and wildlife.

As this book was being written, the EPA was finalizing the Clean Power Plan. It would require deep cuts in carbon pollution from power plants nationwide in an effort to reduce global climate change. The conservation, efficiencies and new fuel sources that would be required to meet those mandates will result in additional reductions in smog and acid rain over the coming decades.

A new management plan

Perhaps our most difficult struggle to protect the High Peaks Wilderness came in the 1970s, 80s and 90s, as we urged the DEC and APA to complete a management plan that would curb its overuse. Incomplete state records made it hard to estimate how many people were visiting through the trailheads in the eastern High Peaks but by 1984, more than 180,000 a year were signing the trail registers. Many more were not bothering to sign in. Most estimated that the total was above 200,000 people per year.

It was becoming clear that we were loving this wonderful place to death. Trails were badly eroded, soils compacted and runoff was silting trout streams. Campsites were being carved in new locations every summer and older sites showed signs of constant use. Firewood was scarce. People started cutting live trees in vain efforts to build fires. Often, the Northway looked like a road rally on summer Friday afternoons. People jockeying for the best camping spots raced one another to their favorite trailhead. Parking lots jammed and overflowed. Keene Valley was experimenting with satellite parking lots and shuttles to relieve pressure on trailhead lots and overflowing roadsides.

After some give and take at a long series of advisory committee meetings and a shorter series of public hearings, the DEC approved a new plan. It closed overused sites; limited the size of overnight camping parties; discouraged at-large camping and creating new campsites; banned campfires—stoves are OK—and encouraged people to try new routes to reach the tall mountains. The entire eastern side of the wilderness is showing signs of recovery since then.

But it was hard to do. It required each of us to remember that, no matter how careful we are, we leave some impact on the woods when we visit. By being conscientious, we can limit that impact significantly. But it was the first place in the Park where wilderness lovers really had to temper their own enthusiasm for recreation in order to save the place they loved.

Nobody likes to realize they are part of the problem. I surely didn't like it. It took me a while to get over it. Lots of people helped to remind me that it wasn't about what I wanted or felt I deserved. It was about the health and sustainability of the wilderness and what was best for the High Peaks. What was best, of course, was less of me stomping through the place, and more of my leaving it for others to enjoy. Besides, there are other pathways to its beauty that don't require me to enter from the popular east. And it's a great, big park out there, with lots of room to explore new places.

Expansion would relieve pressure

Expanding the High Peaks Wilderness would spread out some of the visitor impact over a larger area, giving overused places a chance to recover their vitality. New entryways from the south would spread some economic development too. For example, new expansion of the HPWA boundary would bring it to the doorsteps of North Hudson and Newcomb. Both could use the economic boost that trailheads leading into the High Peaks would bring. At the same time, the new access would relieve pressure on the eastern entrances, where crowds can sometimes diminish the wilderness experience.

In 2007, The Nature Conservancy completed the purchase of 161,000 acres of land in 32 Adirondack towns. Of that, 95,000 acres remains commercial timberland, protected by a conservation easement that prevents its subdivision and development. Of the remaining acreage, half has been added to the Forest Preserve to be managed as non-wilderness. The rest remains to be classified.

Some of the most spectacular of those lands are Boreas Ponds, MacIntyre East and MacIntyre West, all adjacent to the HPWA. Just as amazing are two smaller tracts formerly owned by the Open Space Institute and Elk Lake Lodge—Casey Brook. By classifying the Casey Brook tract as wilderness, the state would connect the HPWA to the Dix Mountain Wilderness Area. This would help the DEC improve its ability to manage wildlife passage and migration as climate change alters local habitat, and as extirpated native species wander back into the Park and attempt to re-establish themselves.

Moose are already beginning to repopulate the area. Twenty years ago, that seemed impossible. Forty years ago, beavers were scarce everywhere in the park. Today, they manage to survive in locations as remote and forbidding as Lake Tear of the Clouds on the shoulder of Mount Marcy.

Who knows what wonders tomorrow will hold?

When we urged the Governor to adopt this wilderness expansion plan in 2015, we were joined by Adirondack Mountain Club, Adirondack Wild: Friends of the Forest Preserve, Audubon NY, Citizens Campaign for the Environment, Environmental Advocates and the Natural Resources Defense Council and the New York League of Conservation Voters.

Through 2016 and beyond the Adirondack Council will commit a great deal of time and money to promoting the benefits of an expanded HPWA. We created the #BeWildNY Campaign to support it, which included boosting the number of advocates for the Park and for wilderness, while launching a major digital, print and video advertising campaign. Once-in-a-lifetime opportunities can't be treated lightly.

Threats to this wonderful wilderness may change over time but they will never cease. As wilderness advocate Bob Marshall said many years ago, what won't ever change is the need for "the organization of spirited people who will fight for the freedom of wilderness."

Heart Lake from Mount Jo
BRENDAN WILTSE

A Sense of Place

By Ross Whaley

Ross Whaley's biography is on page 112

Matt Diskin, Assistant Forest Ranger and former Summit Steward, poses for a photo on the summit of Marcy
NANCIE BATTAGLIA

By education I am an economist with a focus on natural resource policy, by occupation an academic and government administrator, by hobby an outdoorsman, and by good fortune a husband, father and grandfather. During my career we lived in Louisiana, Utah, Colorado, Washington DC, Massachusetts and New York. I mention this only to point out that until moving to New York my involvement in natural resource and environmental policy had largely been an abstraction—in classrooms and board rooms. I didn't quite realize that the task forces or commissions on which I had the honor to serve were dealing with policies that were in general applicable almost everywhere but in specifics were not adequate anywhere. That is an understandable flaw in international, national and at times even state laws and policies. They miss the detail necessary to be just right in this place or that one. Therein lies my excitement for having the opportunity to play a small role in law, policies and regulations impacting the Adirondack Park—a specific identifiable place on the map; big, but small enough to grasp; with the people impacted, my neighbors; the landscape of tremendous ecological importance; and, just perhaps, a model for how protected landscapes, communities and their residents can coexist. Here I began to understand what is meant by "sense of place." How wonderful to focus one's work on the place you call home.

As spectacular as the mountains, lakes and rivers are in the Adirondack Park, there are also precious differences from elsewhere. The day-to-day routine has a different rhythm and feel when you live in the woods. The third of a mile walk to the mailbox means feeling the weather peculiar to that day, the sounds are more subtle than in the city, the dog chasing after something moving in the distance entices you off the road to see what it is, and the seasons wake you up to the miracles of nature. The people differ too. You can't simply get by with a nod and quick hello when you pass an acquaintance. It requires a full stop and a discussion about family and the latest gossip.

Bicknell's thrush
LARRY MASTER

I have touched the Park as administrator of a college that managed a large research forest, a biology station, a forestry summer camp and a forest technician degree program, all located in the Adirondacks. That was the first exposure to the wonders of the place and the people who worked there. Then it really got interesting with the opportunity to serve as Chairman of the Adirondack Park Agency (APA). Chairing a regulatory agency is a different animal than teaching, researching and serving on policy task forces. Clearly, my education was still in its early stages, and it seems as though almost every day was a new learning adventure whether in natural, political or social science.

I would like to share some of the lessons I am still struggling to understand more fully during my sojourn though this special place.

In spite of ourselves, nature is amazingly resilient. Look at many of the pictures of the Adirondack region during the early twentieth century. Some of that landscape which was cut over, burned and stripped of some of its iconic animal and bird species is now public land classified as "wilderness." We could debate the appropriate definition of wilderness and how it should be applied in classifying certain lands in the Forest Preserve but it certainly seems that much of this land is wilderness-in-the-making. So while we struggle to classify lands correctly as mandated by the law creating the APA, I am struck by Mother Nature's power to repair what with hindsight seemed to be mistakes. I mention this not to suggest that the regulatory function of classifying land is unimportant but that we should approach it with humility because nature will win in the long run.

Right action in the world depends on knowing how the world works and what is right (comment by Herman Daly). Knowing how the world works is a matter of science, which is mentioned below, and that's the easier part of right action. "What is right" is the really hard part. I thought Alan Bloom was too cynical when he wrote in *Closing of the American Mind*, "...people really believe in only two things. One is that they believe truth is merely a matter of opinion, and they believe that all morality is merely a matter of preference." Listening to some of the debate over issues of land regulation in the Adirondack Park I may have tempered my opinion about Bloom's observation. I don't think it is too much of a stretch to suggest that "what is right"—even when making land-use decisions—is a matter of ethics. Ethical decisions are easier when you are deciding between right versus wrong. They become really difficult when you are deciding between right versus right—community versus the individual, this community versus that one, short term versus longterm, justice versus mercy. Caring for the ecosystems of the Adirondack Park and nurturing it as a fine place to live, raise children and care for the grandparents is not just politics as usual. It is a challenge in practical ethics of the highest order.

Science is the search for truth. Policy deals with decisions that we have to make whether or not we know the truth. There are propositions grounded in science that absolutely should be considered when making decisions about appropriate use of the land, such as cumulative impacts, carrying capacity and fragmentation. They must be considered when either designing or implementing land-use policies. But often agreed-upon specific metrics which influence the go/no-go decision are elusive not only to the policy maker or regulator but also to the scientific community on which the regulator depends. When this happens, these terms that have their origin in science become pawns for obfuscation in the rhetoric of activists of all stripes. Clearly, we should be allowed our own opinions but we should not be allowed our own facts. And when the facts are elusive, we should be honest and careful.

When asked to write a piece about my experience in the Adirondacks, I was honored. I planned to write mainly about my personal daily life and the marvelous good fortune of living, playing and working here. But I started writing by mentioning I was by training and occupation a policy wonk, and therefore fell into the trap of talking about that part of this place. If I learned anything during this sojourn, it was that my education is in its infancy.

A Picture is Worth a Thousand Words

Nancie Battaglia: Unwitting Historian of Life in the Adirondacks

Award-winning photographer Nancie Battaglia recalls hearing about a "Professor Ketch" from fellow students at Syracuse University where she studied photography and journalism in the mid-1970s. Some fifteen years later the Ketch name resurfaced while Nancie was on a *New York Times* assignment to illustrate a story about the fledgling Adirondack High Peaks Summit Stewardship Program. The story ran in the August 26, 1990, edition and Nancie's accompanying photos of Summit Stewards are reproduced here on page 58.

Another assignment related to the Summit Stewardship Program led to a meeting with Ketch on the seasonal Whiteface Mountain Toll Road at the end of a summer day in 1991. Ketch, the "groundskeeper" of the flora at the peak, had unlimited access and a key to the gate. This allowed their after-hours motorized ascent five miles up the road to photograph while magic light ushered in day's end. That encounter resulted in our evocative cover shot in which Nancie captured her intense subject against a stunning Adirondack sky—a vibrant homage to Ketch and his life's passion. Over the next few years she joined Ketch as he climbed with various groups for summit restoration work or lectures about alpine plants.

Vancouver, January 17, 2010: Lindsey Vonn celebrates gold in downhill
NANCIE BATTAGLIA

Her interest piqued, Nancie has continued to chronicle the summit restoration work. Frequent High Peaks adventures with cameras at hand provide documentation of the Summit Stewardship Program's evolving success. Her decades of photographing everywhere inside the Blue Line has produced a visual library of Adirondack history.

Nancie is an internationally-published photojournalist who began her career working for newswire services. In 1978, she landed in Lake Placid, NY, after being hired by the Lake Placid Olympic Organizing Committee as their official/chief still photographer. Since then freelance assignments have taken her around the Park and across the oceans. Her work has appeared in *Sports Illustrated, National Geographic, Readers Digest, Life Magazine, Adirondack Life, New York Times, Wall Street Journal, Newsweek, TV Guide* and publications throughout the world. Although known for her sports photography, Nancie's photos have also been published in coffee table books, calendars, brochures, cereal boxes and jigsaw puzzles.

An outdoor enthusiast, Nancie is an Adirondack 46er, having climbed all 46 High Peaks not once, but twice, carrying many pounds of photo equipment in her pack. She continues to reside in Lake Placid and explore the Adirondacks thirty-plus years and 11 Olympic Games later.

NANCIE BATTAGLIA

Brendan Wiltse: Connecting People to the Natural World

Brendan Wiltse is a scientist and nature photographer with a passion for the conservation of the Adirondack Park. Brendan's development as a scientist coincided with a growing passion for using photography as a means to connect people to the natural world and establish a conservation ethic within our society. A former High Peaks Summit Steward for several seasons, caretaker and then Property Coordinator at Johns Brook Lodge (JBL) for the Adirondack Mountain Club, he is currently Science and Stewardship Director at the Ausable River Association. He credits his years of summit stewarding for nurturing his love of the High Peaks and the incredible plant life on the summits.

Brendan officially launched his photography business in 2013, marking a new commitment to using this medium to share the beauty and value of the natural world and in particular the Adirondacks. A year later, he crowd-funded a project to document the alpine plants found on New York's highest summits, some of which are published in these pages. Brendan provides images and services free of charge to nonprofits that are dedicated to conservation.

After undergraduate degrees in Environmental Sciences from Hudson Valley Community College and Field Biology from Paul Smiths College, Brendan was accepted into a Master's program at Queen's University in 2008. He ended up staying in Canada longer than originally planned, deciding to enroll directly into a Ph.D. program. He finished his degree while working at JBL where guests were often surprised to see the caretaker working on a computer and even more so upon learning that he was writing a doctoral thesis on the response of lakes to climate change. Brendan has since earned his Ph.D.

It was while attending high school in Watertown, NY, where he grew up, that Brendan developed an interest in photography and could often be found spending study hall time or skipping gym class to work in the darkroom. He made the transition to digital photography many years ago.

Brendan Wiltse carrying rock to build cairns above tree line, Wright 2008
ERIC HAWES

Join Us

We are a nonprofit membership organization that brings together people with interests in recreation, conservation, and environmental education in the New York State Forest Preserve. ADK members choose from short or long outings through local chapters to Adirondack backpacking trips and international treks. Learn through chapter outings or attend one of our workshops or other programs.

We also construct and maintain trails throughout the Adirondacks and Catskills; advocate on issues that affect the wild lands and waters of New York State; and publish guidebooks, field guides, and other books, as well as *Adirondac*, a bimonthly magazine.

For more information and member benefits:
ADK Member Services Center (Exit 21 off the Northway, I-87)
814 Goggins Road, Lake George, NY 12845-4117

Membership: 800-395-8080
www.adk.org

Information Centers

ADK centers in Lake George and on our Heart Lake property near Lake Placid offer ADK publications and other merchandise for sale, as well as backcountry and general Adirondack information, educational displays, outdoor equipment, and snacks.

Information: 518-668-4447
Education (workshops and programs): 518-523-3441

Lodges and campground

- Adirondak Loj, on the shores of Heart Lake, near Lake Placid, offers year-round accommodations in private and family rooms, a coed bunkroom, and cabins. It is accessible by car, and parking is available.
- The Adirondak Loj Wilderness Campground is also located on the Heart Lake property and includes campsites and lean-tos.
- Johns Brook Lodge (JBL), near Keene Valley, is a seasonal backcountry facility located in prime hiking country. It is 3.5 miles from the nearest road and is accessible only by foot.

Both lodges offer home-cooked meals and trail lunches.
For reservations: 518-523-3441

ADK Public Affairs Office

301 Hamilton Street, Albany, NY 12210-1738
Public Affairs: 518-449-3870

Our Mission

The Adirondack Mountain Club (ADK) is dedicated to the conservation, preservation, and responsible recreational use of the New York State Forest Preserve and other parks, wild lands, and waters vital to our members and chapters.

ADK Publications

Forest Preserve Series

1 Adirondack Mountain Club High Peaks Trails
2 Adirondack Mountain Club Eastern Trails
3 Adirondack Mountain Club Central Trails
4 Adirondack Mountain Club Western Trails
5 Adirondack Mountain Club Northville–Placid Trail
6 Adirondack Mountain Club Catskill Trails

Other Titles

Adirondack Alpine Summits: An Ecological Field Guide
Adirondack Birding: 60 Great Places to Find Birds
Adirondack Paddling: 60 Great Flatwater Adventures
An Adirondack Sampler I: Day Hikes for All Seasons
Catskill Day Hikes for All Seasons
Forests and Trees of the Adirondack High Peaks Region
Kids on the Trail! Hiking with Children in the Adirondacks
No Place I'd Rather Be: Wit and Wisdom from Adirondack Lean-to Journals
Ski and Snowshoe Trails in the Adirondacks
The Adirondack Reader
The Catskill 67: A Hiker's Guide to the Catskill 100 Highest Peaks Under 3500'
Views from on High: Fire Tower Trails in the Adirondacks and Catskills
Winterwise: A Backpacker's Guide

Maps

Trails of the Adirondack High Peaks topographic map
Trails Illustrated Map 736: Northville-Placid Trail
Trails Illustrated Map 742: Lake Placid/High Peaks
Trails Illustrated Map 743: Lake George/Great Sacandaga
Trails Illustrated Map 744: Northville/Raquette Lake
Trails Illustrated Map 745: Old Forge/Oswegatchie
Trails Illustrated Map 746: Saranac/Paul Smiths
Trails Illustrated Map 755: Catskill Park

Adirondack Mountain Club Calendar
Price list available upon request, or see www.adk.org